The Paris Review

Founded in 1953.

The Paris Review is published quarterly by The Paris Review, Inc. Vol. 38, No. 138, Spring 1996.
Business Office: 45-39 171 Place, Flushing, New York 11358 (ISSN #0031-2037). Paris Office:
Harry Mathews, 67 rue de Grenelle, Paris 75007 France. London Office: Shusha Guppy, 8 Shawfield
St., London, SW3. US distributors: Random House, Inc. 1(800)733-3000. Typeset and printed in
USA by Capital City Press, Montpelier, VT.   Price for single issue in USA: $10.00. $14.00 in Canada.
Post-paid subscription for four issues $34.00, lifetime subscription $1000. Postal surcharge of $8.00
per four issues outside USA (excluding life subscriptions). Subscription card is bound within magazine. Please give six weeks notice of change of address using subscription card.   *While The Paris
Review welcomes the submission of unsolicited manuscripts, it cannot accept responsibility for
their loss or delay, or engage in related correspondence. Manuscripts will not be returned or
responded to unless accompanied by self-addressed, stamped envelope.   Fiction manuscripts
should be submitted to George Plimpton, poetry to Richard Howard, The Paris Review, 541 East
72nd Street, New York, N.Y. 10021.*   Charter member of the Council of Literary Magazines and
Presses. This publication is made possible, in part, with public funds from the New York State Council
on the Arts and the National Endowment for the Arts.   Second Class postage paid at Flushing,
New York, and at additional mailing offices.   **Postmaster:** Please send address changes to 45-39
171st Place, Flushing, N.Y. 11358.

MFA in Writing
at Vermont College

Intensive 11-Day Residencies
July and January on the beautiful Vermont campus,
catered by the New England
Culinary Institute. Workshops, classes, readings,
conferences, followed by

Non-Resident 6-Month Writing Projects
in poetry and fiction individually designed
during residency. In-depth criticism of manuscripts.
Sustained dialogue with faculty.

Post-Graduate Writing Semester
for those who have already finished a graduate degree
with a concentration in creative writing.

Scholarships, minority scholarships and financial aid available.

For More Information
Roger Weingarten, MFA Writing Program, Box 888
Vermont College of Norwich University
Montpelier, VT 05602   802–828–8840
Low-residency B.A. and M.A. programs also available.

POETRY FACULTY
Robin Behn
Mark Cox
Deborah Digges
Nancy Eimers
Mark Halliday
Richard Jackson
Sydney Lea
Jack Myers
William Olsen
David Rivard
J. Allyn Rosser
Mary Ruefle
Betsy Sholl
Leslie Ullman
Roger Weingarten
David Wojahn

FICTION FACULTY
Carol Anshaw
Tony Ardizzone
Phyllis Barber
Francois Camoin
Abby Frucht
Douglas Glover
Diane Lefer
Ellen Lesser
Bret Lott
Sena Jeter Naslund
Christopher Noel
Pamela Painter
Sharon Sheehe Stark
Gladys Swan
W.D. Wetherell

Skowhegan: A residency program for advanced visual
artists in Maine   *June 15 - August 17, 1996*

An independent program for advanced artists working with
established resident and visiting artists collegially in a rural
Maine community.

Application deadline: February 9th
For information write: 200 Park Avenue South, Suite 1116
New York, NY 10003
Tel. 212 529-0505

Generous financial aid available according to need including aid
based on geographical and cultural backgrounds.

Resident Artists: Tishan Hsu, Jacob Lawrence, Joel Otterson,
Joyce Scott, Jessica Stockholder, Meg Webster
Visiting Artists: Carroll Dunham, Nan Goldin, Gary Hill, Anish
Kapoor
Paul Mellon Distinguished Fellow: Cornel West

THE PARIS REVIEW
announces a
Prize for Poetic Drama

In preparation for our upcoming theater issue, *The Paris Review* will award a prize for the finest previously unpublished poetic drama. Manuscripts may be no longer than thirty pages. The winning piece will be published in *The Paris Review*; its author will receive $2,000.

Submissions must be accompanied by an SASE and be postmarked no later than November 1, 1996.
Submissions should be sent to:
Poetic Drama Prize
The Paris Review
541 East 72 St.
New York, NY 10021

AGENDA

EDITED BY WILLIAM COOKSON AND PETER DALE
EDITORIAL ASSISTANT: ANITA MONEY

'Quite the best and most sane and rational
poetry magazine, with the least axes to grind'
                    JOHN BAYLEY
'... the most important literary magazine in
Britain over the past thirty years'
                    DONALD DAVIE

Just out: IRISH POETRY DOUBLE ISSUE. 320
pages. New poems by Heaney, Kinsella, Mahon,
Montague, Kennelly and many new names.
Price £8 ($16)

Forthcoming (Spring & Summer 1996) Features
on W.D. Snodgrass and Geoffrey Hill.
Autumn 1996: Dante, Pound and the Contemporary
Poet. A double number including new versions
of Dante by Thom Gunn, Charles Tomlinson
and many others. Essays reconsidering La
Divina Commedia and Pound's Cantos. Ronald
Bush contributes an important essay on recently
discovered drafts of cantos Pound wrote in
Italian during World War 2 that shed new
light on the composition of The Pisan Cantos.

We invite readers of THE PARIS REVIEW
to subscribe. Rates: Inland £20. Overseas:
£22 (U.S. $44). We accept credit card
payments by VISA and MASTERCARD.

Orders should be sent to AGENDA, 5 Cranbourne
Court, Albert Bridge Road, LONDON, U.K.,
SW11 4PE. Tel. & Fax 0171-228 0700

"*Valentine Place*
is a Complex Delight."

—John Ashbery

"A profound,
scary and
beautiful
knowledge
of a severe world
truly our own."

—A. R. Ammons

poems

"THIS INCREASINGLY IMPRESSIVE POET
keeps reminding us that putting aside childish things
can be done only wisely and well by keeping in touch
with them, and that American life is best understood and
celebrated by those who are, with Whitman, both in and
out of the game and watching and wondering at it."

—John Hollander

David Lehman

Series editor of
<u>The Best American Poetry</u>

SCRIBNER
150 YEARS OF PUBLISHING

SHENANDOAH

THE WASHINGTON AND LEE UNIVERSITY REVIEW

Betty Adcock

David Baker

Kathryn Stripling Byer

Hayden Carruth

Peter Cooley

Nicholas Delbanco

John Engels

Margaret Gibson

Eamon Grennan

Susan Hahn

Robin Hemley

Michael Longley

Kent Nelson

Mary Oliver

Deborah Pope

Reynolds Price

William Matthews

Scott Russell Sanders

Reginald Shepherd

SHENANDOAH

45/4 $3.50

WINTER 1995

One year (4 issues): $11.00
Sample: $3.50

Name _____
Address _____
_____
City/State _____
Zip _____

                     PR

SHENANDOAH
Troubadour Theater, 2nd Floor
Washington and Lee University
Lexington, VA 24450-0303

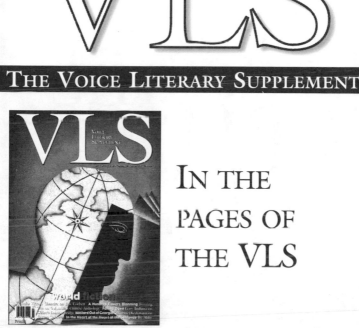

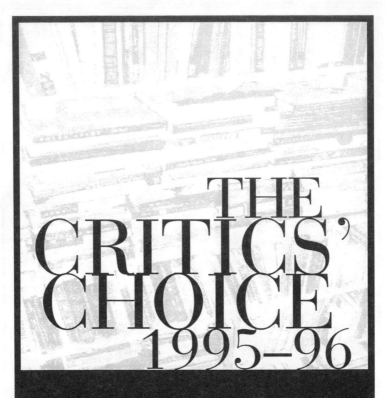

THE CRITICS' CHOICE 1995–96

The Critics' Choice is *the* guide to 1995's best books, as selected by a panel of professional critics from: *The Bloomsbury Review, Chicago Tribune, Esquire, Kansas City Star, Kirkus Reviews, KQED, Los Angeles Times, L.A. Reader, MacNeil/Lehrer News Hour, Miami Herald, The Oregonian, Publishers Weekly*, San Francisco Public Library, *San Francisco Review of Books, The Seattle Times*, and *The Village Voice*.

To order or for more information:
126 South Park
San Francisco, CA 94107
Tel 415.543.7372
Fax 415.243.8514
E-Mail sfreview@aol.com

Compiled by

TODAY'S
FIRST
EDITION

SAN FRANCISCO
REVIEW *of* BOOKS

The Paris Review

Editorial Office:
541 East 72 Street
New York, New York 10021
HTTP://www.voyagerco.com

Business & Circulation:
45-39 171 Place
Flushing, New York 11358

Distributed by Random House
201 East 50 Street
New York, N.Y. 10022
(800) 733-3000

Number 138

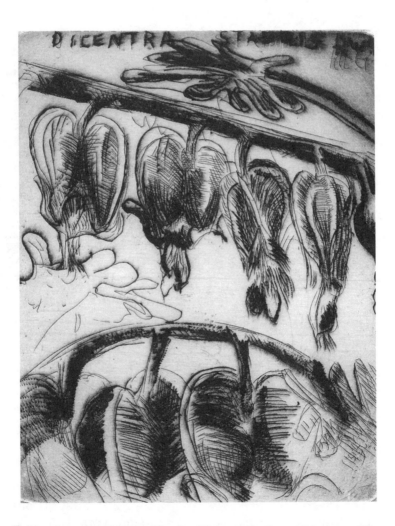

Table of contents illustration by Richard Gaffney, *Dicentra #7*.
Frontispiece by William Pène du Bois.

Notice

Discerning readers of this issue will note that once again we have focused on a single topic — screenwriting in this case. It is the second time we have done a "theme" issue, last fall's number being entirely devoted to humor — poems, short stories, interviews, commentaries. Obviously, such a comprehensive offering is impossible with screenwriting — hardly a subject to be tackled by poets or short-story writers. Nonetheless, the three interviews (with Richard Price, Billy Wilder and John Gregory Dunne) are applicable, and so is the new feature, "The Man in the Back Row Has a Question." As is a feature on Truman Capote's work as a screenwriter of *Beat the Devil.* Lastly, a number of pages have been set aside for a portfolio on the work of the late Terry Southern — a screenwriter of first rank (*Easy Rider, Dr. Strangelove, The Cincinnati Kid*) as well as a distinguished novelist and short-story writer (*Red Dirt Marijuana, The Magic Christian, Texas Summers*). He was a longtime friend of this magazine and its editors; an excerpt from his first novel (*Flash and Filigree*) appeared in the first issue of the magazine, Spring, 1953.

Readers may be interested in the reaction to the first "focused" issue — last fall's "Whither Mirth" humor number. A number of newspapers took notice, which is rare enough: *The Boston Globe* referred to it as "the strongest issue in some time." The *New York Post* commented: "In these often unfunny times *The Paris Review* makes a great contribution to American arts, letters and laughter." The Minneapolis *Star-Tribune* announced: "The highlights are many . . . side-splitting . . . such a success that one hopes there might be more such single-subject issues in the planning stages." The reviewer on *The Washington Post* (Michael Dirda) wrote: ". . . by turns informative, compulsively readable and frequently irritating — what more could any decent literary magazine want?" Actually, Mr. Dirda had a caveat or two. He took exception to my attempts to describe the participants at a conference on humor (written as if informal notes in a diary) which he felt to be in his words "plummy" and an indication that I was either ". . . a snobbish twit or simply a deeply witty man who finds some peculiar kick in pretending to be a snobbish twit." *Plummy* was not a word I knew, as he uses it, though I have seen it elsewhere. W.H. Auden's voice was recently described as "Oxford and plummy." My edition of the Oxford Universal Dictionary defines the word as "full of plums" (big surprise!) "rich, decorative." The OED adds ". . . often to the point of affectation," which I suppose is what Mr. Dirda had in mind. I am reminded that when Martin Gabel, a Brooklyn-born actor, was asked about his cultivated (read "plummy") accent, he would reply, "Affected, my dear sir, affected." As for the "twit" business, I *do* know what that implies, and I would hope that I lie somewhere in the middle of the two extremes Mr. Dirda postulates.

The New Criterion assigned the humor issue to one of its reviewers, Mark Steyn, the London *Spectator's* film critic, who turned in a thoughtful, if somewhat turbulent excercise that takes up five pages in the magazine. He took exception to the rather parochial nature of the *Review's* contents (". . . the narrowness of *The Paris Review's* humor horizons") and thought we would have been better off "chewing the fat" with Mort Sahl, Rush Limbaugh and Howard Stern than inter-viewing Calvin Trillin, Garrison Keillor and Woody Allen. The latter, he felt, were too insulated. Trillin, according to Steyn, is best known for his "small-town chronicles." As for Keillor, Steyn mourns, "there are no blacks or gays or Pakistani taxi drivers in Lake Wobegon." Woody Allen? We were taken to task for not asking Woody Allen about his recent family problems . . . alas, a sure rib-tickler missed!

I'm glad Mark Steyn mentioned Howard Stern. For a while we considered publishing a transcript of an improvised mono-logue in which in a trance Stern is "visited" by Elvis Presley who has "come back" to check on rumors of his daughter's marriage to Michael Jackson. Terrific stuff! Unfortunately, without Stern's brilliant imitation of Presley's accent, the words on the printed page seemed flat and colorless. Nor, finally, did it seem appropriate to include material by Stern (whose agent told me has not opened a book since his high-school days) in an issue devoted to the varities of humor in what Terry Southern used to refer to as the "Quality Lit Game."

"Contemporary comedy," Mr. Steyn writes, "may think of itself as directly descended from Lenny Bruce, but actually it's closer to Ozzie and Harriet." It would seem that fairly lowbrow variety-hall stuff, on-stage jokes, is what concerns Mr. Steyn. Bob Hope, Weber and Fields, David Letterman, Frank Sinatra, Vice President Quayle, Otto the Wonder Poodle are the names that crop up in his piece.

Alas, Hilton Kramer himself, the editor of *The New Criterion*, in the course of an astonishing ad hominem attack on George Steiner, whose interview appeared in the last issue of the *Review*, let on that he too couldn't find anything funny in the Whither Mirth issue. He offered a quip of his own: "Wither Mirth." (*Wow*! Ker-*boom*!)

Frankly, Kramer's inability to find anything of value (or indeed funny) in over 300 pages of short stories, poems, interviews might well suggest something of a lack of humor in that good curmudgeon's sense of things . . . Or could it be that like Alexander Pope he wishes to go through life boasting that he has never laughed.

Ah well. No matter. Obviously, we are grateful for whatever notices, the *Criterion*'s included, the humor issue has engendered.

The reviewer from the Minneapolis *Star-Tribune* said in his piece that he hoped we might schedule additional single-topic issues. We indeed intend to do so — Theater, Biography, Publishing and the Erotic being among the "themes" selected. Subscribers and readers of a literary bent are urged to contribute what they think might be appropriate, even "plummy" work if so inclined . . .

—G.A.P.

from Slowness

Milan Kundera

The room fills gradually, there are many French entomologists and a few from abroad, among them a Czech in his sixties
who people say is some prominent figure in the new regime,
a minister perhaps or the president of the Academy of Sciences
or at least a member of that Academy. In any case, if only from
the standpoint of simple curiosity, this is the most interesting
figure in the assembly (he represents a new period in history,
after Communism has gone off into the mists of time); yet
amid this chattering crowd he is standing, tall and awkward,
all alone. For a while, people were rushing up to grasp his
hand and ask him various questions but the discussion always
ended much sooner than they expected, and after the first
four sentences back and forth, they had no idea what to talk
to him about next. Because when it came down to it, there
was no mutual topic. The French reverted quickly to their
own problems, he tried to follow them, from time to time
he would remark, "In our country, on the other hand," then,
having seen that no one cared what was happening "in our
country, on the other hand," he would move off, his face

veiled in a melancholy that was neither bitter nor unhappy, but reasonable and almost condescending.

As the others crowd noisily into the lobby with its bar, he enters the empty room where four long tables, arranged in a square, await the start of the conference. By the door is a small table with the list of the participants and a young woman who looks as left behind as he. He leans toward her and tells her his name. She has him pronounce it again twice. The third time she no longer dares, and leafs vaguely through her list for a name that might resemble the second she has heard.

Full of fatherly good will, the Czech scientist leans over the list and finds his name: he puts his finger on it:

CECHORIPSKY.

"Ah, Monsieur Sechoripi?" says she.

"It's pronounced 'Tché-kho-rjips-ki.'"

"Oh, that's a tough one!"

"And incidentally, it is not written correctly, either," says the scientist. He takes up the pen he sees on the table, and above the C and the R he draws the little marks that look like upside-down circumflexes.

The secretary looks at the marks, looks at the scientist, and sighs: "It's awfully complicated!"

"Not at all, it's very simple."

"Simple?"

"You know Jan Hus?"

The secretary glances quickly over the list of guest conferees and the Czech scientist hastens to explain: "As you know, he was a great Church reformer in the fourteenth century. A predecessor of Luther. Professor at Charles University, which was the first university to be established in the Holy Roman Empire, as you know. But what you do not know is that Jan Hus was also a great reformer of orthography. He succeeded in making it marvelously simple. In your language, to write what you pronounce *tch* you must use three letters, *t*, *c*, *h*. The Germans even need four: *t*, *s*, *c*, *h*. Whereas, thanks to Jan Hus, all we need in our language is a single letter, *c*, with that little mark above it."

The scientist leans again over the secretary's table, and in the margin of the list, he writes a *c*, very big, with an upside-down circumflex: č; then he looks into her eyes and articulates in a very clear, sharp voice: "Tch!"

The secretary looks into his eyes too and repeats: "Tch."

"Yes. Perfect!"

"It's really very useful. Too bad people don't know about Luther's reform anywhere except in your country."

"Jan Hus's reform," says the scientist, acting as if he had not heard the French girl's gaffe, "is not completely unknown. There is one other country where it is used . . . you know where, don't you?"

"No."

"In Lithuania!"

"In Lithuania," the secretary repeats, trying vainly to recall where in the world to put that country.

"And in Latvia too. So now you see why we Czechs are so proud of those little marks over letters. [With a smile:] We would willingly give up anything else. But we will fight for those marks to the last drop of our blood."

He bows to the young woman and moves to the quadrangle of tables. Before each seat is a small card bearing a name. He finds his own, looks at it a long while, takes it up in his fingers and, with a sorrowful but forgiving smile, brings it to show to the secretary.

Meanwhile, another entomologist has stopped at the entrance table to have the young woman circle his name. She sees the Czech scientist and tells him: "Just one moment, Monsieur Chipiki!"

The Czech makes a magnanimous gesture to indicate, "Don't worry, Mademoiselle, I'm in no hurry." Patiently, and not without a touching modesty, he waits beside the table (two more entomologists have stopped there) and when the secretary is finally free, he shows her the little place card:

"Look, funny, isn't it?"

She looks without much understanding: "But, Monsieur Chenipiki, see, the accents, there they are!"

"True, but they are regular circumflexes! They forgot to

reverse them! And look where they put them! Over the *e* and
the *o*! Cêchôripsky!"

"Oh yes, you're right!" says the secretary indignantly.

"I wonder," the Czech scientist says with increasing melancholy, "why people always forget them. They are so poetic,
these reversed circumflexes! Don't you think so? Like birds
in flight! Like doves with wings outspread! [His voice very
tender:] Or butterflies, if you prefer."

And he leans again over the table to take up the pen and
correct the orthography of his name on the little card. He
does it very modestly as if to apologize, and then, without a
word, he withdraws.

The secretary watches him go, tall, oddly misshapen, and
suddenly feels suffused with maternal fondness. She pictures
a reversed circumflex in the form of a butterfly fluttering
around the scientist and finally settling on his white mane.

As he moves toward his seat, the Czech scientist turns his
head and sees the secretary's tender smile. He responds with
his own smile, and along his way he sends her three more.
The smiles are melancholy yet proud. A melancholy pride:
this would describe the Czech scientist.

— translated from the French
by Linda Asher

Two Poems by Anthony Hecht

To Fortuna Parvulorum

> *Young men have strong passions, and tend to
> gratify them indiscriminately . . . they show
> absence of self-control . . . they are hot tem-
> pered. Their lives are mainly spent not in mem-
> ory but in expectation . . . The character of
> Elderly Men [is different]. They have lived
> many years; they have often been taken in, and
> often made mistakes; and life on the whole is
> a bad business.*
>
> —*Aristotle*, Rhetoric, II, 12.

As a young man I was headstrong, willful, rash,
   Determined to amaze,
Grandly indifferent to comfort as to cash,
Past Envy's sneer, past Age's toothless gnash,
   Boldly I went my ways.

Then I matured. I sacrificed the years
   Lost in impetuous folly
To calm Prudentia, paying my arrears
For heedlessness in the cautious coin of fears
   And studious melancholy.

Now, having passed the obligatory stations,
   I turn in turn to you,
Divinity of diminished expectations,
To whom I direct these tardy supplications,
   Having been taught how few

Are blessed enough to encounter on their way
   The least chipped glint of joy,
And learned in what altered tones I hear today
The remembered words, *"Messieurs, les jeux sont faits,"*
   That stirred me as a boy.

Là-bas: A Trance

From silk route Samarkand, emeralds and drugs
Find their way west, smuggled by leather-capped
Bandits with lard-greased hair across unmapped
Storm-tossed sand oceans drained to the very dregs,

And thence to such ports of call as Amsterdam,
The waters of its intricate canals
Gold-leafed and amethyst-shadowed by the veils
Of cloud-occluded suns, imaged in dim

Hempen mirages and opium reveries
Crowding the mind of a Parisian poet
With jasmine adornments to his barren garret,
The masts of frigates from all seven seas

Moored just outside his window, their bright rigging
What all his neighbors know as laundry lines.
France is as nothing; France and her finest wines
For all this fellow's interest can go begging

As the doors of his perception open wide
Admitting nothing but those nacreous errors
Harvested from unfathomed depths of mirrors:
Harems of young, voluptuous, sloe-eyed

Houris, undressed, awaiting his commands,
Untiring courtyard fountains casting jewels

Thriftlessly into blue-and-white-tiled pools,
Their splashes mingled with languid sarabandes.

Carpaccio's Middle East evokes an airborne
Carpet, a sash and headgear the color of flame
Turned into Holland's tulips whose very name
Comes to him from the Turkish word for turban.

Caroline Knox

Sonnet to the Portuguese

No charts nor maps were accorded
him, so he fabricated a route,
a Maginot Line around the earth.

North he went to Schloss Dreyer-Lindt,
schussing and singing down the isobars
mit mittened nymphs (aw the pwecious dollins):

"He weareth the graph paper by way of shirt;
he doeth his geometry homework upon the tattersall."
They toasted their *après-ski* tootsies on the Sensenbrenner.

South he went to Las Percales,
which is admired for its clement atmosphere,
with Bruce Springsteen and Somerset Maugham,
Gardner McFall and Shelley Winters.

"I'll have a double Branch Rickey, please, with a twist!"
The artisans gathered around him as he spoke.
What was he supposed to do — sit on this hands?

  "Dear Portuguese people, who live in the suburbs
  of Lisbon, painting birds on useful jars
  ultimately sold beside the curbs
  of — gardyloo — the refuse and the cars
  which take no note in haste to the ballet;
  dear civilization that gave us Zurbarán

and a Yankee diaspora thick with snapper blues
in the latitude of the Celestial Snooze:
When Adam delved," he with the feat of Klee
continued, "who was then the gentleman?
   O blessed are they in Portugal who sneeze!
   It's Birthington's Washday, and time to tap the trees."

Two Poems by Mac Hammond

High Art and Low Morals

Fifty Hans Holbein heads
From the Queen's collection:
Wyatt and Surrey so real
You could ask them about
The sonnet (a trick in the eyes
He learned in Art School at
Basel), Basel where he left
Wife and babes to starve
When he sailed off to London
To paint King and courtiers;
Rich, he returned once to
Immortalize their destitution
In a heartrending oil
(and left them nothing in his will).

John Rison Jones, Jr.,
From Huntsville, Alabama,
My classmate, liberated Dachau
And shattered all his Gieseking
78s when he heard that great
Interpreter of Schubert was a
Nazi.

Older now and I still remember
I am a pledge to SAE, in a canoe
With a brother and his fiancée;
Neither can swim. The canoe tips
Over. Which one shall I save?
                    We all drown together.

The Hunt (The Prado)

Lucas Cranach, you have painted yourself
Into a corner where you look out across
The centuries, trying to say something
You have not said in your painting
The Hunt, a tapestry of hounds and deer,
Crossbows and hunters, surmounted
By a medieval pink and white castle
Where no one ever lived. Your self-
Portrait in this corner says: *my heart*
Was with the stags that fell bloody
By the river. I mourned the fallow does.

A.F. Moritz

Nothing Happened Here

Nothing happened here — nothing ever
happened in our city, and yet it was destroyed.
What could the innocent citizens have done?
Heirs to two hundred years of despising whoever wished them
    well,
it had become part of their blood: they could not know
that they were proud and dark and suicidal,
that they had grown content to let their own
houses — with these building paper fronts and gray windows,
wedding receptions on the gravel driveways
and burnt lawns — sink back into
a dusk and trash and landscape God.

                                        Unshaven,
halfway along to work with his rusted black lunch pail,
passing the dusty trees-of-heaven, blinded
by morning sun on concrete walls of the underpass,
on the road to Gate No. 9, the 16-inch rolling mill,
he told me once: "No human wisdom can build a city
and confer a way to live. Or if it does,
if it was the dead who passed down these flaming tracks,
this schedule of peace and steel that evolves more slowly
than the sun bloodies its hands upward and the species un-
    dress,
then it's only because time uses humans the way a flood
sweeps everything down and along,
making it rot, and later spreads some of it on the seeds."

So going around the city while it still struggled
like a beetle half-smashed, I saw
some places that answered to the Louvre,

palaces but built by a feeble, violent desire.
Four white marble urns atop the flat facade
of the long-abandoned discount furniture store.
A stone balustrade before a vista of graceful trees
riven by reflecting water clear to the setting sun,
and in a room behind, redoubled
on a closed piano lid, a painting by Asher Durand
of this same view, though he had never seen it.

And everywhere, strange mutations in the slow
but visible decline. The animals we knew in childhood
were all gone now, and nothing survived
larger than a china figurine on a lamp table:
pigeons and mourning doves with asbestos beaks,
sparrows of creosote that slung their chirps like stones.
At dawn and dusk staggering squads of boys
hunted incompetently for rabid, thieving skunks and
    squirrels,
beat up young husbands, slashed mothers, took
what they wanted, what was there.

                        The river
is quiet now. Ducks have returned. Remember
how we once saw it, in the steady roar and rhythmic
pounding of the mills, changed to a silver pudding
by some powerful process by now long bankrupt and gone?
It looked like melting aluminum, or the gray slurry
that falls from a milkshake machine on humid nights
when the button is punched What did they ever do here
but buy what was put before them at the prices marked?
The great seven-story central tower, all cream-white tile,
of the closed dairy factory stands there, set
into the wooded cliff, and two Gothic dwarves
above its boarded entrance
still bear up the beautiful wall on their crushed backs.

Judy Longley

Brushfire at Christmas

Arkansas, 1993
— *for Lawrence, my brother*

I've followed the crumbs to your feast,
share the table with Father again,

his anger smoldering belly-deep
while Mother smiles, eyes darting,

ready to peck with her sharp words.
In this version of our lives

I'm Sis and you're Sonny, once children
of a powerful king. You serve platters

of spiral-sliced ham while I butter
my tongue, trapped in my wish

to become an angel of peace, to swallow
lies past the lump in my throat.

Hands schooled to the courteous
passing of bowls, I'm the daughter

Mother intended, silent when her sugarplum
version of the past clashes

with my memory of dishes flying: Mother
hurling china into the dark that cowers

outside our kitchen steps, a crash
and a curse for each year since my birth

until strawberries clotted on our last
unshattered plate. Now we're polite,

mouth good-byes into the stiff wind
worrying a Christmas angel on your door,

hot-pink gown blazing against a pine
swag, horn mute at her lips.

Then a neighbor shouts, smoke writhes
from the broom he beats at crumpled

Christmas wrapping ribboned in flame,
the field between us unraveling with fire.

You mount your tractor, plow a firebreak
around your house, the dependency

where our parents tremble, caught
in the witch's spell of illness, old age.

Overdressed for a fire in my purple silk,
the mauve felt shoes that won't return me

to Kansas or even my youth, I'm released
into a more exuberant self, brandish

the hose, spray water into a dragon's mouth
hissing back. My pulse a castanet

I stamp errant sparks until firemen arrive,
save the forest of tall pine where creatures hide,

no river to halt the angelic choir of flame,
should it rise, sentient, over everything.

Two Poems by Mark Wunderlich

Suture

Someday you will leave this town and not look back
but for now you keep hurtling toward
the red center, the road unfolding,

the ice raining down in crystals
while the bridge heaves itself onto the bank;
river of mud, river of sad oily pleasures

where a kingfisher cuts through the water's brown skin
clean as math, and you want to say
this is like logic, but something fails you.

Listen to the unforgivable birds
piercing cold sky and singing like needle and thread
and feel for the scar splitting your eyebrow.

(You remember the doctor tying his knots, don't you.)
This is always yours—the shadow of an animal,
smell of newly shorn wool, the workhorse pawing air

and stomping in his stall. Somewhere in the marsh
cress sharpens green in this age of stunted miracles.
Do you know how to get there from here?

Take Good Care of Yourself

On the runway at the Roxy, the drag queen
fans herself gently, but with purpose.
She is an Asian princess, an elaborate wig
jangling like bells on a Shinto temple,
shoulders broad as my father's. With a flick

of her fan she covers her face, a whole
world of authority in that one gesture,
a screen sliding back, all black lacquer
and soprano laugh. The music of this place
echoes with the whip-crack of 2,000

men's libidos, and the one bitter pill
of X-tasy dissolving on my tongue is the perfect
slender measure of the holy ghost,
the vibe crawling my spine exactly,
I assure myself, what I've always wanted.

It is 1992. There is no you yet for me
to address, just simple imperative. *Give
me more. Give.* It is a vision, I'm sure
of this, of what heaven could provide — a sea
of men all muscle, white briefs and pearls,

of kilts cut too short for Catholic girls
or a Highland fling. Don't bother with chat
just yet. I've stripped and checked my jeans
at the door. I need a drink, a light, someplace
a little cooler, just for a minute, to chill.

•

There is no place like the unbearable ribbon
of highway that cuts the Midwest into two unequal
halves, a pale sun glowing like the fire

of one last cigarette. It is the prairie
I'm scared of, barrelling off in all directions,

flat as its inhabitants' *As* and *Os*. I left
Wisconsin's well-tempered rooms
and snowfields white and vacant as a bed
I'd wished I'd never slept in. Winters
I'd stare out the bus window through frost

at an icy template of what the world offered up—
the moon's tin cup of romance and a beauty,
that if held too long to the body,
would melt. If I'd felt anything for you then
it was mere, the flicker of possibility

a quickening of the pulse when I'd imagine
a future, not here but elsewhere, the sky
not yawning out, but hemmed in. In her dress
the drag is all glitter and perfect grace,
pure artifice, beating her fan, injuring

the smoky air, and in the club, I'm still
imagining. The stacks of speakers burn
and throb, whole cities of sound bear down
on us. I'm dancing with men all around me,
moving every muscle I can, the woman's voice

mixed and extended to a gorgeous black note
in a song that only now can I remember—
one familiar flat stretch, one wide-open vista
and a rhythm married to the words standing
for what it was we still had to lose.

Nicole Cuddeback

Son of Medea

Sunlight sang through the thick door's crack.
  And I heard her words,
    yet chose not to wake my brother,

the one content to toss his ball
  eternally. Sad
    is what they called me, wandering

the streets far as I was allowed,
  and then I would go
    one more. Both mother and father,

but more mother, dark of eye, hand.
  My face: hers, they'd say.
    Unworried, forgetful brother,

sleep on. Your death is dead. Mine spreads,
  ravels like spring clouds.
    Mother/father, sky/field, wave/rock,

when will men see how unions are
  impossible, birth
    proof of nothing, not link, bond, life,

marriage bed's harvest. Soft and small
  likeness, but hollow:
    a mere ring around the failure

to incarnate. Imaginings
  can't agree with flesh.
    Too free, they are what I've become:

the stuff of betrayal. Father
   gone. That's when we died.
      How could we have lived? Invalid

promises. What else are children?
   He brought toys, gold lambs:
      blank, unkissing sacks of feigning —

children are lied to — wool and beans
   sewn to suck and suck
      love, painted, bounced, thrown, stained and rent,

teaching what it is to love. Loved
   by two who despised.
      They, fleece borne into the hearth fire.

We, the hot, dislodged bones, the joint
   dissolved. They survive,
      wither, wander. Forever child,

I live in the black nut of death.
   The garden at night,
      a buried thousand-year-old egg.

No unmelting candy ichor
   catches in my throat.
      I am gift gown, burnt crown, distance

of the distance, volume of wrath,
   the girth of passion.
      Severed breath, long evanished blood,

a canyon for a gut, a child
   of divorce, a grave.
      But the grand, shaggy, yellow clouds —

sun-warmed, I waved and waved with arms
   I could not move. Wisps
      of flame-lit cirrus couched our craft.

As if drowsed, I strained to admire
   the jade sun dragons,
      the approving blue of the sky.

I wished to sit up, to reach for
   those splendid serpents!
      Mother's arm cradled my small back.

I could not feel it there. Pretty
   feathery sun ram —
      yes, my death was full of daylight —

dazzling spiral of horns, you came
   late. And finally
      I am alone here. The awful

symbols gone. I am no longer
   damned as their love. Freed
      from belief in what cannot be.

Three Poems by Christopher Bakken

Cliff Lullaby

Though the rest of us remains closed, tired,
we go on hoping for what we know,
the essence of it enclosed in a dream—
we never know more. The massive trees
are wistful in the flash of our passing,
lit like a field of deplorable ice
then plunged back into their own birdlessness.
We follow yellow roadsigns, the dark
curves ahead, echoes of names undressing
the petty sufferings we desire
and acts of premeditated grief,
suspending, on the highway, our belief
in sheer emptiness around the bend,
the symmetry we adore in the end.

Daughter

Some freezing afternoons the fireplace
chirps a tree full of birds up the chimney
and I wander around on the ceiling
in my funeral clothes among the gaudy
mushrooms of lightbulbs until I am struck,
falling with a half-turn, like a stone
into river water, as my daughter would turn
in sleep, sighing to remember my face
hovering still above her dream's fading
mosaics before she forgets it all and returns,
unborn, to an impermanence of her own.

Dido

Tossing lit matches over her shoulder
into a jumbled pile of sap-soaked pine,
the queen, fired by her recognition,
flails at the cliff, cursing the Trojan ships.
As for disappointments she's had her share,
joining now with the horizon's grief,
the wide sea stretching to Italy.
The waves slip out: *Aeneas leaving*.
Wind raises, then lets fall her golden hair—
the swift south wind that raises, too, the fire:
mere props in a divine psychodrama,
the bloody blade and the diriment pyre,
utterly defeated, the lamenting woman's pain,
his will, the sunset, her orange tears in vain.

WILLIAM HOLDEN
GLORIA SWANSON
ERICH VON STROHEIM
Sunset Boulevard
BOULEVARD DU CREPUSCULE
Production
CHARLES BRACKETT
avec
NANCY OLSON
FRED CLARK
LLOYD GOUGH · JACK WEBB
Mise en scène
BILLY WILDER
C'est un film Paramount
DE LAAN DER SCHIMMEN

Billy Wilder

The Art of Screenwriting I

Billy Wilder, one of American cinema's premiere writer-directors, has always maintained that movies are "authored," and has always felt that much of a film's direction ideally should take place in the writing. Like many of the medium's great filmmakers, Wilder began his career as a writer, yet he is unique in the extent of his involvement in the development of the material he has directed. Indeed, he has cowritten all twenty-four of his films.

Samuel "Billy" Wilder was born June 22, 1906 in Vienna, in the Austro-Hungarian Empire. After years as a reporter—highlighted by a single day during which he interviewed Rich-

ard Straus, Arthur Schnitzler, Alfred Adler and Sigmund Freud — Wilder gravitated to Berlin. There he worked as a crime reporter, drama critic and (so he claims) gigolo, before he began to produce scenarios for the booming German film industry, finally writing over two hundred, including the nota- ble precursor of neorealism, People on Sunday *(1929). Wilder, driven by Hitler's ascendancy, left Berlin; his mother, grand- mother and stepfather, who stayed in Vienna, perished later in the Holocaust. He arrived in Hollywood, with only a tempo- rary visa and almost no English, to share a room and a can of soup a day with the actor Peter Lorre. Later he upgraded his quarters to a vestibule near the woman's restroom at the Chateau Marmont on Sunset Boulevard.*

Wilder began his American career at a moment when stu- dios had begun to let some screenwriters direct their own scripts — or, as one film executive said, "Let the lunatics take over the asylum" — a phenomenon that sparked the careers of a number of remarkable writer-directors (Preston Sturges, John Huston, Joseph Mankiewicz). At the time, Ernst Lubitsch, an emigree from the earlier, silent, period, was head of produc- tion at Paramount, where Wilder first flourished, the only time a filmmaker has been in charge of a major studio.

As a contract writer at Paramount, Wilder cowrote a number of films with Charles Brackett, among them Ball of Fire, *di- rected by Howard Hawks,* Bluebeard's Eighth Wife *and* Ni- notchka, *directed by Lubitsch. Although he credits the experi- ence of working with Lubitsch for teaching him much of what he knew about film, Wilder grew increasingly exasperated by the misinterpretation of his work by lesser filmmakers. He resolved to become a director himself.*

Wilder's films show an extraordinary range, from film noir to screwball comedy. Although he claims that as a director he aspired to an unobtrusive style of shooting, all his films, nonetheless are marked by a singular vision — elegant dramati- zation of character through action, distinctive dialogue, and a sour/sweet, or even misanthropic, view of humanity — quali- ties which stem, for the most part, from the writing. Wilder's credits as a director and cowriter include Double Indemnity,

Sunset Boulevard, Sabrina, Ace in the Hole, Stalag 17, The Lost Weekend, Some Like it Hot *and* The Apartment. *Four films directed and cowritten by Wilder have been selected by the National Film Registry of the Library of Congress for recognition and preservation. Only director John Ford, with five, has more.*

The office where he goes every weekday is a simple suite on the second floor of a low-rise office building. On the wall across from his desk, in gilt letters eight inches high is the question HOW WOULD LUBITSCH DO IT? *A day bed, like an analyst's couch, is set against one wall. The opposite wall is decorated with personal photos, including a number of him with some of cinema's other great writer-directors – John Huston, Akira Kurosawa and Federico Fellini. Wilder points out a Polaroid collage depicting a paper-strewn desk – "David Hockney's portrait of my office" – and then, with mercurial amusement, a number of his own creations, a goofy series of plaster casts of a bust of Nefertiti, each painted and decorated with the distinctive features of a number of cultural figures – a Groucho Nefertiti, an Einstein Nefertiti, a Little Tramp Nefertiti. Wilder mentions with some pride the "one-man show" of these figurines that had been presented at a gallery nearby.*

Asked about his noted art collection, Wilder says, "I didn't get rich as a director, I got rich selling art. Thirty-four million dollars to be exact, when it went on sale at Christie's." When asked for tips on collecting he says, "Sure, don't collect. Buy what you like, hold onto it, enjoy it." Later he would offer a number of other get-rich tips: "Back some pornographic films and then, as a hedge to balance your investment should family values rise, buy stock in Disney." Also, "Bet consistently against the Los Angeles Rams."

A restless man, taller than expected, Wilder wears large black-framed glasses, and conducts himself with the air of a benevolent, even exuberant, dictator. When firmly settled in a large chair behind his desk, he says, "Now, you wanted to ask me a question."

INTERVIEWER

You're known as a writer and director for your sharp eye. Could that have anything to do with your sense of yourself as an outsider?

BILLY WILDER

Everything was new to me when I arrived in America, so I looked closely. I had arrived in the country on a six-month visitor's visa, and I had great difficulty obtaining an immigration visa that would allow me to stay on. Also, the status of my English was rather poor. I couldn't rearrange the furniture in my mouth — the tonsils, the curved palate. I've never lost my accent. Ernst Lubitsch, who came in 1922, had a much heavier accent than mine, as did Otto Preminger. Children can get the pronunciation in a few weeks, but English is a tough language because there are so many letters in words that are totally useless. *Though* and *through*. And *tough*!

INTERVIEWER

Coming to the American movie industry at a time when many distinguished German directors were working, did you feel part of a special group?

WILDER

There were some excellent German directors, led by Mr. Lubitsch, but I simply met him and shook his hand; he had no interest in me when I arrived. In fact, he was very reluctant to give jobs to Germans; it was only four years later that he hired me. I had written some pictures in Germany, usually working alone. But when I came here I had to have a collaborator on account of my unsteady English and my knowledge of only about three hundred words. Later I found that if I had a good collaborator it was very pleasant to talk to somebody and not come into an empty office. The head of the writers' department at Paramount had the good idea to pair me with Charles Brackett, a distinguished man from the East, who had gone to Harvard Law School and was about fifteen years older than I. I liked working with him. He was a very good man. He was a member of the Algonquin round table. He had been the movie critic or theater critic on *The New Yorker* in the beginning, the twenties.

One day, Brackett and I were called in to see Lubitsch. He told us he was thinking vaguely about doing an adaptation of a French play about a millionaire—a very straightforward law-abiding guy, who would never have an affair with a woman unless he was married to her. So he married seven times!

That would be Gary Cooper. Claudette Colbert was to be the woman who was in love with him, who'd insist, "I'll marry you, but only to be the final wife." As the meeting was being adjourned, I said, "I have a meet-cute for your story." A meet-cute was a staple of romantic comedies back then, where boy meets girl in a particular way, and sparks fly. "Let's say your millionaire is an American who is very stingy. He goes to a department store in Nice on the French Riviera where he wants to buy a pajama top, but just the top, because he never wears the pants. She has come to the same counter to buy pajamas for her father, who as it happens only wears the pants." That broke the ice, and we were put to work on that picture, which became *Bluebeard's Eighth Wife*.

Lubitsch, of course, would always find a way to make something better. He put another twist on that meeting. Brackett and I were at Lubitsch's house working, when during a break he emerged from the bathroom and said, "What if when Gary Cooper comes in to the store to buy the pajama top, the salesman gets the floor manager, and Cooper again explains he only wants to buy the top. The floor manager says, 'Absolutely not,' but when he sees Cooper will not be stopped, the floor manager says, 'Maybe I could talk to the store manager.' The store manager says, 'That's unheard of!' but ends up calling the department store's owner, whom he disturbs in bed. We see the owner in a close shot go to get the phone. He says, 'It's an outrage!' And as the owner goes back to his bed you see that he doesn't wear pajama pants either."

INTERVIEWER

When you first met Lubitsch over lunch, did you think of that meet-cute on the spot?

WILDER

No, I already had that. I had been hoping to use it for something, and when he told us the story of the picture I saw how it might fit. I had dozens of meet-cutes. Whenever I thought of one I'd put it in a little notebook. Back then they were *de rigeur*, a staple of screwball comedies. Every comedy writer was working on his meet-cutes; but of course we don't do that anymore. Later, I did a version of the meet-cute for *The Apartment*, where Jack Lemmon and Shirley MacLaine, who when they see each other every day have this little routine together. And in *Sabrina*, where she reappears and the younger Larrabee, William Holden, doesn't recognize her — him not recognizing her becomes a kind of meet-cute. When Sydney Pollack was remaking that movie, I told him they should make the Larrabee family's company a bankrupt company, and Sabrina's competition for the younger Larrabee the daughter of a Japanese prospective-buyer.

INTERVIEWER

You have a gold-framed legend on the wall across from your desk. HOW WOULD LUBITSCH DO IT?

WILDER

When I would write a romantic comedy along the Lubitschian line, if I got stopped in the middle of a scene, I'd think, "How would Lubitsch do it?"

INTERVIEWER

Well, how did he do it?

WILDER

One example I can give you of Lubitsch's thinking was in *Ninotchka*, a romantic comedy that Brackett and I wrote for him. Ninotchka was to be a really straight Leninist, a strong and immovable Russian commissar, and we were wondering how we could dramatize that she, without wanting to, was falling in love. How could we do it? Charles Brackett and I wrote twenty pages, thirty pages, forty pages! All very laboriously.

Lubitsch didn't like what we'd done, didn't like it at all. So he called us in to have another conference at his house. We talked about it, but of course we were still, well . . . blocked. In any case, Lubitsch excused himself to go to the bathroom, and when he came back into the living room he announced, "Boys, I've got it."

It's funny, but we noticed that whenever he came up with an idea, I mean a really *great* idea, it was after he came out of the can. I started to suspect that he had a little ghostwriter in the bowl of the toilet there.

"I've got the answer," he said. "It's the hat."

"The hat? No, what do you mean the hat?"

He explained that when Ninotchka arrives in Paris the porter is about to carry her things from the train. She asks, "Why would you want to carry these? Aren't you ashamed?" He says, "It depends on the tip." She says, "You should be ashamed. It's undignified for a man to carry someone else's things. I'll carry them myself."

At the Ritz Hotel, where the three other commissars are staying, there's a long corridor of windows showing various objects. Just windows, no store. She passes one window with three crazy hats. She stops in front of it and says, "That is ludicrous. How can a civilization of people that put things like that on their head survive?" Later she plans to see the sights of Paris — the Louvre, the Alexandre III bridge, the Place de la Concorde. Instead she'll visit the electricity works, the factories, gathering practical things they can put to use back in Moscow. On the way out of the hotel she passes that window again with the three crazy hats.

Now the story starts to develop between Ninotchka, or Garbo, and Melvyn Douglas, all sorts of little things that add up, but we haven't seen the change yet. She opens the window of her hotel room overlooking the Place Vendôme. It's beautiful, and she smiles. The three commissars come to her room. They're finally prepared to get down to work. But she says, "No, no, no, it's too beautiful to work. We have the rules, but they have the weather. Why don't you go to the races. It's Sunday. It's beautiful in Longchamps," and she gives them money to gamble.

As they leave for the track at Longchamps, she locks the door to the suite, then the door to the room. She goes back into the bedroom, opens a drawer, and out of the drawer she takes the craziest of the hats! She picks it up, puts it on, looks at herself in the mirror. That's it. Not a word. Nothing. But she has fallen into the trap of capitalism, and we know where we're going from there . . . all from a half page of description and one line of dialogue. "Beautiful weather. Why don't you go have yourselves a wonderful day?"

INTERVIEWER

He returned from the bathroom with all this?

WILDER

Yes, and it was like that whenever we were stuck. I guess now I feel he didn't go often enough.

INTERVIEWER

You've indicated where Lubitsch got his ideas. Where do you get yours?

WILDER

I don't know. I just get them. Some of them in the toilet, I'm afraid. I have a black book here with all sorts of entries. A little bit of dialogue I've overheard. An idea for a character. A bit of background. Some boy-meets-girl scenarios.

While I was working with Mr. Lemmon for the first time on *Some Like It Hot*, I thought to myself, "This guy's got a little bit of genius. I would love to make another picture with him, but I don't have a story." So I looked in my little black book and I came across a note about David Lean's movie *Brief Encounter*, that story about a married woman who lives in the country, comes to London and meets a man. They have an affair in his friend's apartment. What I had written was, "What about the friend who has to crawl back into that warm bed?"

I had made that note ten years earlier, I couldn't touch it because of censorship, but suddenly there it was — *The Apartment* — all suggested by this note and by the qualities of an actor with whom I wanted to make my next picture. It was ideal for Lemmon, the combination of sweet and sour. I liked it when someone called that picture a dirty fairy tale.

INTERVIEWER

Sunset Boulevard?

WILDER

For a long time I wanted to do a comedy about Hollywood. God forgive me, I wanted to have Mae West and Marlon Brando. Look what became of that idea! Instead it became a tragedy of a silent-picture actress, still rich, but fallen down into the abyss after talkies. "I am big. It's the pictures that got small." I had that line early on. Someplace else I had the idea for a writer who is down on his luck. It didn't quite fall into place until we got Gloria Swanson.

We had gone to Pola Negri first. We called her on the phone, and there was too much Polish accent. You see why some of these people didn't make the transition to sound. We went to Pickfair and visited Mary Pickford. Brackett began to tell her the story, because he was the more serious one. I stopped him. "No, don't do it." I waved him off. She was going to be insulted if we told her she was to play a woman who begins a love affair with a man half her age. I said to her, "We're very sorry, but it's no use. The story gets very vulgar."

Gloria Swanson had been a big star, in command of an entire studio. She worked with DeMille. Once she was dressed, her hair done to perfection, they placed her on a sedan and two strong men would carry her onto the set so no curl would be displaced. But later she did a couple of sound pictures that were terrible. When I gave her the script, she said, "I *must* do this," and she turned out to be an absolute angel.

I used stars wherever I could in *Sunset Boulevard.* I used Cecil B. DeMille to play the big important studio director. I used Erich von Stroheim to play the director who directed the first pictures with Swanson, which he in fact did. I thought, "Now, if there is a bridge game at the house of a silent star, and if I am to show that our hero, the writer, has been degraded to being the butler who cleans ashtrays, who would be there?" I got Harry B. Warner, who played Jesus in DeMille's biblical pictures, Anna Q. Nilsson and Buster Keaton, who was an excellent bridge player, a tournament player. The picture industry was only fifty or sixty years old, so some of the original people were still around. Because old Hollywood was dead, these people weren't exactly busy. They had the time, got some money, a little recognition. They were delighted to do it.

INTERVIEWER

Did you ever feel disappointed with your results, that the picture you had imagined or even written hadn't turned out?

WILDER

Sure, I've made blunders, for God's sake. Sometimes you lay an egg, and people will say, "It was too early. Audiences weren't ready for it." Bullshit. If it's good, it's good. If it's bad, it's bad.

The tragedy of the picture maker, as opposed to the playwright, is that for the playwright the play debuts in Bedford, Massachusetts, and then you take it to Pittsburgh. If it stinks you bury it. If you examine the credits of Moss Hart or George Kaufman, no one ever brings up the play that bombed in the provinces and was buried after four shows.

With a picture that doesn't work, no matter how stupid

and how bad, they're still going to try to squeeze every single penny out of it. You go home one night and turn on the TV and suddenly, there on television, staring back at you, on prime time, that lousy picture, that *thing*, is back! We don't bury our dead; we keep them around smelling badly.

INTERVIEWER

Is there one you have in mind?

WILDER

Don't make me. I may lose my breakfast.

Now, I do have to admit I was disappointed by the lack of success of some pictures I thought were good, such as *Ace in the Hole*. I liked the movie very much but it did not generate any "must-see" mood in audiences.

On the other hand, sometimes you'll have a rough time, and the film will turn out all right. On *Sabrina* I had a very rough time with Humphrey Bogart. It was the first time he'd worked with Paramount. Every evening after shooting, people would have a drink in my office, and a couple of times I forgot to invite him. He was very angry and never forgave me.

Sometimes when you finish a picture you just don't know whether it's good or bad. When Frank Capra was shooting Claudette Colbert in *It Happened One Night*, after the last shot she said, "Will that be all Mr. Capra?"

"We're all done."

"All right. Now why don't you go and fuck yourself." She thought the picture was shit, but she won the Academy Award for it.

So you're never quite sure how your work will be received or the course your career will take. We knew we'd gotten a strong reaction at the first big preview of *Sunset Boulevard*. After the screening, Barbara Stanwyck went up and kissed the hem of Gloria Swanson's robe, or dress, or whatever she was wearing that night. Gloria had given such an incredible performance. Then in the big Paramount screening room, Louis B. Mayer said loudly, "We need to kick Wilder out of America if he's going to bite the hand that feeds him." He was with his contingent from MGM, the king then, but in front of all his department heads, I told him just what he could do. I walked out just as the reception was starting.

Although the movie was a great success, it was about Hollywood, exaggerated and dramatized, and it really hit a nerve. So on the way down the steps I had to pass all those people from MGM, the class studio . . . all those people who thought this picture would soil the taste of Hollywood.

After *Sunset Boulevard*, Brackett and I parted friends. Twelve years together, but the split had been coming. It's like a box of matches: you pick up the match and strike it against the box, and there's always fire, but then one day there is just one small corner of that abrasive paper left for you to strike the match on. It was not there anymore. The match wasn't striking. One of us said, "Look, whatever I have to give and whatever you have to offer, it's just not enough. We can end on the good note of *Sunset Boulevard*." A picture that was revolutionary for its day.

INTERVIEWER

How do collaborators work together?

WILDER

Brackett and I used to share two offices together with a secretary in between. When we were writing he always laid down on the couch in my office while I would walk around with a stick in my hand.

INTERVIEWER

Why the stick?

WILDER

I don't know. I just needed something to keep my hands busy and a pencil wasn't long enough. He always had the yellow legal tablet, and he wrote in longhand, then we'd hand it to the secretary. Brackett and I would discuss everything, the picture as a whole, the curtain situations — first act, second act and then the end of the picture — and the curtain lines. Then we would break it down and go to a specific scene and discuss the mood and so forth, then we'd figure out what bit of the story we'd tell in those ten pages of the scene.

INTERVIEWER

Was it the same working with I.A.L. Diamond?

WILDER

Pretty much the same as with Brackett. Discuss the story, break it down into scenes, and then I would dictate and he would type. Or he would sit there thinking, and I would write on a yellow tablet and show it to him.

"How's this?" I'd say.

"No. No good," he'd say. Never in an insistent way, however.

Or he might suggest something to me, and I'd shake my head. He'd just take it, tear it up and put it in the wastebasket, and we'd never come back to it.

We had a great deal of trust in each other. But sometimes with writing you just can't tell, especially if you're writing under pressure. Diamond and I were writing the final scene of *Some Like It Hot* the week before we shot it. We'd come to the situation where Lemmon tries to convince Joe B. Brown that he cannot marry him.

"Why?" Brown says.

"Because I smoke!"

"That's all right as far as I'm concerned."

Finally Lemmon rips his wig off and yells at him, "I'm a boy! Because I'm a boy!"

Diamond and I were in our room working together, waiting for the next line — Joe B. Brown's response, the final line, the curtain line of the film — to come to us. Then I heard Diamond say, "Nobody's perfect." I thought about it and I said, "Well, let's put in 'Nobody's perfect' for now. But only for the time being. We have a whole week to think about it." We thought

about it all week. Neither of us could come up with anything
better, so we shot that line, still not entirely satisfied. When
we screened the movie, that line got one of the biggest laughs
I've ever heard in the theater. But we just hadn't trusted it
when we wrote it; we just didn't see it. "Nobody's perfect."
The line had come too easily, just popped out.

INTERVIEWER

I understand your collaboration with Raymond Chandler
was more difficult?

WILDER

Yes. Chandler had never been inside a studio. He was writing for one of the hard-boiled serial magazines, *The Black
Mask* — the original pulp fiction — and he'd been stringing ten-
nis rackets to make ends meet. Just before then, James M.
Cain had written *The Postman Always Rings Twice*, and then
a similar story, *Double Indemnity*, which was serialized in
three or four installments in the late *Liberty* magazine.

Paramount bought *Double Indemnity*, and I was eager to
work with Cain, but he was tied up working on a picture at
Fox called *Western Union*. A producer-friend brought me
some Chandler stories from *The Black Mask*. You could see
the man had a wonderful eye. I remember two lines from
those stories especially: "Nothing is emptier than an empty
swimming pool." The other is when Marlowe goes to Pasadena
in the middle of the summer and drops in on a very old man
who is sitting in a greenhouse covered in three blankets. He
says, "Out of his ears grew hair long enough to catch a moth."
A great eye . . . but then you don't know if that will work
in pictures because the details in writing have to be photo-
graphable.

I said to Joe Sistrom, "Let's give him a try." Chandler came
into the studio, and we gave him the Cain story *Double Indemnity* to read. He came back the next day — "I read that story.
It's absolute shit!" He hated Cain because of Cain's big success
with *The Postman Always Rings Twice*.

He said, "Well, I'll do it anyway. Give me a screenplay so I can familiarize myself with the format. This is Friday. Do you want it a week from Monday?"

"Holy shit," we said. We usually took five to six months on a script.

"Don't worry," he said. He had no idea that I was not only the director but was supposed to write it with him.

He came back in ten days with eighty pages of absolute bullshit. He had some good phrases of dialogue, but they must have given him a script written by someone who wanted to be a director. He'd put in directions for fade-ins, dissolves, all kinds of camera moves to show he'd grasped the technique.

I sat him down and explained we'd have to work together. We always met at nine o'clock, and would quit at about four-thirty. I had to explain a lot to him as we went along, but he was very helpful to me. What we were doing together had real electricity. He was a very, very good writer—but not of scripts.

One morning, I'm sitting there in the office, ten o'clock and no Chandler. Eleven o'clock. At eleven-thirty, I called Joe Sistrom, the producer of *Double Indemnity*, and asked, "What happened to Chandler?"

"I was going to call you. I just got a letter from him in which he resigns."

Apparently he had resigned because, while we were sitting in the office with the sun shining through, I had asked him to close the curtains and I had not said "please." He accused me of having as many as three martinis at lunch. Furthermore, he wrote that he found it "very disconcerting that Mr. Wilder gets two, three, sometimes even four calls from obviously young girls."

Naturally. I would take a phone call, three or four minutes, to say, "Let's meet at that restaurant there" or "Let's go for a drink here." He was about twenty years older than I was, and his wife was older than him, elderly. And I was on the phone with *girls*! Sex was rampant then, but I was just looking out for myself. Later, in a biography he said all sorts of nasty things about me—that I was a Nazi, that I was uncooperative and rude, and God knows what. Maybe the antagonism even helped. He was a peculiar guy, but I was very glad to have worked with him.

INTERVIEWER

Why have so many novelists and playwrights from the East, people like F. Scott Fitzgerald and Dorothy Parker, had such a terrible time out here?

WILDER

Well, because they were hired for very big amounts of money. I remember those days in New York when one writer would say to the other, "I'm broke. I'm going to go to Hollywood and steal another fifty thousand." Moreover, they didn't know what movie writing entailed. You have to know the rules before you break them, and they simply didn't school themselves. I'm not just talking about essayists or newspapermen; it was even the novelists. None of them took it seriously, and when they would be confronted by their superior, the producer or the director, who had a louder voice and the weight of the studio behind him, they were not particularly interested in taking advice. Their idea was, "Well, crap, everybody in America has got a screenplay inside them — the policeman around the corner here, the waiter in Denver. *Everybody*. And his *sister*! I've seen ten movies. Now, if they would only let me do it my way . . ." But it's not that easy. To begin to make even a mediocre film you have to learn the rules. You have to know about timing, about creating characters, a little about camera position, just enough to know if what you're suggesting is possible. They pooh-poohed it.

I remember Fitzgerald when he was working at Paramount and I was there working with Brackett. Brackett, who was from the East, had written novels and plays, and had been at Paramount for years. Brackett and I used to take breaks and go to a little coffee joint across the street from the studio. "Oblath's!" we used to say. "The only place in the world you can get a greasy Tom Collins." Whenever we saw Scott Fitzgerald there, we'd talk with him, but he never once asked us anything about writing screenplays.

Pictures are something like plays. They share an architecture and a spirit. A good picture writer's a kind of poet, but a poet who plans his structure like a craftsman and is able to tell what's wrong with the third act. What a veteran screenwriter produces might not be good, but it would be technically correct; if he has a problem in the third act he certainly knows to look for the seed of the problem in the first act. Scott just didn't seem particularly interested in any of these matters.

INTERVIEWER

Faulkner seemed to have his difficulties too.

WILDER

I heard he was hired by MGM, was at the studio for three months, quit and went back home; MGM never figured it out and they kept sending the checks down to Mississippi. A friend of mine was hired by MGM to do a script and he inherited the office where Faulkner had been working. In the desk he found a yellow legal pad with three words on it: "Boy. Girl. Policeman." But Faulkner did some work.

At some point he worked with Howard Hawks on *To Have and Have Not*, and he cowrote *The Land of the Pharaohs*. On that movie they went way over schedule with production and far past their estimated costs. On screen, there were thousands of slaves dragging enormous stones to build the pyramids. It was like an ant heap. When they finally finished the film and screened it for Jack Warner, Warner said to Hawks, "Well, Howard, if all the people who are in the picture come to see it, we may break even."

But there were other writers out here who were clever and good and made a little fortune. The playwrights Ben Hecht and Charles MacArthur, for example. Hecht truly endeared himself to the people he worked with. A producer or director would be in a jam . . . the set built, the leads hired, the shooting begun, only to admit to themselves finally that the script they had was unusable.

They would bring out Hecht, and he would lie in bed at
Charles Lederer's house and on a yellow tablet produce a pile
of sheets, a screenplay ready to go. They'd take that night's
pages from Hecht's hands, forward them to Mr. Selznick,
who'd fiddle with them, have the pages mimeographed and
put in the actor's hands by morning. It was a crazy way to
work, but Hecht took the work very seriously, though not as
seriously as he would a play of his. They call that sort of thing
script doctoring. If Hecht had wanted, he could have had
credit on a hundred more pictures.

INTERVIEWER

Does the script you've written change as you direct it?

WILDER

As someone who directed scripts that I myself had cowritten, what I demanded from actors was very simple: learn
your lines.

That reminds me. George Bernard Shaw was directing a
production of his play *Pygmalion*, with a very well-known
illustrious actor, Sir Something. The fellow came to rehearsal,
a little bit drunk, and he began to invent a little. Shaw listened
for a while and then yelled, "Stop! For Christ's sake, why the
hell didn't you learn the script?"

Sir Something said, "What on earth are you talking about?
I know my lines."

Shaw screamed back at him, "Yes, you know *your* lines,
but you don't know *my* lines."

On a picture, I would ask the actors to know their lines.
Sometimes they would study the part at night and might ask
me to come by to discuss things. In the morning, we would
sit in chairs around a long table off to the side and read the
day's scene once more. It was wonderful to work with some
actors. Jack Lemmon. If we were to start at nine, he'd be there
at 8:15 with a mug of coffee and his pages from the night
before. He'd say, "Last night I was running lines with Feli-
cia" — his wife — "and had this wonderful idea. What do you

"The Paris Review remains the single most important little magazine this country has produced."

—T. Coraghessan Boyle

THE

PARIS

REVIEW

Enclosed is my check for:

☐ $34 for 1 year (4 issues)

(All payment must be in U.S. funds. Postal surcharge of $8 per 4 issues outside USA)

☐ Send me information on becoming a *Paris Review* Associate.

Bill this to my Visa/MasterCard:

Sender's full name and address needed for processing credit cards.

_____

Card number   Exp. date

☐ New subscription   ☐ Renewal subscription

☐ New address

Name _____

Address _____

City _____ State _____ Zip code _____

Please send gift subscription to:

Name _____

Address _____

City _____ State _____ Zip code _____

Gift announcement signature _____

call (718)539-7085

Please send me the following:

☐ The Paris Review T-Shirt ($15.00)

Color _____ Size _____ Quantity _____

☐ The following back issues: Nos. _____

See listing at back of book for availability.

Name _____

Address _____

City _____ State _____ Zip code _____

☐ Enclosed is my check for $ _____

☐ Bill this to my Visa/MasterCard:

_____

Card number   Exp. date

BUSINESS REPLY MAIL

FIRST CLASS   PERMIT NO. 3119   FLUSHING, N.Y.

POSTAGE WILL BE PAID BY ADDRESSEE

THE PARIS REVIEW
45-39 171 Place
FLUSHING NY   11358-9892

No postage
stamp necessary
if mailed in the
United States

BUSINESS REPLY MAIL

FIRST CLASS   PERMIT NO. 3119   FLUSHING, N.Y.

POSTAGE WILL BE PAID BY ADDRESSEE

THE PARIS REVIEW
45-39 171 Place
FLUSHING NY   11358-9892

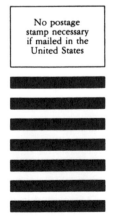

think here?" And he'd go on. It might be wonderful and we'd
use it, or I might just look at him, and then he'd say, "Well,
I don't like it either." He worked hard and had many ideas
but he never was interfering.

Sometimes I'd have an actor so stubborn that I'd say, "All
right, let's do it two ways." We'd do it my way, and I'd say
to my assistant, "Print that." Then to the actor, "All right,
now your way." We'd do it his way with no celluloid in the
camera.

INTERVIEWER

What was it like working as a writer for a studio?

WILDER

When I was a writer at Paramount, the studio had a swarm
of writers under contract — 104! They worked in the Writers
Building, the Writers Annex and the Writers Annex Annex.
All of us were writing! We were not getting big salaries but
we were writing. It was fun. We made a little money. Some,
like Ben Hecht, made a lot of money. All the writers were
required to hand in eleven pages every Thursday. Why on
Thursday? Who knows? Why eleven pages? Who knows? Over
a thousand pages a week were being written.

It was all very tightly controlled. We even worked on Saturdays from nine until noon, knocking off half a day so we could
watch USC or UCLA play football in the Coliseum. When
the unions negotiated the work week back to five days, the
executives ran around screaming the studio was going to go
broke.

There was one guy at the studio whom all the writers turned
in their work to — a Yale man, who was at *Life* when his classmates Henry Luce and Briton Haddon founded the magazine.
Everyone at the start of the magazine had the option of getting
something like seventy-five dollars a week or part of his salary
in *Time* stock. Some buildings at Yale were built by people
who went for the stock. Our guy at Paramount used to say
proudly, "I went for the cash."

INTERVIEWER
What happened to the thousand-plus pages a week that were being generated?

WILDER
Most of the writing just gathered dust. There were five or six producers, each specializing in different kinds of pictures. They would read the writing over the weekend and make comments.

INTERVIEWER
What were the producers' comments like?

WILDER
I was talking once with a writer who had worked at Columbia who showed me a script that had just been read by Samuel Briskin, one of the big men at that studio. I looked at the script. On every page, there was at the bottom just one word: "Improve!"

INTERVIEWER
Like the *New Yorker* editor Harold Ross's imperative, "Make better."

WILDER
That would be one word too many for these producers. Just "Improve."

INTERVIEWER
What about the "Scheherezades" one hears about?

WILDER
They were the guys who would tell producers stories, or the plots of screenplays and books. There was one guy who never wrote a word but who came up with ideas. One of them was, "San Francisco. 1906 earthquake. Nelson Eddy. Jeanette Mc-Donald."

"Great! Terrific!" Cheers from the producers. A film came out of that sentence.

Do you know how Nelson Eddy ended up with his name? He was Eddie Nelson. He just reversed it. Don't laugh! Eddie Nelson is nothing. Nelson Eddy was a star.

The studio era was of course very different from today. There were many different fiefdoms scattered around town, each producing its own sort of picture. The Paramount people would not converse with the MGM people; wouldn't even see each other. The MGM people especially would not consort for dinner or even lunch with the people from Fox.

One night before I was to begin *One, Two, Three* I had dinner at the home of Mr. and Mrs. William Goetz, who always had wonderful food. I was seated next to Mrs. Edie Goetz, Louis Mayer's younger daughter, and she asked what sort of picture I was going to make. I told her it was set in Berlin and we'd be shooting in Germany.

"Who plays the lead?"

"Jimmy Cagney." As it happens, it was his last picture except for that cameo in *Ragtime*.

She said, "Who?"

"Jimmy Cagney. You know, the little gangster who for years was in all those Warner Brothers . . ."

"Oh! Daddy didn't allow us to watch Warner Brothers pictures." She had no idea who he was.

Back then, each studio had a certain look. You could walk in in the middle of a picture and tell what studio it was. Warner Brothers were mostly gangster movies. For a while Universal did a lot of horror pictures. MGM you knew because everything was white. Mr. Cedric Gibbons, the head of production design, wanted everything white silk no matter where it was set. If MGM had produced Mr. Scorsese's *Mean Streets*, Cedric Gibbons would have designed all of Little Italy in white.

INTERVIEWER

Film really is considered a director's medium, isn't it?

WILDER

Film's thought of as a director's medium because the director creates the end product that appears on the screen. It's that stupid auteur theory again, that the director is the author of the film. But what does the director shoot — the telephone book? Writers became much more important when sound came in, but they've had to put up a valiant fight to get the credit they deserve.

Recently, the Writers' Guild has negotiated with the studios to move the writer's credit to a place just before the director's, a more prominent position, bumping aside the producers. The producers are screaming! You look at an ad in the papers and they are littered with the names of producers. "A So-and-So and So-and-So Production, Produced by Another Four Names! Executive Producer Somebody Else." Things are slowly changing. But even so the position of a writer working with a studio is not secure, certainly nothing like a writer working in the theater in New York. There a playwright sits in his seat in the empty parquet during rehearsals, right alongside the director, and together they try to make the production flow. If there is a problem, they have a little talk. The director says to the writer, "Is it all right if the guy who says 'Good morning. How are you?' instead enters without saying anything?" And the playwright says, "No! 'Good morning. How are you?' stays." And it stays.

Nobody consults the movie writer. In production, they just go wildly ahead. If the star has another picture coming up, and they need to finish the picture by Monday, they'll just tear out ten pages. To make it work somehow, they add a few stupid lines.

In the studio era, screenwriters were always on the losing end in battles with the director or the studio. Just to show you the impotence of the screenwriter then, I'll tell you a story from before I became a director. Brackett and I were writing a picture called *Hold Back the Dawn*. Back then, no writer was allowed on the set. If the actors and the director weren't interpreting the script correctly, if they didn't have the accent on the right word when they were delivering a gag, if they

didn't know where the humor was, a writer might very well
pipe up. A director would feel that the writer was creating a
disruption.

For *Hold Back the Dawn*, we had written a story about a
man trying to immigrate into the U.S. without the proper
papers. Charles Boyer, who played the lead, is at rope's end,
destitute, stranded in a filthy hotel — the Esperanza — across
the border, near Mexicali or Calexico. He is lying in this lousy
bed, holding a walking stick, when he sees a cockroach walk
up the wall and onto a mirror hanging on the wall. Boyer
sticks the end of the walking stick in front of the cockroach
and says, "Wait a minute, you. Where are you going? Where
are your papers? You haven't got them? Then you can't enter."
The cockroach tries to walk around the stick, and the Boyer
character keeps stopping it.

One day Brackett and I were having lunch across the street
from Paramount. We were in the middle of writing the third
act of the picture. As we left our table to walk out, we saw
Boyer, the star, seated at a table, his little French lunch spread
out before him, his napkin tucked in just so, a bottle of red
wine open on the table. We stopped by and said, "Charles,
how are you?"

"Oh, fine. Thank you."

Although we were still working on the script, Mitchell Leisen
had already begun to direct the production. I said, "And what
are you shooting today, Charles?"

"We're shooting this scene where I'm in bed and . . ."

"Oh! The scene with the cockroach! That's a wonderful
scene."

"Yes, well, we didn't use the cockroach."

"Didn't use the cockroach? Oh, Charles, why not?"

"Because the scene is idiotic. I have told Mr. Leisen so, and
he agreed with me. How do you suppose a man can talk to
some *thing* that cannot answer you?" Then Boyer looked out
the window. That was all. End of discussion. As we walked
back to the studio to continue to write the third act, I said
to Brackett, "That son of a bitch. If he doesn't talk to the

cockroach, he doesn't talk to *anybody!*" We gave him as few
lines as possible . . . wrote him right out of the third act.

INTERVIEWER

Was that one of the reasons you became a director, the
difficulty of protecting the writing?

WILDER

That was certainly one of the reasons. I don't come from
the theater or any dramatic school, like the Strasberg school,
and I didn't particularly have ambitions to be a director, to
be a despot of the soundstage. I just wanted to protect the
script. It's not that I had a vision or theory I wanted to express
as a director; I had no signature or style, except for what I
learned from when I was working with Lubitsch and from
analyzing his pictures — to do things as elegantly and as simply
as possible.

INTERVIEWER

If you'd always had more respectful directors, such as Lubitsch, would you have become a director?

WILDER

Absolutely not. Lubitsch would have directed my scripts
considerably better and more clearly than I. Lubitsch or Ford
or Cukor. They were very good directors, but one wasn't always
assured of working with directors like that.

INTERVIEWER

I see Federico Fellini on your wall of photos.

WILDER

He also was a writer who became a director. I like *La Strada*,
the first one with his wife, a lot. And I loved *La Dolce Vita*.
   Up above that picture is a photo of myself, Mr. Akira Kurosawa and Mr. John Huston. Like Mr. Fellini and me, they too
were writers who became directors. That picture was taken at

the presentation of the Academy Award for best picture some years back.

The plan for the presentation was for three writer-directors to hand out the award—John Huston, Akira Kurosawa and myself. Huston was in a wheelchair and on oxygen for his emphysema. He had terrible breathing problems. But we were going to make him get up to join us on stage. They had the presentation carefully orchestrated so they could have Huston at the podium first, and then he would have forty-five seconds before he would have to get back to his wheelchair and put the oxygen mask on.

Jane Fonda arrived with the envelope and handed it to Mr. Huston. Huston was to open the envelope and give it to Kurosawa. Kurosawa was to fish the piece of paper with the name of the winner out of the envelope and hand it to me, then I was to read the winner's name. Kurosawa was not very agile, it turned out, and when he reached his fingers into the envelope, he fumbled and couldn't grab hold of the piece of paper with the winner's name on it. All the while I was sweating it out; three hundred million people around the world were watching and waiting. Mr. Huston only had about ten seconds before he'd need more oxygen.

While Mr. Kurosawa was fumbling with the piece of paper, I almost said something that would have finished me. I almost said to him, "Pearl Harbor you could find!" Fortunately, he produced the slip of paper, and I didn't say it. I read the name of the winner aloud. I forget now which picture won — *Gandhi* or *Out of Africa*. Mr. Huston moved immediately toward the wings, and backstage to the oxygen.

Mr. Huston made a wonderful picture that year, *Prizzi's Honor*, that was also up for the Best Picture Award. If he had won, we would have had to give him more oxygen to recover before he could come back and accept. I voted for *Prizzi's Honor*. I voted for Mr. Huston.

—James Linville

Lorna Simpson

Nine Props

An Interview and Art Portfolio

Amid the coffeehouse clatter of cups, saucers and water glasses, Lorna Simpson recently discussed her own resonant vessels created for the photographic series Nine Props. *Simpson is known for her sparse images that suggestively play photographs off text to explore issues of identity and the instant assumptions formed through visual cues. In* Nine Props, *Simpson uses the photographs of James Van Der Zee (1886-1983) as a starting point. Working largely out of his Harlem photography studio, Van Der Zee spent more than fifty years chronicling the lives around him in stylized portraits of sitters ranging from young housewives to luminaries of the Harlem Renaissance. In what follows Simpson shares her thoughts on the process of making* Nine Props.

INTERVIEWER

Tell me about the genesis of *Nine Props*.

LORNA SIMPSON

Well, I was invited to an artist-in-residency program at Pilchuck, a glassblowing school in Seattle, where I had the opportunity to work with glassblowers; and I came up with the idea of having the glassblowers recreate shapes of vases that appear in James Van Der Zee's photographs, which I would then accompany with text. So first the piece evolved as actual vases accompanied by texts, and then I flopped it and remade the piece as a photographic still life that was a kind of homage to various Van Der Zee photographs.

INTERVIEWER

Why did you decide to work from a two-dimensional image, recreate it three-dimensionally and then flatten it back to a two-dimensional image?

SIMPSON

Because I was slow! Because the idea didn't come to me the first time around! After being at Pilchuck, I had the work shipped to my studio, and as I sat there arranging the objects and looking at them in terms of the text, I discovered that to involve myself as a photographer with this work would be to recast it as a photographic still life.

INTERVIEWER

Do you continually move back and forth between installation work and photography?

SIMPSON

Yes. I guess I do go back and forth between wanting to use objects and thinking about a space and its volume, and then being very, very flat and two-dimensional. When I work one to death, I go back to the other. So it is kind of back and forth movement.

INTERVIEWER

Did you arrive at Pilchuck with your mind set on working with Van Der Zee's images?

SIMPSON

Well, I'm really familiar with his work and have always admired his portraits, but quite frankly the idea developed while sitting among all of these people pouring things with glass into big molds or making these gigantic vases — so it was then that I was really thinking about how I could connect my photographic interests to working with these glass artists.

INTERVIEWER

Van Der Zee is known for his idealized portraits and his generous retouching of images. Are you commenting on his conception of the ideal?

SIMPSON

In a sense, by commissioning or having someone fabricate something exactly from an image, that kind of exactness is still in play. I try to bring out Van Der Zee's obsession with details and how they portray class and wealth and the character of an individual.

INTERVIEWER

These photographs have a Steichenesque feel to them.

SIMPSON

Yes, just a very traditional still life, a nice line and shadow, kind of playing on a traditional photographic genre. The work I just completed plays with landscape, so I'm using these different conventions in photography but doing a little twist on them.

I'm highly interested in seducing the audience, even in works I've done that might have spoken about the politics of sex and race. In the way that the photograph is taken, there is a kind of beauty and gorgeousness to the figures, so I am touched by that, and that's the way I suck the others in.

INTERVIEWER

Are you trying to engage a particular moment in art history?

SIMPSON

To me, *Nine Props* has historical content. For instance, many people within the art world don't even know who James Van Der Zee is. Not that these works position his work in a way that allows a lot of information to be gleaned, but on a certain level it's engaging a part of art history that does not seem of interest to the contemporary art world. The academy's canon has nothing to do with James Van Der Zee.

INTERVIEWER

How do you think of your work in relation to the documentary tradition?

SIMPSON

My work is and always has been about deleting information.

INTERVIEWER

It's exactly what is *not* going on in the image.

SIMPSON

Right.

INTERVIEWER

So is this style a direct reaction to the documentary photography that you were doing early on in your career?

SIMPSON

Yes, I wanted to dismantle or kind of play with all of those assumptions about modes of interpretation and the way that you decipher an image, and read it — all those sociological and physiological cues about how you read an image in terms of emotion or what's going on.

INTERVIEWER

I've noticed, in this series and in past works, that you seem to have a fixation with vessels, and particularly with water and water jugs.

SIMPSON

And a vast collection of glassware. I don't want to go too deep! No, really I collect them, and they seem to find their way into the work. There's something very anthropomorphic about the shapes of vases, some certain sensuality about them, which I guess the ones that I've chosen for my work really show. Especially in the case of the Van Der Zee, it's almost like associating the vase with the person or the situation that's described.

INTERVIEWER

There is that odd vase in *Beau of the Ball*, a very phallic shape . . .

SIMPSON

But that was in the picture!

INTERVIEWER

Did you deviate from the original shapes of the props at all? Did you emphasize the phallic nature of that vase?

SIMPSON

No, because I would make a drawing and hand it to someone and say, "Make that," and that's what they came up with. And that's just the nature of vases, which is why it was very nice to play off them because they do have this human sense. And in referring to the photographs I would refer back to the vase, and then it kind of takes on the attributes of who is described. Although there literally isn't any connection made by James Van Der Zee, and I'm not really making that connection, there's just that presence that those objects have in the world. At some point it's nice to have a description of something that is absent, yet is still present in the world somewhere.

— Maria Christina Villaseñor

Nine Props

Lorna Simpson

Beau of the Ball,
1926
James VanDerZee
S/he is dressed in a skirt and small jacket with bell sleeves. The neck, sleeves
and bottom of the skirt is trimmed in fur, and her/his silk stocking legs and with and satin shoes are
crossed at the ankle. She/he is seated and rests her/his left elbow on the table, and her/his right hand
on her/his hip. A painted backdrop of a window and a landscape appears behind her/him. A vase
with flowers and a phone are on the table.

Dinner Party with boxer Harry Wills,
1926
James VanDerZee
Harry Wills aka "The Black Panther," boxer, businessman- sits with
seven other men and women, mostly women with champagne glasses raised as a
woman on his left makes a toast in his honor. There are three bottles of champagne,
a crystal decanter, a bottle of port, an arrangement of flowers and fruit, and before
each guest an untouched china place setting.

Woman with a goldfish bowl,
1923
James Van Der Zee
A woman wearing pearls stands behind a bouquet of flowers and goldfish bowl.
Her right hand rests on the rim of the bowl, as she gazes at a painted
image of a butterfly in flight.

Benny Andrews,
1976
James VanDerZee
Artist (b.1930). Wearing a trench coat, he is seated with
his right leg crossed and holds it with his right hand. To his
left is a small table with a circular top and a vase with
Chrysanthemums. A wooden folding screen stands behind him.

Max Robinson,
1981
James VanDerZee
News correspondent of ABC World News Tonight
(1939-1988). He is seated with his legs and hands crossed
wearing a tuxedo and white bow tie with medals. To his left is a
table and a vase with flowers. Behind
him is a painted back drop of a wall and window.

A man in his bedroom,
1931
James VanDerZee

A man stands on the far left of the room with a pipe in his mouth. He is dressed in a smoking jacket with a shirt and tie, with his right elbow resting on a dresser and a ring on his finger. The bed has a satin cover with a small stuffed animal positioned at the center of the pillows. Behind the bed hangs a rug, off of the backboard a fringed lamp, and above hangs an chandelier. In front of a curtained window a standing lamp shines on the portrait of a full figured woman. On the right side of the room is a dresser with an ashtray, small boxes, a candle and vase.

Reclining nude,
date unknown
James Van DerZee
A smiling woman rests her face on her right arm as her left arm
crosses her breasts. Fabric is draped over the edge of the couch,
around her hips and continues to the floor. Her legs are exposed,
knees bent, and her left foot is tucked under her right. Flowers
are strewn over the edge of the couch and on to the floor. An
upside down vase sits on the floor, as if its' position and the
arrangement of flowers had been disturbed.

Tea time at Madame C.J. Walker's Beauty Salon,
1929
James VanDerZee
Sarah Breedlove Walker (1864-1919) developed a hair care product that
was very successful, and set up the Walker Manufacturing Company in Indianapolis as well as the
Walker College of Hair Culture in Harlem. Seventeen elegantly dressed women appear seated and
standing, seven are holding tea cups.

Just Before the Battle,
1920's
James VanDerZee

Calendar image for the Elks Convention taken in an apartment on 135th street. A woman a wearing a Kimono is seated in a rocking chair with a cigarette in her left hand and a rolling pin in her right, with legs crossed. A fringed lamp positioned behind her lights her face. Hand painted smoke, trails from the tip of the cigarette. A deer's head is mounted on the wall with two framed images of figures bathing, a floral design and a mirror at the center of the arrangement. At her feet are an array of objects - three milk bottles, several cups and saucers stacked, and four irons. "Her husband would get home that night late, and if his explanation wasn't satisfactory, well, she had all that ammunition there to blast him with."

Ellen Hinsey

The Sermon to Fishes

He was struck with awe at the sight of them:
a shoal lifting above the water's surface;
each head trained to his voice's timbre,
each spine anchored for the moment's purpose.

For the sea-dark flock, he fixed his words,
he the shepherd above them.
In the distance the itinerant waves obeyed
by ritual motion. Words flew from him —

How he had rehearsed such a miracle!
Before the silver of their scales, and
the heads in seeming infinite number,
he was great and gathered them in his hunger.

Yet, once lulled, how quiet this multitude —
that like quarter notes broke the water's line
as if hovering above the stillness where the lowest
staff separates music from endless silence.

Though his words had touched their hearing
and their heads above the water were tamed
he was pinned by his eye in water.
Arms outstretched, his figure remained

rooted, and would never master what, in one
movement turning round, they did, descending
guiltless into water, which glimmered darkly
as they fanned out, flying downward.

Two Poems by Lise Goett

Red Vision

> *What one wants in this world isn't so*
> *much to "live" . . . as* be *lived, to be*
> *used by life for its own purposes.*
> *What has one to give but oneself?*
> > —James Merrill

> *after Leonor Fini*

A time comes of silence and secret Sargassos,
the desolation of tourists and billboards,
a time of seamless ennui:
the bride all dressed for the cotillion,
the groom feigning repose
as he contemplates a future with no visible horizon,
prays for a sailable breeze.

Then into the hurricane's eye
comes a god wearing a mask of the most crushable petals
who fathoms their wish to be changed,
a god whose grace braises even the most reluctant among
    them—
they who are trapped in the hurricane's center of calm.

And this is how they ready themselves to receive him—
their fans carved of ivory, their stays made of bone:
into the furnace of long-waiting they climb,
discarding the immaculata's white gown
for the shimmering blow
of a god who arrives in the guise of a devil or a clown.

Oh then how they yearn for his swagger,
his spangles of silk,
desire etching its word in their bone.
For what comes in the stealth of this hour,
this caesura that harbors the moment of change,
but the wish to be shaped,
to feel the impress of the old gods
like a burning seal into wax?

Then he'll come hovering,
his arms incandescent with blossom,
his sacred red
staining their trumpets of silk,
his entrance a fissure of light
cleaving now from the past—
with the wish, the kiss, the embrace!

Convergence

Matthew 25:1-13

When first you came to Paris,
you attended saturnalian balls
in chandeliered rooms with faux-marble walls,
French doors giving out onto jade copses.
Men, versed in the sports of the body,
fingered cigars in velour cases, eyed
you as gristle for their boiling oil,
the net of good fortune catching you in the nick.

You no longer grieve for the past;
but there are days, you admit,
when you yearn for the future.
Still, a burning persists in the gut,
all winter the doctor the only man you unveil for,
your niggling diseases sentencing you
to some final apprenticeship
before the purest happiness comes.

Now your body resounds, taking the bus across town,
your body gliding slightly above it
as you survey the chestnut blossoms' tiered crowns,
a light haze coming into the treetops—
the reception of something so delicate
that if it isn't received it will die.
A frail insistence now emerges
into the effulgence of broad daylight.

Discarding the pallor of shrouds, of linen,
the earth's inner clocks releasing alchemical forces,
you will meet this fine day.
There will be oil enough to wait for the bridegroom.
There will be oil enough when the inner and outer align
to see your illumination in the face of the beloved,
all lanterns lit
like the raging garden of your father's old age—

delphiniums, nasturtiums—
the masterwork of the last stage, the last flowering,
born of a diligence so light-filled
that its equal is summoned again.

David Wojahn

Before the Words

—for Mark Doty

The companion Enkidu is clay. Sharp March dawn
at my study window, at my view of twenty-seven
budless lakefront elms. By May the water vanishes,

blurred green, embowered, lost beyond
the fat arcs of the leaves. The companion Enkidu is clay
and not even the godlike Gilgamesh

shall retrieve him from the world below.
I set the book down, to the white cat's
white-noise purr, and half a continent away

my friend wakes alone, to Cape light's blue-glass sheen,
and one more morning beyond his lover's death.
There the dog's nails click the wooden floor

and the sun through the curtains
in the hypnogogic dawn begins
its etches and erasures—nightstand, dresser,

photographs, ox-eye daisies in a fluted jar.
The bright diagonals lap the room. Is this
how the day prepares its naming, the hesitant tongue

to the gateway of the mouth?
Before the words can be inscribed
they issue from the throat, and song of a kind is invented,

a crumbling harp from the burial pits at Ur,

to testify first to lamentation.
From the throat to the tablets, crosshatched

to point the way, crosshatched in clay and baked
in Euphratian sunlight. The voice
raised first in lamentation, and the voice

entombed, seven hundred generations buried.
But also the voice reborn, its dry bones ablaze.
To cleanse the tablets with a fine horsehair brush

selah. To photograph by silver emulsion
the excavation where they're piled selah. Burnooses
of the grinning Fellaheen. To sort the lamentation

onto wooden crates, catalogued and labeled,
hoisted on a river barge for Baghdad, its sky
a hundred years from the black, infernal poppy heads

of antiaircraft fire, elided wail of siren
selah. Istanbul, then London selah or Berlin.
A basement room, the lamentation shuffled

under gas lamps. The sudden pince-nez glint
as Herr Von Dobereiner rubs his eyes,
the inkwell dipped, the letters molten

on the notebook page, unscrolling as the cry
emerges selah from its clay. The Elamite,
the Hittite and the proto-Babylonian,

and the cry as it hovers and its music sweetens.
And the lamentation selah fills the pages,
fills too oh Lord the vaulted caverns of the world

below. The companion Enkidu is clay.
Selah selah selah. The tablets have been broken
and the tablets now shall be restored.

Three Poems by Madeline DeFrees

Surgery Waiting

Supine on a gurney below the Acropolis tacked
to the ceiling, my right leg slowly turning
cement, I'm an accidental artifact of Pompeii
preserved in the cast of history. This is
the way I solidify my position: fully awake
except for the limb no longer connected
to my brain, chatting with the anaesthesiologist.

Here in the shadow of the Parthenon, hair veiled
from view like a medieval nun, what I really need
is a hard hat for this major foot reconstruction.
Pale curtains drawn around me for the epidural
or the nerve block. They are like the virginal
curtains of the novices' dormitory
fifty-eight years ago. Now it's IV time

and a member of the team, with a single thrust
boldly enters my bloodstream. I am wheeled out
feet first, to the operating theater, delivered up
to scalpel and saw. Before the cock crows
three times, I will be struck as foretold
from the ground I stand on, my log of a leg lifted
for the thigh-high tourniquet. *What you have to do*

do quickly. Betrayer and betrayed, I carry the Parthenon
with me, its colonnade of perfect form, record of
shifting attachments: Athena, Santa Sophia, the Virgin
Mary, and the Turkish mosque. Twelve of us gathered
in the narrow chamber, I feel the cut, remember to ask,
Is it I, Lord? Is it I? already swayed by the outcome,
the processional frieze over the Judas foot.

Balancing Acts

At 47, Hope's driven to find her feet in construction.
She crawls the hip roof of her house like a cat burglar,
gives herself plenty of rope, lashed to
the chimney. In her left hand, she carries a loaded
staple gun. Her right grips the insubstantial.

Cordless phone in my lap, I watch at 74, from my rented
wheelchair, fingers tattooing *9-1-1*.
Let me hop with the help of the Sunrise Medical Guardian
to the open door to rehearse
our common fate. We are Siamese joined by a bungee

cord at the inner ear, that delicate point of balance.
Every day we devise new methods
of locomotion. When my walker, upset by a comforter,
collapses to the floor and takes me
with it, I want to reverse the digits:

four and seven, seven and four. Yesterday, Hope wrestled
the circular saw over the edge
where she clung to the ridge and tripped on the safety
cord. It was then I heard the Sirens
wooing Ulysses tied to the mast. Twilight hangs fire

in the west, then snuffs it out. Behind the slant roof
of a dormer, Hope disappears. Two ladders
reach into the void. Is that white flash a sneakered
foot in search of a rung? I conjure a cloudy head
between the smokestack and the evergreen.

No matter how I strain, I cannot bring her back.
Reluctantly, I fiddle with the blind,
hear a tune old as the burning of Rome as I weave

between the cave and the whirlpool for a saving
equilibrium. What if I call her Faith,
the evidence of things unseen?

Metempsychosis

After a week, unbalanced on one foot, I know why
they call the great blue heron
Big Cranky. Some farmers call them cranes, as if
they were mere weight lifters, which
in a sense, they are.

                            I watch the big bird from
an evil star, honking across the sky. Every day
I drag my plaster-of-paris leg past the archer
on one knee lying in wait, past hunters
riding full tilt across the Karastan rug to their
hounds. I would have made a great

                            heron with my
movable metatarsal, shifting my bulk to the front of
my foot, although my surgeon implies
that I'm not a fully evolved human. He saws through
the joint, cleans out arthritic
bone, inserts

                    three screws to help it fuse and pins
four toes to point them in a northerly
direction. Why do I think of animal rights and tales
of vivisection? When I fly south in my wheelchair,
appendages neatly folded, at other
times extended,

           my wingspread matches the Great Blue's.
We are, in truth, the upper crust of
heronry, brooding and solitary. Days go by as we
flap towards bodies of water,
our croaks and calls

                    too often unreturned. I am worn
down to a wren, to the hollow
bone and broken flight that will not mend. Beyond
the riverbank, my semicircular canals
refuse to balance. Yet I do my best to sing, my

last year's nest under the wing of nine full choirs
of pagan muses and Christian
angels. Each day I put my trust in transmigration.

Six Poems by Stephen Sandy

Field and Stream

They want one of every kind and they
can't help it, it's an addiction,
the house full of novelty radios,
snow domes, stickpins, aquarium furniture,
Depression glass, Flow Blue. An example
of everything there is in the category
of your choice, mint copies of all the variant
bindings of *November Boughs*

or take aunt Nell, her toothpick holders—
and then her last great passion, nut cups.
Just try to get a run of something,
they call you a completist. So
what if it is a desire to have—
if not *it all*—then all of one
shelf, or slice of it! But I
am not one of those who buys bears

chainsawed from logs by the roadside.
If I could have any Greuze in the world,
why bother to choose, for who these days
has even heard of Greuze! I'd rather
skim the cream off the top of the jug;
I am after high spots, I follow
the plough along the mountainside
and pause for a smile, or a mouse. I go

for field and stream and may have
terminal panolepsy; open
spaces afflict me like a passion.
I have done the physical things;

I take some bike rides so far out
in the country it might surprise you. I keep
stores of garlic, parsley, and ginseng
in the hollow trunk of yon ancient oak.

Even though a dark plank tilts
into the maw of earth just here
by the tar pits, and there is every danger
that my collection will slip into
that sinkhole, dire fosse, I fear
no evil but opening my mouth
and going on about the origins
of the sacred; the bounty of nature.

Overhead

Now half asleep he heard the sonic boom
Knock his window, burly legerdemain;
He felt it in his bed, across the room,
Rattle the window pane
                          once — and only once — as if
It did not ask but kicked the door with steel-toed boot
And took possession, one of the roughs: tough,
                     vertiginous, destitute.
The possession it announced was nothing final
No knock of Linz brimming with doom; but

As if new neighbors, after the flush and lull
Of first possession, stopped with shears and cut
The survey pins, re-drawing lines with braggadocio;
        entered to ogle — & dance their angry drag.

Elixir

On Mao Shan did Tao Hongjing a fabulous
Pharmacopeia decree: of cinnabar
And orpiment, mica and malachite;
Dragon foetus, liquid gold, realgar, lead—

Ingesting which sent one to bed; and soon
To be one with earth and sky. You ate and went
Immortal, one of the cloudy sages of air;
Saw jasper mountains, found Peach-blossom spring,
Rode with the starry crane. But they didn't. They—

Just died. A kind of suicide, assisted
By the swank of alchemy, rank faith in fancy's
Medicine: red bole, white lead, Six-One cement.

They breathed; poisoned by nostrums, they perished thinking
Untimely death was apotheosis.

Pretzel

Topiary before we got to Winding Hill
and other songs—Death Valley, Old
Depot, Bald Mountain, and the like.
Life is just full of coincidences
especially if you are wearing the right shoes
and get there on time without
too much confusion, timidity, or gnats.
At Mortar & Pestle Dry Cleaners we got

Tour de France dusters the owners never collected.
Looking for veronica and a whiff of elbow
you came laden with camera equipment
hanging out waiting for your scoop

going off with your smart apertures.
I flew onward alone, north
in my Mallard Sprinter, accompanied
by charm and ignorance and that old American

pie, this hankering for the open road.
When I got there the pretzels had been
picked over, though at the sidewalk sale
an occasional fuschia love boat, or magenta,
showed up on the rack, if usually the wrong
size, not mine not yours. I bought a floppy
and headed for the Historic District.
At a basket barn I found an electric one;

handled the fuzz dreamily, fondled
the rust of my old life again and heard memory's
loose muffler barking hot ones
underneath. I loved you once, and for years, but now
the trees have stopped giving and the maple
syrup has been cut with corn. Can't do anything
about it because I don't even notice; can't
taste the difference, having forgotten you.

If Winter Comes

A redhaired man in a rusty salt & pepper van

If you want to do something you have to do it yourself

Your mother said it was all right for you, he said

Your gift is your own responsibility

You can ride to school with me, he said

You have to do what you have to do

She described him as a Caucasian

An idle dalliance in Hades' playground

She said he had a New York or a Spanish accent

The essence of making is invention

She bolted toward a nearby elementary school

A stitch in time saves nine

Prior attempted abductions Troy area by a redhaired man

Most remanded, soonest mended

The man's hair was described as being cherry red

If higher powers won't help, the lower will

People phoned in license numbers on salt & pepper vans

You can swing it if you wing it

She said the van had no windows

A Walk-in Orrery

—for John Swan

I'm here to see this model of the spheres
where our planets make a cosmos that just fits
inside the circular room; a folly

of the Enlightenment. But your bout with death
is what I'm thinking of, resistlessly as gravity
holding you like a moon in thrall to its

sovereign mass while we, a little out of breath,
like lightweight meteors flit and skitter,
trail sparkles of reflexive fear across
the dark. And you, not lonely and (you said) not bitter
and not (I thought) afraid, too soon will make
your move. But enough of melancholy!

I'm here with an old friend. We're out
to show me a good time, and music plays,
if not the music of the spheres; some moody violins
romance us. A button beckons, red, ablaze
with inner light. I touch it, and the dim-bulb sun
goes even dimmer. We sit back. The show begins.

Across the cosmic mock-up, metal quarrons ride
in cold pursuit, seeming to importune
each other. Everything rotates—save for Saturn, which
inches along so slowly we decide
they didn't throw his switch.
Green-landed, sea-blue Earth with her white moon

spins furiously, showing off. And Mars
is racing, furtive, like a baseball caught
in the drag of something else's gravity.
A recorded voice intones the facts with practiced awe.
And then the whole contraption crashes with a
clunk. Is heaven kayoed—seeing stars—

or what? The planets one by one
shake lightly on their spindles of black wire
like ornaments on a tree that shudders
when the dog brushes against it. Well, this was fun.
The music starts to fade. And you'll be gone
before I write the lines you asked me for.

But poems are only a raid
on the inevitable. The machinery of my life,
you said last month, is slowing
and when the stress becomes too great
for those who keep it going,
adjustments will have to be made.

Our lines do not have answers, framed
and cunning as may be. Not to phrase
too many questions may be best; and steer for home
clear of ignorant hankering. Let your wishes
like those baubles near the dome
go their entropic ways. And have good days.

Two Poems by Pimone Triplett

Tiresias to Penelope

. . . Then you must take up your well-shaped oar and go on,
  I said, and I admit he took it well,
  hampered as he was by my kind of sight.
True, my words, though absolute, weren't always winning.

Don't you think I knew every night he'd see nothing
  (even in your arms) but that wooden form,
  both sacred and handled by slaves: the branch
that carved a sea's distance, smoothed by the rash water?

Forgive me, since I was only the blind seer
  and not without my sympathy for you.
  A prophet's business is always brutal —
feeling the throat flood, then parch, only to fill

once again with the god's desires, insisting I
  instruct him: *journey until you come*
  where there are men living who know nothing
of the sea . . . I was anchored to their points of view . . .

Yet I knew something of how a hero's wife lived,
  the marble throne of patience at her back.
  Tell me, wasn't there, in your privacy
(where, let's face it, the threads kept fraying in silence)

a nervous edge to things that pinned me as the cause
  of his quick departure? I could see you,
  alone again at your loom, scissoring,
fingering, out to find the whole picture now.

From my vantage below, I watched you watching him
   the morning of his imminent exit.
   His arm holding a water jug to the light,
that small injury at his wrist (where he'd slipped on

a door frame — when?) the scrape's rough edges uplifted,
   like cut seams, the underside of stitches.
   Meanwhile, his eyes glowed: a pair of cities
as seen from the sea . . . Why must a hero go on

barging against the everyday, you must have thought,
   leaving you to nuisances and slipknots,
   the thread of wedded life starting to
stall and stiffen? Forgive me. What else could you have

done then, the god-like wife always moored to his gap,
   other than weave him walking in your frame,
   in your one outlook? Still, I envied you.
It's only devotion, a vow, that makes you fill

what's empty with its warp of shape and color —
   a love most of the dead must forget.
   What I'd give to live as you've done, my friend!
Discovering with your art what I got by a hard

grace — each with our visions of him toward the end.
   Are we right to be fond of those hours
   spent in the voyeur's trances? How I loved
the oar! — its bruise on his white shoulder as he walked

through dryness trying to pay an old debt, give back
   some honor to that ocean, angry god
   and wounded father. I saw guilt
somewhere, not in killing the untamed, one-eyed son

(which was called for), so much as, in his infinite
   arete, a thread of pride which only
   the rulers (who've ruined me) would love to
unravel . . . It's their craft to snip us with a prank,

you know, like sending that servant girl to mistake
   his ship's wing for a winnowing fan,
   fresh from her race that never tasted salt.
Did you see how the child laughed that time he sacrificed

the bull, the ram, the creaking pig? All forcing him
   to say the oar was not a thing of slaves,
   bent to thresh their kernels to a world,
but the rod of progress warped and wholly human,

to be set against the flirting, god-perfect waves.
   In time, her people will believe him. Still,
   a joke to such divinities is how
a man pays for his life with the shape of his life —

and, just so, you can see how seldom we shall change
   our devotions, my sister — laboring
   even now at your daily weave. Someday,
soon, you'll know my mind. And I shall witness your skills,

such as they might be in the darkness of this world,
   where you'll choose the one right thread,
   the silver line of sight in which we live,
watching him die, moment by moment, in the quick . . .

The Siren Parthenope: On Odysseus

Listen, with chaos and harmony contrapuntal,
with our knowing over all the earth everything
that happens, the open throated eddies, the one

man moving forward, and we three interrupting,
piling jetties to his current, breaking against
the story's wave. With him on course, hemmed at the mast,

and our wide intermezzo, wanting to knock down, uproot,
start diluvials, windy frets and choral fortes,
each voice, in jubili, departing from the tune.

All the while wanting this wreckage, the adagios
flung from the beach that only we made indelible
with men's bones, craving the tethered hero,

his wrists throbbing under tight-bound cords,
the slender joints reddening, each of us hoping
to catch his other-blooded kind of time.

Still, of course, it was a call without answer,
though we kept up the scattering, scuttling (we thought)
his half-expected arrival, as if his longing

to know could match the longing to be known,
as if it could be enough—or too much—
our trebled echoes, underscores of everything

to come . . . Then we saw the white staves of his ribs,
infrangible beneath the steady jib, and the men's
ears mute with wax, arms bent to oars, to history,

their blades whitening the water, a spume'd path of
desire and choice. As I stepped into the sea,
I thought I saw the islands' cliffed layers of silt

change tense, with each tier a shifted era,
ochre making its inroads into brick red,
dried russets of the suitors' blood . . . His gift:

this sense of an ending. Story goes, the mask he wore
as we went under matched the one I wore going
under, each hard face upturned, pocked with wood

shards, sea-glut, garbage, buoyed and slicked with
brine. Perhaps. Who can remember absolutely?
I know there were days of floating, a fusion of

white sea spiders and diamond glints of time,
adrift with me in the silent fermata,
the pause without measure, and the rowers leading him on.

Kenneth Rosen

The Work of Life

In all honesty, saying this
As if reaching out to hold your hand
And attest to a truth, my tongue
Naked as a palm, but extended
And without fingers, it's five
After three A.M., I should be
In bed, we should be
Asleep, its grotesque
To have the tongue
Outthrust as in a handshake,
Attempting to taste what a hand
May firmly squeeze without
Attempt to possess, rolling
As in dice, the tongue out
Without trying to swallow,
In all honesty, think of yeast,
How in wet flour it holds
Its breath and swells into bread,

If this were Paris
At this hour, or Monte Carlo,
Or Roquebrune, being the low red
Tip of the Appennines, its
Granite streets by certain
Basements, bulkheads or casements,
Would smell of the endeavor
Of a *boulanger* turning wheat
Into wands of fool's gold,
The work of life, a butcher
Putting an ox's tongue on ice
In a window, a candlestick maker,

Hanging flickering wands
Of candor and light, in all honesty,
The work of life, whether wax,
Ox or yeast, is a gamble
That hangs by its wick, and we
Could be followed by police.

Bruce Bond

Pomegranate

—*for L.K.*

You could be turning it in your fingers like a planet.
A knife would do, if you're good with knives,
bracing the hard fruit in your slender hand;
a knife and a narrow gaze to guide it.
You brush a fly from your lip, quiet your breath.

Then there's the sound a vow makes when it shatters
and the shallow fissure splits and reddens.
And all for this: a stain running out of a maze,
its honeycomb filled with dead sweet bees.
Your hunger is a straight line, pinned and singing.

It's only now you realize what you craved,
how shyly you ripened into a panic.
As for the shiny rivulets of juice
you close your eyes to drink, who's to say
it was their freshness that drew you? All those times

you slipped your tongue into the bright tomb
the way a moth enters a jar of lamplight.
You know the place, how its mouth meets yours.
And now wherever you leave, it's winter.
You go to the window and wait, stare, turn away,

and the long night trails you like a gown.
Even in March as you return to all
your name's sake, what flowers you see are the tips
of buried fingers, each red flame bursting
through the earthly crust, calling you down.

Letting Loose the Hounds

Brady Udall

Goody Yates was a mess. He shambled along the side of the road, slump-shouldered and bleeding from the mouth, his head stuffed with cotton, pain and delirium duking it out in the pit of his mind. He didn't know where he was or what he was doing, barely knew *who* he was, but the one thing he did know was this: if he didn't get some relief soon, if the pain in his head continued to attack him like the firebreathing beast it was, he was going to throw himself under the wheels of a passing car, just go right ahead and end the whole damn thing.

There had been something keeping the agony in check, something that had numbed everything, settled over his brain like heavy mist, white and soothing, but now it seemed to be wearing off. Goody whimpered like a baby and swallowed a mouthful of blood.

A primer-gray El Camino pulled over next to him, spraying gravel. "Why are you standing in a ditch?" somebody inside the car wanted to know.

Goody hadn't realized that he was in a ditch, but he looked down and sure enough, there he was in a weed-clogged ditch.

"You okay?" the person in the El Camino said. "Did somebody lay you upside? Your face looks like a pumpkin."

Goody tried to tell the guy to fuck off but he couldn't seem
to talk. He made a try at opening his mouth, which set the
nerves in his jaw smoldering like lit fuses.

"Stand up out of that ditch and get in the car," the man
said. "I'll give you a lift. You appear to me like a person who
needs help."

Goody had to agree. He got in the car and was able to get
a view of this guy for the first time—a squat, grizzled version
of General Custer: the handlebar mustache, the longish
golden-blond hair waving out from under a stained Peterbilt
baseball cap. Cool green hungover eyes.

They started back onto the road, the El Camino belching
and shuddering. Empty beer cans and rifle shells rolled around
on the floor.

"Where to?" Custer said, his voice full of cigarettes. "Hospitals are good in situations like this."

Goody shook his head, which was a mistake; fireworks went
off in front of his eyes. He didn't want to go to a hospital.
If he knew anything at all, it was that hospitals cost money
and one thing he did not have in this world was money.

He leaned back and put his head against the top of the
seat and watched the pine trees zipping past. The steady *lug-
lug-lug* of the car's engine soothed him. He heard Custer
talking but couldn't make out the words. He felt like he was
falling down a very deep hole and before he had time enough
to be grateful, he'd passed into sleep.

When Goody woke up he found himself in a whole new
universe of pain. The haze in his head had cleared up considerably, which was not a good thing; everything was clear and
excruciating. He was so hot it felt like his clothes were rotting
off him. Custer helped him out of the car, and the only thing
Goody could think was: *I want to die, I really would prefer
to die*. Custer stood him up, waited for him to get his balance
and led him onto the porch of a small house, a cabin really,
by itself in the middle of a saltgrass meadow, set up on blocks
off the muddy ground and surrounded by ponderosa pines.
Next to the house was an orange Le Mans sedan and a large,
chain-link kennel where a bunch of hounds—fifteen or
twenty—stretched out in the afternoon sun.

Custer rattled the handle on the screen door, which was
stuck, and finally, unable to get it to work, yanked the entire
door off its hinges and sailed it over the porch railing and into
the mud. Inside there were various broken objects scattered
around: a splintered chair, a coffee table that appeared to
have been sawn in half, an old-time jukebox with its electronic
guts spilling out. In one corner of the living room were stacked
a bunch of wooden milk crates filled with odds and ends.
After helping Goody onto a small couch missing its cushions —
the only intact piece of furniture in the room — Custer handed
him a pink slip of paper and said, "You dropped this in the
car when you fell asleep."

The paper was a crumpled sheet of stationery and at the
top was printed: *H. Felix Manderberry, D.D.S. 149 South
Mountain Road, Alpine, Arizona. (602) 337-2093.* Underneath, in the kind of indecipherable longhand doctors and
dentists are known for, was a prescription for something,
Goody couldn't tell what. As soon as he saw the prescription
he remembered, as if recalling a dream: earlier today, possibly
only an hour or so ago, this dentist, this H. Felix Manderberry,
had fed sodium pentobarbital into his veins and removed
four impacted wisdom teeth from his mouth. He remembered
waking up in the chair and a nurse looming above him in the
harsh light, asking: *Are you awake Mr. Yates, can you open
your eyes?* She handed him the prescription and went on,
giving her prepared speech on what foods he could eat, when
to take the medication, etcetera. Goody hardly got any of it;
he thought he heard everything, but the moment the words
entered his brain they just fell away. She left him, telling him
to stay put for awhile until he felt fully himself, but Goody
got right up and off he went, still caught in a fuzzy sleepworld,
floating past the reception desk and the jittery, hand-wringing
folks in the waiting room, opening the door to the outside,
the mountain sun slapping him hard in the face. The next
thing was getting into the El Camino and now here he was,
in a remote cabin with Custer.

"First I thought you were a handicapped person that somebody had knocked around. I almost did something really crazy
like call the police, but then I saw this paper. Did they yank
out all your teeth? Seriously, friend, you should see this; you've
got a dirty dinner plate for a face."

Custer stomped around, looking for something, then went back into the bathroom. Goody heard a loud, wrenching groan and Custer came out with a mirrored medicine chest, plaster dust still falling from the screws that had secured it to the wall. He held the mirror in front of Goody.

"Take a look," Custer said. "They must have done some butcher work on you."

Goody's face was an unrecognizable lump of puffed-up flesh. Purple bruises had begun to show under his eyes and his face was so swollen his jaws were clamped shut.

Custer said, "You didn't pick up your prescription, did you? I can tell you're ailing. Tooth pain is the worst there is."

Goody tried to form words without moving his jaw, but his tongue was as thick and dry as a balled-up tube sock and there was blood-clotted gauze still packed into the craters where his teeth used to be. "Uhhggl Gaawwd," was the best he could do. Finally, using half-assed hand gestures, he asked for something to write with. Custer searched but the only writing utensil he could come up with was a fat blue marker. There wasn't a sheet of paper in sight.

"Just go ahead and write on the wall," Custer said, lighting up a cigarette. "I'm going to burn this place down soon enough anyway. Can't even stand the sight of it anymore."

With only a slight hesitation, Goody turned and wrote on the wall above the couch, *wisdom teeth no drugs you got anything?*

Custer squatted, opened the medicine cabinet, which was now on the floor and surveyed its contents. "She took most of her pills with her when she left. Oh, she loved her pills, by God." He began picking up small brown bottles, squinting to read their labels. "Something for toenail fungus, stool softener, Demerol, Dexetrin something-or-other—shit, I don't know what this stuff is. I've never swallowed a pill in my life. Hold on a second." He went into the kitchen and came back with a bottle of Wild Turkey, took a swig before handing it to Goody. "See if you can get some of this into you, and I'll give this dentist a call so we can find out what in hell to do." He took the prescription and went back in the kitchen where the phone was.

Goody unscrewed the cap on the bottle, tilted back his head

and did his best to pour some whiskey through his teeth, but there was still the problem of the clumps of gauze trapped in his mouth. *Fuck it*, he thought and gagged the gauze down. Misery had pushed him into a state of complete disregard.

One thing was certain: if he ever saw this Manderberry character again he'd reciprocate some of this pain. He'd known people who'd had their wisdom teeth out and were running around chewing on pretzels and candy apples the next day. Sure, sometimes there was some swelling, a little discomfort, but, good Lord, how could it be this bad?

Just the thought of it all, the whole twisted junk heap of his life, made him want to puke. Goody was twenty-eight years old, slashed, burned and abandoned by his girlfriend of seven years, up to his eyebrows in debt, and going into the Army — the *Army* — in two weeks' time. Once there was no longer any doubt in his mind that his life was an irretrievable failure he'd considered suicide but decided on the Army instead.

It was his father, a World War II vet with a wide and varied collection of medals, ribbons and patriotic lies, who convinced him to sign up. His father had told him that the Army dentists were assembly-line hack artists, and if he needed any dental work done he should do it before he joined. Manderberry owed a favor to his father, who arranged the surgery at no cost to his son. In the carefree, oblivious years following high school, Goody's parents had supported him almost completely, but six years ago pulled the plug on him, telling him it was time to make his own way. His father had even helped him take out a loan to start his own landscaping business, but the whole thing went belly-up. He tried again, this time with a pawn shop and with the same result: out of business in less than a year. Now he was the janitor at Speaking Pines Country Club, earning two dollars over minimum wage and cleaning up after puckered old men (including his father) who, when they pissed, had great difficulty reaching the urinal. He lived in the basement of a hardware store and his meal of choice was rice with ketchup on top. He was drunk much of the time, always lonely (all his high-school friends gone away, moved on) and his most common fantasy consisted of punching out just about everyone he knew. Nights, when he wasn't haunting the bars, he sat at his rickety table in the posture of some sullen, self-taught philosopher, writing long fuming letters to his ex-girlfriend, Dottie, who, just over a year ago, had become pregnant by him, aborted the baby without letting him know and had run off to Phoenix to live in a big ranch-style house filled with feminists and lesbians, taking his torn and bleeding heart with her.

This is what was left of his life: he would give his four years to Uncle Sam, make enough money on the GI Bill to pay for college and maybe by the time he was forty he'd be able to get a good job so he could start paying off all his debts. It seemed entirely fitting that such a sad and ridiculous fuck-up as himself could go in for a simple dental procedure and end up like this.

He heard Custer tell Manderberry's secretary that he didn't give a good goddamn that the dentist was on his way out at this moment. He needed to speak with him right away. It was a *bona fide* emergency.

"Mr. Dentist?" Goody heard him say. "Well, my friend here . . ." he dragged the phone and its cord out into the living room, and Goody wrote *Goody Yates* on the wall— ". . .Goody, he's been given the dirty deal. Apparently you did a hatchet job on his wisdom teeth and then let him wander out into the street still loopy on the gas. I picked him up on fifth north, didn't know where he was, bleeding out of the mouth. Now his face is so swole up he can't open his mouth and he's suffering like a goddamn Christian. I guess you didn't give him any painkillers, either."

Just then there was a long howl and the scratch-and-snarl sound of dogs fighting. It sounded like only two or three dogs to begin with then escalated into a kennel-wide brawl: growling and yelping and clicking teeth. Goody could hear Custer trying to talk over the racket for a good thirty seconds before slamming down the phone, sticking his head out the window—the stench of dog shit coming through—and bellowing, "Hah, hah, hah, hah, HAH!"

Instant silence. One of the dogs ventured a weak whine, but that was it. Custer, red-faced and fierce, went back to the phone but nobody was on the line. "I told him to wait a second but the chickenshit must have run off. I was truly prepared to lay into that sucker. Seems like I can't do anything without having some kind of commotion from them," Custer said, pointing to the window. "I've been off the mountain eight days now and they're going stir-crazy. I've got a black-and-tan bitch out there, Lucy, she's the one causing all the calamity. She has to be out on a trail every few days or she gets bored and starts bullyragging the boys."

Goody kept tipping up the whiskey, getting it all over his face, letting it run down his neck. He was practically showering in it. He was feeling a little better now. The pain was there, red-hot as ever, but he didn't seem to notice it as much. He offered the bottle to Custer who took another stiff swallow.

"You and me, Goody," Custer said, wiping his mouth. "Been a good three months since I had someone to swap the shit with. Even if you have to write your comments on the wall like a graffiti artist." He pulled a milk crate from the corner, emptied out its contents on the floor — a blow-dryer, a box of Kleenex, dozens of bottles of nail polish — and sat down in front of Goody. "I should tell you, before your dentist buddy got away I told him what drugs we had in the house and he said Demerol, one tablet every four hours, should get you through until you can make it to the pharmacy. He said it's your fault for walking out still under the gas. He said he won't accept responsibility for anything because he has the best lawyer in the county."

Goody wrote, *I'll piss in his gas tank.*

"There you go. Yes. Subversive activity, they call it. That's the way you have to conduct these things." He found the bottle of Demerol and opened it for Goody. It took all the whiskey-fortitude Goody had to fight back the ache in his jaw, to open his mouth just wide enough to get the tiny BB-sized pills past his teeth. Once he had downed the pills he relaxed, quit tensing himself against the pain. Just the possibility of relief was enough for him.

Goody wrote on the wall, *God bless the pharmacy.*

Custer took a long drag on his cigarette. Even though the dogs had quieted down, Goody could still hear them, just outside the window, breathing and shifting, a single lurking presence.

After awhile Goody wrote, *Why so many dogs?*

"I hunt lions," Custer said.

Goody raised his eyebrows, and Custer explained that he hunted and killed mountain lions for a living, that he had a permanent camp up in the Blue Wilderness Area where he stayed seven months out of the year. Right now the place was crawling with lions, lions that were killing an inordinate number of livestock: the Arizona Fish and Game had done a lousy job of wildlife management over the past few years, issuing multiple deer permits and severely limiting the lion hunts. Now everything was out of whack; the lions, without much choice, admittedly, were taking livestock — even the shy black bears were coming out of the woods to drag calves away — and the ranchers were paying good money to have the predators killed.

Goody hadn't noticed until now, but it seemed that Custer spoke with a slight southern drawl. *You from Texas?* he wrote.

"Please, Lord, no," Custer said. "Louisiana. When we moved out here I had it in my head I was going to join the forest service, you know, driving around in a Jeep with a goofy hat on, being kind to trees. And now look at me. I practice violence on wildlife. Just last week my dogs got a big she-cat in a juniper tree and the branch broke out from under her. She killed four of my boys before the rest tore her to pieces. By the time I got there the only recognizable thing they'd left me to verify the kill was a right foreleg. I just about didn't get my money on that one, but that rancher ended up paying me because he knows I've got the best-trained dogs around, and he might need us again. These dogs, loud and obnoxious as they are, are the best pack in the southern Rockies. They'll go after any scent I set them to — bear, bobcat, lion — don't matter, and they'll kill it if they can. They know I don't like the killing part so much so sometimes they take care of it for me."

Goody didn't know what to say to that, so he just sat there, rolling the marker between his palms.

"Yeah, shit," Custer said, standing up and walking in a tight circle, smoothing his mustache with both forefingers. The sun was dipping behind the trees and shadows were beginning to eat up the room.

They sat there for awhile, facing each other, and Goody wrote, *You live with somebody else here?*

Custer seemed to read the sentence over five or six times.
At first his face was blank but then it fell into a broken,
cheerless smile. "Used to," was all he said. He got up again
and stared at a spot on the wall. Goody was immediately sorry
he'd asked the question.

"I'm still trying to get a hold on this." Custer kicked the
wall and tried to laugh. He looked ready to tear the house
apart with his hands. "I come home off the mountain last
Sunday, tired and dirty and ready for a little female attention,
and Mary is *gone*, along with most of her stuff. She is now, at
this moment, shacked up with Wallace Greer, a big worthless
layabout with the mind of a shrieking Chihuahua. The year
Mary and me moved here from Baton Rouge, before I started
up on the mountain, we'd go bowling Friday nights, and he
was always there, and I'd catch him looking at her. I noticed,
but I didn't think twice. I'd been saying to myself: I'm gone
a lot, we've had our problems, our shouting matches, but
Mary is good and faithful, Mary would never do such a thing,
Mary wouldn't let a creeping Jesus like him come and steal
her away. Mary is my *wife*." Custer went over to the stack of
milk crates and picked up a blue flannel shirt that was draped
over one of them, held it out in his bony fist. His green eyes
were burning in his head. "This is his shirt. I come home off
the mountain, and this man's *shirt* is on my bed. Right now,
up on the mountain, lions are coming out of the trees and
killing innocent calves, and I'm down here, drinking too much
and trying to find the guts to do something about this."

Custer took an antique-looking glass kerosene lamp off the
table and fiddled with it, trying to bring the wick up, his
battered fingers trembling. It was almost full dark now.

"Damn, I'm sorry," Custer said. "I didn't bring you here
to air out my sorrows. I'm mouthing off like a lunatic. Why
don't you tell me something about yourself? Only thing I
know about you is your name is Goody and you have a shitty
dentist."

Goody just stared up at him and Custer said, "Do you have
a job or something?"

Cleaning toilets, Goody wrote.

Custer nodded. "Girlfriend?"

Left me high and dry.

"Hell," Custer sighed.

Goody wrote, *You said it.*

The fact of it was, Goody didn't know what to say to Custer. He had only questions of his own: was it really this bad? was the world chock-full with the frustrated and betrayed? Everybody he met these days—mostly in bars, it was true—seemed to be stricken with heartache and fracture and fallen hopes. Goody could tell him something like, *Hey, I can relate to what you're going through*, but that would be about as comforting as a glass of ice water in the face. Goody thought about what he might say about his life, about his father, king of the country club, and his alcoholic mother and his insurance-salesman brother and wife and her beautiful, fake breasts and capped teeth. He thought about Dottie and the little lost baby, fetus, whatever it was, that they had made together, and he began to write it all on the wall, tried to make it come out with some sense so Custer could understand, but what came out instead were phrases and names and words and tangled scribbles that had no meaning at all except to express the blackness inside him; now that the Demerol had taken care of the pain in his mouth he could focus without distraction on the pain in his soul. He knew, as he wrote, that it was a jumbled mess, but he couldn't stop himself, he had that same driven feeling that came over him when he wrote fifteen-page furious, ranting letters to Dottie late at night; he wrote about plagued lives and human failure and our hapless attempts at fulfillment and the slow burn of anger and bitterness. He wrote all over the damn wall, standing up from the couch, his arm moving with a jerking twitch. Phrases such as *the milk of hatred* and *so many awful pleasantries* showed themselves; words like *trash* and *mockery* and *outrage* popped up occasionally, but mostly it was just a dark impulsive scrabbling that continued, almost with a life of its own, until the marker ran out of ink.

Goody hadn't noticed that the shadows in the room had fused together and night had moved in. Custer took a Zippo from his pocket and lit the kerosene lamp, holding it up to the ink-covered wall like an archaeologist getting his first look at ancient hieroglyphics in a cave.

"Damn," he said in a low voice, putting his hand on Goody's shoulder. "What the fucking hell."

Goody sat slumped on the couch feeling nothing at all. He could hear Custer outside, clomping up and down the porch steps, loading things into the trunk of the Le Mans. He came into the house, his skin slick with sweat even though it had turned into a cool night. Goody could tell, even in the indefinite light, that an unnatural calm had come over Custer. "I believe I've come to a decision here," he said, his features a patchwork of shadows. "I hate to ask, with the condition you're in, but I could use a little assistance."

Goody nodded: of course, anything at all. This man had gone out of his way to help him, and even though he'd known him for only a few hours, and not under the best of circumstances, he felt closer to Custer than he had to anyone in quite awhile.

Outside the crickets were going mad, an almost deafening sound, and the air was piney and sweet. He followed Custer to the gate of the kennel and the dogs were gathered there, the whole clustered pack of them, yapping and wagging their entire bodies, saliva swinging from the loose folds of their mouths. There were eighteen of them in all—black and tans, blue ticks, treeing walkers, redbones, a couple of bloodhound mixes—and their coats were oiled and sleek and their molten eyes like dozens of tiny perfect moons.

Goody helped Custer clip leashes to each of the dogs' collars, and Custer put nine of them into the back and front seats of the Le Mans and nine into the bed of the El Camino. "When she left, she took the pickup," he explained, a little embarrassed. "Technically it's hers. Her daddy gave it to us before we left. Anyway, I'm going to need you to drive one of the cars. Just follow behind—we won't be going too far."

Goody sat in the El Camino and watched Custer go into the house one last time. When he came out, he lingered in the doorway, looking into the house for a moment, then pitched the kerosene lamp into the middle of the living room. Goody could hear the sound of the lamp's glass breaking, followed by the *thwump* of the kerosene igniting, and through the porch window he could see a blaze leap up, a flash that lit up the whole house, quickly died down, but didn't go out.

By the time they were out on the highway after driving one

or two miles on a muddy two-track, Goody looked back and couldn't see flames, but there was definitely a smoky yellow glow lighting up the sky just over the tops of the trees. They drove north on the highway, eight or nine miles, up through Quemado Pass, until Custer pulled over next to a shiny red Dodge pickup parked at the side of the road.

A cool breeze was coming down off the peaks, rustling the grass in the meadow that was stretched out until it reached a dense line of ponderosas. The only sound in Goody's ears was the fierce thump of his heart.

Custer gathered the dogs, knotted their leashes together and handed them over to Goody. The dogs snapped and pranced and yowled, their own tiny mob. "Stand there real firm and they won't get away from you," Custer said. "They're a little crazed tonight. I haven't fed them in three days."

Custer went around to the passenger side of the Le Mans, reached through the window and came back holding Wallace Greer's shirt, a ratty old flannel shirt that now seemed terribly significant in the blue mountain light. "I've been following him around the past week," Custer said, his face grim and alive. "He comes out here every night to pick the mushrooms that grow along the river about a half mile down that little valley. Kind of mushrooms make you see crazy things. He makes a bit of money selling them to the high-school kids and keeps the rest for himself. This is the son of a bitch my wife ran off with."

Goody and Custer stood there for a moment, staring at each other, and something like agreement or acceptance passed between them. It felt to Goody like his insides, his brain, all of him, was vibrating like a tuning fork.

Custer squatted down and held the shirt in front of the dogs' noses and said, in a low growling voice, "Seek out, seek out," over and over again, almost like a chant. At the sound of the command the dogs went haywire, sniffing and biting the shirt until one ripped it out of Custer's hand, and all of them dove on it, slashing it to tatters. They were pulling so hard the leather was biting into Goody's hands—it was all he could do to hold on—but when Custer released them from their leashes, one by one, it was as if something loosened and

gave way inside Goody, and he stepped forward and shouted —
a strangled cry that barely made it past his tongue and clenched
teeth — urging the dogs on, feeling a strange, hot thrill run
through him as he watched their black shapes moving across
the meadow, howling like demons, charging through the dark
beautiful night and into the trees.

Truman Capote, Screenwriter

Beat the Devil

*In Italy in the summer of 1952 Truman Capote was asked
by the director John Huston (on the recommendation of David
Selznick, who had admired Capote's work on an ill-fated Vitto-
rio De Sica movie entitled* Indiscretion of an American Wife)
to collaborate with him on the script for a movie called Beat
the Devil. *For an adventure-thriller something along the lines
of* The Maltese Falcon, *a cast had been assembled which included Humphrey Bogart (who had financed the film), Jennifer Jones, Peter Lorre, Robert Morley and Gina Lollobrigida.
The reminiscences that follow are edited from a forthcoming
oral biography on Truman Capote.*

TRUMAN CAPOTE [undated, typed letter to Andrew Lyndon]
*The last few weeks here have been filled with peculiar adven-
tures, all involving John Huston and Humphrey Bogart,
who've nearly killed me with their dissipations . . . half drunk
all day and dead-drunk all night, and once, believe it or not,
I came to around six in the morning to find King Farouk
doing the hula-hula in the middle of Bogart's bedroom. Jack
[Dunphy] was disgusted with the whole thing; and I must
say I breathed a sigh when they went off to Naples.*

JOHN HUSTON I met Truman at a party at Bennet Cerf's.
He was the party-giver of New York at that time. Truman's
picture had appeared in various magazines—the famous one
of him reclining in a sofa looking very feminine. Sure enough,
when I met him, he was the only male I'd ever seen attired
in a velvet suit. It would have been a very easy thing to have
laughed at him had it been anyone except Truman. I immediately fell for him—it didn't take me five minutes to be won
over completely, as was everyone I ever saw him encounter.
He had a charm that was, to coin a phrase, ineffable. He
exerted this charm freely. We planned then and there to do
a picture together "one day." I hadn't read his book—I didn't
get it the same night because there were no bookstores open—
but I had one the first thing the next morning.

Next, I met him in Rome. I was there to do *Beat the Devil*.
I didn't have a very good script, well, practically no script at
all. It occurred to me to get Truman to write on it with me.
I said, "Truman, we spoke back in New York about our one
day doing a film together, here's the big chance." He agreed.

STEPHEN SONDHEIM Huston did a lot of standing around
musing. I had a feeling that this was not a serious movie they
had, in any way, shape or form. Huston took a liking to me.
I was trying with my little 16-millimeter camera to shoot a
documentary on what happens to a small town when it gets hur-
ricaned by a movie company, but I didn't have enough film
or money, enough time, that sort of thing. But Huston acted
for me. I wanted a shot of Huston pondering. So he walked
back and forth in front of the camera pondering for me.

JOHN BARRY RYAN Before moving on to Ravello, we all arrived at Rome. There was no script. We would go out every
night to the Caffè del Orso, already two weeks after the start
date of the movie: Humphrey Bogart, Jennifer Jones, Huston,
Peter Viertel, who had written the original script that no one
liked, and Jack Clayton, who was the production manager.
It was the hottest place to go in Rome. It had a bar on the

ground floor, a restaurant on the second, and a dance floor. It is indescribable how much we all drank. One night we were leaving, and Huston grabbed Jack Clayton and said, "See that piano player over there? He would be great as the purser in the picture." So, Clayton went over to this piano player and asked, "Do you speak English?" The piano player said yes. Two and a half weeks later when we all got down to Ravello we discovered that that *yes* was the extent of the piano player's English. But Huston decided his face was so perfect for the part of the purser that he got the dialogue director to train him to speak enough English in the next few days to deliver his line. Truman was writing the movie in a sequential order. Well, the first scene in the movie is a shot of Bogart sitting outside the cafe and the purser comes to see him. Truman wrote a line for this purser who speaks *no* English at all that I will remember to my dying day: "Mr. Danruther, the captain of the SS *Niagara* presents his compliments and wishes to inform you that, owing to failure of the oil pump, the sailing will be delayed." I swear to you that Truman did this intentionally. If we had stayed in Ravello for five *years* the piano player never would have been able to say these lines! So we spent three days in the square of Ravello with John Huston listening to the purser repeat his lines "Mr. Danruthah, the captain . . . compliments of the SS *Niagara*." And then we would start all over again.

JACK CLAYTON I had met Truman at a nightclub in Rome. He was with David Selznick, a little lilac shawl around his shoulders. We started the film with three pages of script. The old script had been torn up by John Huston about three weeks before we started shooting, and he had hired Truman. It was bewildering to work on the picture. The pages for the next day would arrive at 10:30 at night, if we were lucky — more often, 7:30 the next morning. David Selznick, who was in Italy because his wife, Jennifer Jones, was in the cast, used to send me at least five letters a day. I wish I had kept them. All on yellow pages, they were absolutely brilliant. He knew more about producing a film than anybody I've ever met in my life. He kept complaining about the things that were wrong but could not be helped because without a script you can't plan. He was always complaining about how Jennifer's dress didn't suit a particular scene. So I would reply, "David if I knew what the scene *was* going to be . . ." I kept pleading with Huston, saying, "Listen, give me an idea, even if the scene is not set yet. Just give me an idea where exactly it's going to be — the boat, or the palace, or the grounds, just so I can prepare."

JOHN HUSTON   Truman and I worked on the script. We tried to stay ahead of shooting. If it caught up to us, I'd give the crew a very complicated setup — to put together dolly tracks, take out walls and such . . . While this was going on Truman and I would go back to the hotel and write a scene. We hoped the company wouldn't know of our desperation, how close the dragon was breathing on our necks.

WILLIAM STYRON   I saw Truman a little down in Ravello. Rose and I had rented a small villa that was attached to this hotel. Truman, Humphrey Bogart, Gina Lollobrigida, Robert Morley, Jennifer Jones, John Huston and Peter Lorre. Can you imagine that gang? They were all living in this hotel, and the movie evolved as Truman wrote the script each day. They didn't have a real script at all; Truman just invented the dialogue, and the movie shows it. Rose and I saw a little bit of Truman then, but we more or less stayed away from them. I didn't have much to do with them, or they with us.

JOHN BARRY RYAN   There was this big poker game associated with *Beat the Devil*. Selznick, Huston, Bogart, Jack Clayton, occasionally, and Truman. Truman didn't know three of a kind could beat a pair when he sat down. He'd never played poker in his whole life! He thought it was hilarious to sit down with these people. Then Selznick's lawyer came to town and took everybody's money for three nights until Bogart and Huston went to Selznick and said, "Get this man out of town, or we'll find some nice mafioso to take care of him."

STEPHEN SONDHEIM   It was a very macho game — Huston, Bogart, Selznick and the lawyer. The stakes were very high — $1500-2000 a pot at least, I'd say. Truman asked to play. He'd never played. I remember the first night. I sat on the outside. Obviously they were playing for stakes I couldn't play. At one point Truman said, "I'll match the pot." He must have had a wonderful hand. Somebody said, "You can't do that. You don't have enough money." Truman said, "Oh well, then I'll fold."

STEPHEN SONDHEIM   I was witness to a wrestling match between Truman and Humphrey Bogart on the floor of the hotel. I don't know how it started — it wasn't really a violent or angry fight, more in fun — two bears wrestling each other.

JOHN HUSTON   Truman was a little bulldog of a man. One night, he and Bogey were arm wrestling. Funny picture, Truman and Bogey arm wrestling! Truman put Bogey's arm down! And the next thing, they were wrestling on the floor, and Truman again put Bogey down! Bogey wasn't all that husky a number, but you don't see Truman in the role of a wrestler. A little bulldog. His effeminacy didn't in any way affect his strength or his courage.

STEPHEN SONDHEIM   Actually we didn't see much of Truman and Huston because they were writing all the time. They were working.

JOHN HUSTON   There were only a few interruptions I remember. One was when Truman hurried back to Rome to see his bird, Lola. He said that this bird — I think it was some kind of crow or raven, black in any case — wouldn't talk to him over the phone. It was either ill or sulking. It turned out it was neither: it had flown off the balcony and disappeared . . .

WILLIAM STYRON   Truman had taught it a few obscenities like "screw you," that was all. It sort of sat there and clucked and suddenly it would come out with a "fuck you" every now and then.

JOHN HUSTON   Two weeks into shooting the picture, I came back down one day. Truman was staying in his room writing, trying to keep up with my shooting. I'd come back at night, and we'd work together. This evening, Truman's face was twice its normal size. He had an impacted wisdom tooth; it was frightening to look at him. I said, "You've got to get to the hospital."

He said, "But John, we have work to do . . ."

When Jack Clayton saw him, he sent for an ambulance. We helped Truman down the stairs. He must have been in dreadful pain. Typical of Truman: he said, "Bring me my shawl. Don't forget my shawl." Jennifer Jones had given him a Balmain shawl; he needed his shawl to go to the hospital? He worked that night in the hospital. That's Truman.

JOHN BARRY RYAN   Only Truman knew what he was going to write. John had no idea. Selznick had no idea. You should see the script, if there is such a thing. Drink had a lot to do with it.

JACK CLAYTON   Truman had the gift of dialogue. Narration doesn't really come into films because the narration part is done with the camera. The story was there, and all that had to be filled in was the dialogue. He had absolutely a brilliant sense of dialogue. You may not think it from *Beat the Devil* . . . he did a wonderful script for me on *The Innocents*. Although he only got half-credit, he wrote the whole script, really. Bearing in mind it was a very difficult script to do because you had to keep the Victoriana and at the same time bring the dialogue up to date. It was brilliant.

JOHN HUSTON   *Beat the Devil* came out to absolutely wretched reviews. No one came to see it. The other day I saw Jennifer Jones and she said, "They don't remember me for *The Song of Bernadette* but for *Beat the Devil*."

JACK CLAYTON   I am one of the few people who are not attached to that clique who think *Beat the Devil* is a masterpiece. I view it with enjoyment, but only enjoyment that the thing could happen. It's a film that shouldn't have been made. That's the whole point.

JOHN HUSTON   Afterward Jack Clayton gave him a bulldog that he adored. Truman had expressed his liking for the breed, and I don't wonder at that because, as I say, Truman himself was one.

LAUREN BACALL   He swam into my life after *Beat the Devil*. I had been making *How to Marry a Millionaire* in California and when I was finished I met Bogie in London. He told me about Truman. "When you meet him, you can't believe that he's real. And then after a while, when you get to know him a little bit, you just want to put him in your pocket and take him home." He said he'd never seen anyone who worked harder than Truman. In those days he was really nose to the grindstone. Then I finally met him when he came to California. He came to the house. And of course I *didn't* believe him. That little voice; "Hello dear." He was totally infectious because of his incredible brain and his wit; this was before any of the bad stuff happened. We developed a great friendship. He adored Bogie. The unlikeliest couple in the world were Bogart and Truman Capote. They respected each other as professionals.

As might be expected Beat the Devil opened to mixed reviews. The critics rather liked it. Time magazine called it a "screwball classic." The public did not agree. One theater owner in Michigan took out a paid advertisement in a local paper apologizing to his patrons for showing it. But the film has had its enthusiasts. Gerald Clarke in his biography Capote *quotes Charles Champlin of the Los Angeles Times: "However antic and loopy the circumstances of its making may be, Beat the Devil holds up as a fast and disciplined comedy, with a richness of invention which even now, after fifteen or twenty viewings, I find astonishing."*

—G.A.P.

IM GONNA WANT YOU TO WALK ME THROUGH the scene you think you CAN DO THAT?

"We're gonna go back to Armstrong now, ~~see what we can do~~" he said pulling ~~onto~~ out onto JFK Boulevard, the reflectors tape clothing fad strobing the ~~darkness~~ street corners. ~~with the lostless~~

"NO.. I don't WANT TO ~~DO THAT..~~ ~~too~~ she's not there.."

"Most likely not, Sub.."

"What do you think of my dream ?" ~~she just asked it flatly, almost like a demand~~

"What do I think?" Andre talking associating dreams more with ~~Old Testament~~ Bible stories than with analysis

"IS IT ~~Do you think it~~ true?"
~~"you cant think that Brenda..."~~
~~you got to be positive about?"~~
"Brenda ~~you got to be~~ positive ATTITUDE.." HAVE A

go
"I want to look for the car."
She blurted, abruptly twisted then around as if someone might be hiding in the rear seat.

Andre had seen that funnel-hipped anxiety in victims before, that adrenalyzed helplessness, people ~~dealing with~~ a clock that had no hands
I'M PRISONER STARING AT

I
"No ~~I~~ cant do that right now, because if we run up on ~~the guy~~ it? I cant get involved in a apprehension with you setting next to me.."

Richard Price

The Art of Fiction CXLIV

Richard Price has proven that there can indeed be a third
act in the career of an American writer. After a distinguished

debut as a novelist, with The Wanderers, *and a subsequent literary faltering that led to his recasting himself as a screenwriter of studio-produced movies, Price returned in recent years to fiction with* Clockers, *a monumental work that is both a murder mystery and a descendant of literary naturalism.*

In fact, at the time of this interview, as Price was finishing a spate of screenplays, script-doctoring assignments and embarking on a new novel, this member of the first generation of writers who grew up as much with television as with books seemed poised to shuttle back and forth between the composition of capacious and highly regarded novels and what is often seen by writers as the devouring maw of the motion-picture industry.

Price's fiction has always been cinematic. The Wanderers, *a novel about an eponymous gang he wrote while in the Columbia University writing program, was an evocation and exaggeration of his childhood in the Bronx housing projects, and was made into a film soon after publication. That novel was followed in quick, almost annual, succession by* Bloodbrothers, *also adapted for the screen,* Ladies' Man *and* The Breaks, *this last harkening back to his college experience at Cornell.*

While contending with a cocaine addiction, having produced two unfinished novels and feeling that he had cannibalized his own life as a subject matter, Price accepted a screenwriting assignment that, though never made into a film, became a kind of calling card. Since then his prolific screen credits include The Color of Money *(1986, a sequel to 1960s* The Hustler, *directed by Martin Scorsese),* "Life Lessons," *a half-hour segment of* New York Stories *(1989) directed by Scorsese,* Sea of Love *(1989, a quasi-adaptation of his novel* Ladies' Man), Night and the City *(a 1992 remake of the Jules Dassin film),* Kiss of Death *(a remake of the 1947 noir),* Mad Dog and Glory *and the forthcoming* Ransom.

In researching his movies and finding that worlds beyond his own experience could feed his imagination, Price discovered that "talent travels" and determined to return to the novel. After immersing himself in the diverse lives of Jersey

City housing projects, a nightmare version of the terrain of his childhood, he wrote Clockers, *which takes its name from lower-echelon crack dealers. In many ways that novel is an answer to the challenge Tom Wolfe laid down in his essay "The Billion-Footed Beast" for writers to enlarge the scope of the novel through engagement in the larger social issues.* Clockers *was widely recognized as a dispatch from the asphalt combat zone of the American underclass, but Price, having stalled earlier as a novelist, seems prouder of its artfulness.*

On meeting Price, one is struck first by his extreme verbal intensity. His earlier career ambition to be a labor lawyer is easy to imagine. Although one might not notice, even after a number of meetings, that Price's right hand is imperfect — a result of complications during his birth — his physical self-consciousness is apparent, and he goes to some effort in managing new acquaintances to avoid shaking hands.

The first two sessions of this interview were conducted in the summer of 1993 at a loft on lower Broadway in New York where Price lived with his wife, Judy Hudson, a talented painter, and their two daughters, a home he would soon be moving from. We conversed in the kitchen area of the open central space. The walls were hung with paintings by Hudson and her contemporaries — Bachelor, Linhares, Taafe.

Price has since moved to a new home, where the third session of this interview took place. He now lives in a brownstone near Gramercy Park, which still bears many effects from a previous owner, a member of FDR's brain trust, who decorated it with art-deco details, including a bathroom featuring huge double bathtubs and a deep-sea motif. In the living room hangs one of the better examples of Julian Schnabel's work — a gift for Price's consulting on the script of that artist's forthcoming biopic of Jean Michel Basquiat.

The whole suggests a place decorated with the grace and tasteful eye of downtown artists into whose lives a great deal of money has recently flowed. During the interview, signs of the couple's young daughters were in evidence; twice they buzzed on an intercom to demand, not without charm, the family's video-account rental number. Friends of the couple

had remarked that Judy Hudson was the secret to Price; attrac-
tive, accessible and funny, she seemed surprisingly uncompli-
cated for an artist.

Price's office, the first he has had in the place he lives, is
dominated at one end by a large desk where he writes, at
the other by a fireplace blocked with the poster of the movie
Clockers. *A large Chinese box. A many-drawered chest, like*
an old typesetter's case. A Jonathan Borofsky print. A Phillip
Guston print. A Sugimoto photo of a theater screen, with a
proscenium decorated by Botticelli's Venus on a Half Shell.
Leaning against a wall is an Oscar-nomination certificate for
his screenplay of The Color of Money. *Price says, "You're*
supposed to hang that in the bathroom where everyone who
comes to your home will be forced to stare at it and see how,
since you keep it there, you don't take it very seriously."

One senses that the writer is proud of the domesticity he
has achieved, but that he is not particularly attached to the
material objects of the world he and his family have created.
At the center of the room is a coffee table surrounded by a
couch and chairs — on its surface as if arranged for inspection,
are three stacks of Day-Glo orange notebooks, the startling
color of a traffic cop's safety vest. Placed before the notebooks,
front and center, is a typescript, shy of a hundred pages. As
Price sits down to talk, he glances intently for a moment at
the novel-in-progress perhaps to reassure himself that it is still
there.

INTERVIEWER

What started you writing?

RICHARD PRICE

Well, my grandfather wrote poetry. He came from Russia.
He worked in a factory, but he had also worked in Yiddish
theater on the Lower East Side of New York as a stagehand.
He read all the great Russian novelists, and he yearned to say
something. He would sit in his living-room chair and make

declarations in this heavy European accent like, "When the black man finally realizes what was done to him in this country . . . I don't wanna *be* here." Or, "If the bride isn't a virgin, at some point in the marriage there's gonna be a fight, things will be said . . . and there's gonna be *no* way to fix the words."

I mean I didn't even know what a virgin *was* but I felt awed by the tone of finality, of *pronouncement*. He wrote little stories, prose poems in Yiddish; my father translated them into English, and they'd be published in a YMHA journal in Brooklyn. I remember a story about a dying wife, a husband's bedside vigil, a glittering candle. The candle finally goes out the minute the wife draws her last breath. He was kind of like the O. Henry Miller of Minsk. I was seven, eight years old and I was fascinated by the idea of seeing my grandfather's name and work on a printed page. Later, in college, I always went for the writing classes. I'd get up at these open readings at coffeehouses, read these long beat/hippy things and get a good reaction from people. It was like being high. Back then, I would take a story, break it up arbitrarily and call it a poem. I had no idea where to break anything. Rhythm, meter, I didn't know any of this stuff. I just had a way with words, and I also had a very strong visceral reaction to the applause that I would get.

INTERVIEWER

Were books an influence?

PRICE

The books that made me want to be a writer were books like Hubert Selby's *Last Exit to Brooklyn*, where I recognized people who were somewhat meaner and more desperate than the people I grew up with, but who were much closer to my own experience than anything I'd ever read before. I mean, I didn't *have* a red pony. I didn't grow up in nineteenth-century London. With *Last Exit to Brooklyn*, I realized that my own life and world were valid grounds for literature, and that if I wrote about the things that I knew, it was honorable—that old corny thing: "I searched the world over for treasures, not realizing there were diamonds in my own backyard."

INTERVIEWER

How old were you when you read *Last Exit*?

PRICE

I was sixteen or seventeen. I was a major screwup in school, but I always read. Libraries. Paperbacks. I read *City of Night* and all the Evergreen and Grove Press stuff. I read a lot of horror stuff. I read Steinbeck. Although my experience wasn't Okie, rural, there was something in the simplicity of his prose that was very seductive. It made me feel that I didn't have to construct sentences like a nineteenth-century Englishman to be a writer.

INTERVIEWER

You intended to go to law school, but you ended up a writer . . .

PRICE

I always wanted to be a writer, but coming from a working-class background it was hard to feel I had that right. If you're the first generation of your family to go to college, the pressure on graduation is to go for financial security. The whole point of going to college is to get a *job*. You have it drilled into your head: job, money, security. Wanting to be an artist doesn't jibe with any of those three. If you go back to these people who have "slaved and sacrificed" to send you to school, who are the authority figures in your life, and you tell them that you want to be a writer, a dancer, a poet, a singer, an actor, and to do so you're going to wait tables, drive a cab, sort mail, with your Cornell University degree, they look at you like you're slitting their throats. They just don't have it in their life experience to be supportive of a choice like that.

Because I came from that kind of background, it was a scary decision not to go to law school. Maybe one reason *The*

Wanderers got the attention it did was that nobody coming from my background with such an intimate knowledge of white housing-project life was writing about it. The smartest minds of my generation in the projects became doctors, lawyers, engineers, businessmen; they went the route that would fulfill the economic mandate.

INTERVIEWER

Had you ever met a writer before you decided to be one?

PRICE

At Cornell the class of 1958 or 1959 was amazing — with Richard Farina, Ronald Sukenick, Thomas Pynchon, Joanna Russ, Steve Katz, all of whom are working writers now in various degrees of acclaim or obscurity. When I was at Cornell from 1967 to 1971 two or three of them came back to teach. It was the first time I sat in a room with a teacher who wasn't as old as my father. Here was a guy wearing a vest over a T-shirt. He had boots on, and his hair was longer than mine. A novelist! I couldn't take my eyes off him. I felt, "Ah, to be a writer! I could be like this teacher and have that long, gray hair . . . boots up on the table and cursing in class!" It made me dizzy just to look at the guy. I don't remember a thing he said to me, except that he usually made encouraging noises: "You're good. You're okay, keep writing, blah, blah . . ." He gave us this reading list that ranged from Céline to Walter Abish to Mallarmé and Rimbaud, names I'd never even heard of. The books looked so groovy, so cool and so hip. I bought every one of them. I walked around with Alfred Jarry and Henri Michaux under my arm, but I didn't understand what they were trying to do, to *say*. I had no context for any of them. The only one I could get through on the list was Henry Miller. One writing teacher gave us his own novel, and frankly, I couldn't understand that either.

INTERVIEWER

What kinds of things did you write for him?

PRICE

I had a talent for making ten-page word soufflés that were
sort of tasty. In the late sixties anything went. Everybody was
an artist in the late sixties. Sort of like punk music in the
seventies.

INTERVIEWER

You once mentioned some pancake poems.

PRICE

Some crazy Hungarian guy wrote those. He'd write them
on round paper, bring them to class, read them, pour syrup
on them and then eat them. The sixties. I will be eternally
grateful to Richard Brautigan for *Rommell Drives on Deep
into Egypt* and *A Confederate General from Big Sur.* I'd look
at this stuff: "Jesus . . . If this could get published, I can get
published . . ."

INTERVIEWER

Could you tell me how you work?

PRICE

It's important to me to have a place to work outside of
where I live. So I have always found myself an office. I go off
to work as if I had a clock to punch; at the end of the day I
come home as if I had just gotten off the commuter train. I
need to impose a structure on myself. Otherwise I can go three
or four days without looking at a piece of paper. I try to keep
it as close to a nine-to-five job as I'm able, probably closer to
ten to four. I spend the first hour reading the *Daily News*,
answering phone calls, lining up paper clips, doing anything
but working. Toward the end of the end of the morning, I
realize I have no choice but to finally get to work. Sometimes
I'll be transported by the work; sometimes it just won't come.
The most painful part of the day is getting to the moment
when I see I have no choice but to do it.

INTERVIEWER

During that typical ten-to-four writing day how much time are you actually creating something new?

PRICE

About half of the time. Typically, what I'll do is write a page, reread it, edit it, write half a page more, and then I'll go back to the very first thing I wrote that morning. It's like the nursery rhyme "The house that Jack built," where you go back to the first line of the poem and go all the way through, adding a line each time, and then back to the first. So, I don't know whether I'm editing, reediting or writing something new, but it's kind of a creeping, incremental style of writing. I always sort of half-know where I'm going.

INTERVIEWER

How much revising did you do for *Clockers*?

PRICE

About a year and a half's worth. I had an endless, interminable draft, well over one thousand pages, with no ending in sight. I gave it to John Sterling, my editor, and with him I went back and started on page one and attacked the manuscript for a number of things: consistency of tone, a narrowed point of view, filling in all the holes in the plot. I tried to weed out excessive writing and cut down on the personality of the narrative voice. We wound up going back to page one three times and working our way through to page one thousand-plus—eighteen months of rewriting. Sterling would say, "You have too many speakers, too many points of view and your narrative voice is too florid. There are still some big-time problems with consistency of tone. Let's start on page one again." It was like wrestling a zeppelin.

INTERVIEWER

That must have been time-consuming for an editor.

PRICE

Very. Earlier, writing the first draft, I went through a process
with him in which every day for a solid year I read to him
over the phone everything I wrote. It seems I needed to do
that . . . to hear, "Good dog." His goal in humoring me like
this was to get me to the end so he could have a manuscript
to work with. For him it must have been like talking to a
headjob or a child, coaxing and comforting, saying, "Ooh,
that's good. Wow. Oh, you're such a good writer. Very good.
What page are we on? How many pages do you think you
have left? What time is it? March?"

INTERVIEWER

No criticisms?

PRICE

Every once in a while he couldn't help it. He'd see I was
taking a dogleg somewhere into the woods. But basically he
understood that his role on the phone was almost that of a
psychiatric nurse.

INTERVIEWER

You were just fortunate in finding the right editor for
Clockers.

PRICE

We sort of grew into this relationship. Before I wrote a word
of *Clockers* I had arranged to tell the story aloud to a number
of publishers. Whoever was interested could bid against the
others. I didn't trust my prose at that moment in time, because
I had been writing movie scripts for eight years. I said, "At
this point I can talk so much better than I can write. Let me
just talk. If it's inadequate, don't bid." I was confident enough
in my story that if they could hear it, they would have the
faith to go with it. If not, fine. Worse comes to worst, I would
actually have to start writing something. But I wanted a setup
where I knew someone was literally waiting for pages, because

what I feared in going back to fiction was the isolation: the phone not ringing, no hugger-mugger, no emergency meetings, no "Clint has an idea . . ." I wanted someone waiting, someone keeping the light burning in the window. As it was, we had about nine publishing houses bidding. John Sterling of Houghton Mifflin was the last guy to hear the story. Every time I'd tell the story I'd tell it a little differently. I would always ad-lib a bit. I'd hear myself say something that I'd never said before and I'd think, "Whoa, I'd better write that down." I was continually working out the story verbally in front of people. I keep hearing these days that nobody edits anymore, that editors are basically in-house expediters, but I've been lucky, always getting these guys who like to get into the trenches and duke it out over everything from punctuation to psychological consistency. I've since started a new novel, and I went with Sterling from Houghton Mifflin to Broadway Books . . . like the story of Ruth, "Whither thou goest . . ."

INTERVIEWER

How'd you learn to do this — walking into a publisher's office and telling them a story?

PRICE

It's from the studios. The way you get work with them is by being a salesman, by walking into an office where people have the power to commission projects and saying, "Have I got a story for you!" Then you try to tell them the story as succinctly and as seductively as possible so they can envision the movie and the stars they might snag. It never occurred to me that you don't do this with a publisher.

INTERVIEWER

Do you act out the characters' parts or just describe the characters?

PRICE

Well, I'm not going to sit in front of some publisher and do black dialect, or New Jersey–cop dialect. I'd quote to them an imagined exchange that symbolized the type of dynamic that I wanted to write about. "This is what this guy said, and this was the reaction." In a way, I would act it out. Given the fact that I wasn't giving anything on paper to these people, I wanted them to know that while it's one thing to have an idea for a story, you've also got to get across that you know your stuff.

Let me tell you how *Clockers* got me back to fiction. First, I had had my own painful experience with cocaine, although I had been clean for about eight years by the time I started on the novel. In 1986-1987, crack hit the newspapers. You couldn't pick up a newspaper and *not* find the word *crack* in every article, including the weather report and the sports page. It seemed crack was this new nihilistic monster that was going to destroy us, the ultimate thing that was going to lead to the undoing of civilization. My own drug experience was such that I fell apart on your typical middle-class sniffing cocaine. But after I straightened out, this demon, this *crack* came along, ten times more potent, addictive and debilitating. It seized my imagination because, although I was clean, I was still having nightmares. This new thing seemed like kryptonite, and to make amends for being a coke-jerk all those years, I began teaching in a rehab center in the Bronx. My students were adolescent crack addicts or crack dealers — many of them from broken homes, homes in which some of the parents had crimi-nal histories, homes in which there were intravenous drug problems, sexual abuse, physical abuse, suicide attempts. Some of these kids going home to a house where, if the father was there and not in Rikers, he was chopping up lines on the table. And there *I* was, educated, mainstream, in my early thirties, financially solvent, professionally established, having almost fallen through the earth on pedestrian coke-sniffing, looking out at a room full of adolescents with nightmare back-grounds who had fallen prey to the same drug that almost killed me, but who were taking it in a form *ten* times more pernicious, and they were saying to me that they they smoked crack in order to *cope*? That made me crazy. So *Clockers* came about through the teaching experience, the crack epidemic, my not too ancient memories of drugs and, last but not least, returning to the world of housing projects from which I came.

The first time I went back was with the police, when I was doing research for *Sea of Love*. We went to these projects looking for a witness to a homicide, and that night I looked around, and even though I'd spent the first eighteen years of my life in buildings like these, I felt like I had landed on a distant planet. They had turned into such tiger pits. The only things that looked familiar to me were the bricks. I felt this disorientation; it made me feel like, "I know this, but I don't know this. Actually, I don't know *anything*." And I was seized by the desire to understand what happened to the projects. I felt compelled to return to the world I came from to find out what happened.

INTERVIEWER

What year was this?

PRICE

About 1985. I had stopped doing drugs in 1982. The funny thing is, once you stop doing drugs, you don't see it anymore because you're not around the people who have it. You don't even have to do that by design. It's sort of like when you're single everybody you know is single, when you get married everybody you know is married and when you have a baby everybody you know has a baby. You move into the circle of what your status and commitment are at that moment. I hadn't been around drugs for years; I literally hadn't seen any. The first time I saw it again was about a year and a half into the book, when one of the guys I was running with brought out a kilo of coke, like a loaf of bread, and this giant wok and began chopping rocks with a bowie knife, mixing it with Italian baby laxative, what they call "stepping on it." Well, the last thing I wanted was to be high right then. A guy with a bowie knife chopping up his kilo? I'm not going to get strung out around here. Anyway, the urge was no longer there.

Did you ever try writing under the influence of cocaine?

I'm not Thomas de Quincey or Coleridge. I'm not William
Burroughs. I don't feel anything creative for me can come out
of writing under the influence of a drug. One danger is that
cocaine gives you the illusion of being creative; you get into
this vicious circle of feeling so inspired by this chemical in
your system that you do write. Then you come down, and
the next day you look at what you wrote and get depressed.
What you see before you is yesterday's rush transformed into
burbly bullshit, at which point you start to panic because now
you're *really* behind your deadline or whatever and you better
get cracking, but you're too depleted, physically and mentally,
and therefore what you realize is, in order to jump-start yourself, maybe just a wee hair of the dog would be in order, so
you go out and score again.

And here comes another day's worth of deluded flop-sweat
trying to pass for art. I mean, you might be able to squeeze
out a dazzling paragraph or two, but it's the law of diminishing
returns. In the end, the coke will overwhelm the work. I got
to the point where I had to do a line to write a line. You
might do coke in order to write, but by the end you're writing
in order to do coke.

I've never written anything good on coke. I mean, I've written good paragraphs and good pages, but if I were to write a
story for one hundred days on coke, I might write one hundred
good pages, but they wouldn't be pages that belonged together — one hundred pages for one hundred different books.
Unfortunately, with a novel they're all supposed to be for the
same story. Nobody can write well using cocaine. It's the worst
drug of all for an artist.

Take marijuana: when you're stoned you know you're stoned
and you stop smoking. When you're shooting heroin, you
don't keep shooting. You don't think, "Maybe I should shoot
some more." You're nodding. You stop. You put down the
needle. When you're drinking, you can't drink endlessly.

You're going to vomit or you're going to pass out. You stop. Cocaine is the only drug that you can take and take, and nothing stops you except running out of the stuff. And when you're blasted you don't realize that you've got garbage for brains.

One of Elmore Leonard's characters came across with the awful realization that addiction not only destroys your body and brain, but also dominates your consciousness. Twenty-four hours a day an addict is thinking about where they are in relation to their drug. They are thinking about how high they are. They're thinking about the fact that they're not high. They're thinking about scoring. They're thinking about cleaning up. They're thinking about cutting back, about getting better stuff. Endlessly thinking, 24-7-365. It simply dominates your thoughts around the clock.

INTERVIEWER

To get off it . . .

PRICE

It got to the point where I wanted to do something about it. I quit through self-disgust.

INTERVIEWER

Did you find a substitute?

PRICE

Baseball cards—1955, 1956, 1957.

INTERVIEWER

What's the prize of the collection?

PRICE

A first year Mickey Mantle, which should be worth thousands of dollars, except somebody sat on it. So now I just use it to scrape crumbs off the table.

To get back to *Clockers*. Did the story evolve as you wrote it?

PRICE

The more I hung out doing research, the more the story changed, the more specific and the more intimate it became, and also the more daunting and endless. You're hanging out with drug dealers; the world of the drug dealers impinges on the world of poverty-in-general; the world of poverty-in-general impinges on the world of welfare, which impinges on criminal justice, which impinges on social work, which impinges on the world of education. So everything I learned naturally led to something else.

Also, seeing the world through cops' eyes, all you see are situations among people in which police are required, and that is wild on a day-in, day-out basis, that's addictive. You have a backstage pass to the greatest show on earth. As one cop said, "One thing about God, he had to have been a genius to invent this job." But it wasn't like I was pulling a Margaret Mead number here. I'd known guys like these ever since I was a kid. So I was out there day and night, compiling, compiling, compiling. I couldn't stop. I felt like a degenerate gambler who gambles until he craps out. I felt if I went out with these guys just one more time, something *so* phenomenal was going to happen, something so epiphanic . . . and I got hooked on hanging out waiting for this tomorrow that I was afraid of missing.

At one point, I had a stack of notebooks two feet high of overheard things, sights, descriptions, sounds. Six months after Houghton Miflin had bought the book, I was still coming in with anecdotes, snatches of conversation, war stories. The novel was taking shape, shaping *me*, but I hadn't written a word. So, for my fortieth birthday my editor took me to lunch and he hit me with this hideous question: "Well, this is all good and well. This stuff is amazing. This is going to be a phenomenal book. Let me just ask you . . . What's the first sentence?"

I was simply afraid. Actual writing is no fun for me. Going out and hanging out and getting impressions out there on the streets, that's fun. I was running with everybody. I was like one of those guys who jumps off the stage into the audience and gets passed around. I got myself passed around for three years. So you've got all these good lines in a notebook, but then what? I think it was Norman Mailer who said that the fact that something really happened is the defense of the bad novelist. At some point I got so hooked on research that after a while it seemed out of the question to make things up. Ultimately, everything in *Clockers* was pure fiction, but in the beginning I had to learn enough about the texture of *truth* out there in order to have the confidence to make up lies, responsible lies.

INTERVIEWER

Incidentally, why do you think these people spoke to you?

PRICE

First of all, I was completely honest with everybody. Nobody really has an audience for their life. If you're a drug dealer or a cop or a woman on welfare with four kids, and suddenly here I come, a writer, saying, "Look, I want to write a book. What you do and how you make it through the day is mysterious to me. I would like to learn how you make it from dawn to dusk and then back to dawn." People want to talk. People have a lot to get off their chests. "You want to know how I survive in my life? Well, somebody should write a *book*; let me tell you." I was a guest in the house of their life. People took me in. I made no judgements.

INTERVIEWER

Did you ever get into a dangerous situation?

PRICE

Sometimes I'd go out with the cops, and it would get kind of hairy, not because they were doing a "Well, tonight we raid Mr. Big," but they'd get their load on, and stuff would happen. I could never be left alone. I had to run when they ran. It can be pretty scary to get lost in a building. You're with the cops. Everybody *hates* the cops. Once there was a drug dealer, Earl, who had seen me in the company of the cops when they were stripping him down, harassing him, breaking his balls. Then the next night I come around to his turf with another drug dealer at three o'clock in the morning to be introduced to him, this big four-hundred pound Bluto. Since Earl had seen me with the cops, I needed the second drug dealer to front for me and explain to Earl that I was not a cop. I was a *writer*, somebody who wanted to hang out with drug dealers *and* the cops. The front guy says, "Yeah, I'll take care of it. I'll take care of it." First thing, he leaves me in the car. He jumps out of the car and he gets into kind of a shadow-boxing, slap-boxing fistfight with Earl, their way of saying hello to each other. "How you doing you fat motherfucker? Hey, when's the last time you saw your dick?" They're cursing each other out like this when some girl comes up, and my escort — the guy who's supposed to be explaining why I hang with cops — leaves Earl and goes off around the corner to dry hump her, and they're like *whup*, *whup*, *whup*, up against the wall when Earl, this big four-hundred pounder, comes over and looks at me in the car. He goes, "Oh, shit, there's that cop! Willie! you brought a motherfucking cop!" All the guys come running, reaching for their pieces, gold chains jangling.

"Wait a minute!" I say, "No! I'm a *writer*!" I held out my books and started speed-rapping my way out of God knows what kind of payback. But, I was very lucky. A couple of good war stories was the worst that happened.

INTERVIEWER

When you're writing a book do you tend to avoid reading other books?

PRICE

I'm very protective of myself. I once made the mistake of reading *Sophie's Choice* while I was trying to to write *The*

Breaks. It was like trying to sing while somebody else is singing another song in the background. I just got completely off course, not that I had much of a course to begin with. So, when I'm writing a book all I read is genre stuff; I'm very careful not to read anything too good, that's going to make me anxious. When I was writing *Clockers* I would not read anything about urban experience. A nonfiction book on exactly the same subject might have been a source of information for me, but I wouldn't have been able to stand the anxiety of not having covered an area that its author found essential.

INTERVIEWER

Do you show your work to other writers?

PRICE

Not anymore. In the beginning I was so enraptured by everything I wrote, I thought I was the cat's pajamas. I just couldn't wait to read my stuff to people. I'd read to a fire hydrant. And if the reaction was negative, I would just shrug it off. These people are wrong. The end. I had three novels out before I was thirty and I just felt like everything I did was great. I wasn't interested in what I didn't know. It's when you're older that you realize how ignorant you are. The older I get, the more insecure I feel about my work, although I do think it's better. I'm glad for whatever my early work got me, but it's painful to reread.

INTERVIEWER

Your first book was *The Wanderers*.

PRICE

I wrote *The Wanderers* when I was still in school. The book started out basically as assignments for my creative-writing classes at Columbia. Being published almost felt like the prize for handing in the best term paper. I didn't even know I was working on a book. I was just writing. "It's time to write another one of these stories about these guys, the Wanderers."

In class I read what turned out to be the first story of *The
Wanderers*, and everybody hated it. Then Dan Halpern, who
had started the literary magazine *Antaeus* and was a student
in class with me, said, "Well, I like it. I'd like to publish it.
Can I have it?" I'd never been published. It took a year for
it to come out. Meanwhile, I had gone off to Stanford on a
fellowship in their creative-writing program. Out there in Palo
Alto, I felt so isolated from my past life that a great need
came over me to crystallize my memories of the Bronx, my
adolescence, the textures of a life to which I knew I'd never
return. So my need to write about these *mooks* kicked into high
gear—it was all tied into homesickness and disorientation. I
was writing in the same manner and for the same reason that
someone would whistle a tune as they navigated a dark and
creepy forest.

When it was published in *Antaeus*, an editor at Houghton
Mifflin wrote me a letter saying, "I'd like to see more stuff
like this if you have it." By the time I got that letter I had
ten stories, about two-hundred pages. Houghton Mifflin
bought the book for like four thousand bucks. My editor
straightened out the grammar. I didn't even know I was doing
what I was doing. I was twenty-four when it was published.

INTERVIEWER

You make it sound effortless.

PRICE

If I had known what I was doing, truly known what I was
doing, I might not have been able to do it. Sometimes, things
come easy. You're oblivious to the statistics, the big picture.
No book since has been that easy for me.

The first book is always the most fun, because when you
write your first book you're just a writer. Then you get published. Then you become an author, and once you're an author
the whole thing changes. You have a track record. You have
a public. A certain literary persona. You can become very self-
conscious and start to compete with yourself. No fun at all.

INTERVIEWER

How did your novel *Ladies' Man* come about?

PRICE

Ladies' Man came out of an assignment from *Penthouse*. They wanted a series of three articles about public places in which you can go and either participate in or observe actual sex: massage parlors, back-room gay bars, Plato's Retreat-type places, even singles bars. At the time I had never been to any of these places, not even a singles bar. So I went to a singles retreat in the Catskills—just the most desultory, horrific, depressing place. Fourteen guys and three women. Pocked handball courts. Dead birds in the swimming pool.

Then an old friend of mine who is gay took me to the back rooms of bars like The Anvil, The Toilet, The Ramp, The Strap, The Stirrup, The Eagle's Nest and God knows what. I started writing about this stuff and I couldn't stop. It was so freaky, such a sense of anarchy, anything goes. It's like you go crazy. You don't need amyl nitrite; just being in there is like a giant popper. My first reaction in those leather bars was, "Christ, I hope nobody makes eye contact with me." Then, after about forty-five minutes, I found myself wondering, "How come nobody's making eye contact with me? Am I that ugly?" And it hit me that under all the cruising and anonymity of the back-room bars, there existed the same undercurrent of desire and neediness that I experienced at the singles weekend in the Catskills. Well, obviously there were a lot more people getting their rocks off in the backrooms, but . . .

So I realized I wanted to write a story about a guy who goes to a place like The Eagle's Nest, then the Catskills place, singles bars, massage parlors. Like *Lost Weekend*, but about sex, not alcohol. So I bought back the articles from *Penthouse* because I wanted to use the material for a book. That's how *Ladies' Man* began.

INTERVIEWER

Writing became more difficult later?

The hardest book for me ever to write, and the least satis-
fying, was *The Breaks*. I was writing in a blind panic because
I couldn't think of anything to write about. I had published
three books, one every other year. All of a sudden I ran out
of autobiography and I started spinning my wheels. I began
two books I never finished and never sent out because they
were empty. You can write because you have something you
want to work with, or you can write because you're desperate
to keep your name out there. If you write because the subject
intrigues you and challenges you and makes your life as a
writer engaging, and then you get to a place where you realize
that, at this moment in time, you don't have anything to write
about, you're going to stop. But if you're writing because you
haven't been published, and your star is dimming, then you
write regardless. And if you have enough talent you'll deliver
readable page after readable page after readable page, but all
of it will add up to nothing because you're just treading water.

In *Ladies' Man* I had the whole book outlined. It was an
easy structure: seven days. In seven days I wanted the guy to
go here, here, here and here. I plotted out his week. It just
fell into my lap. Afterwards, I thought, "If that took me three
weeks, maybe the next one will take me a week. This is great.
Then, after that I'll write a book a day. I'll be like Georges
Simenon, seventy-four books a year!" No such luck.

The first draft of *Ladies' Man* took me three weeks. It was
the opposite of the Judeo-Christian work ethic: "The harder
you work the greater the reward." Sometimes what's easiest
is the best simply because you're in complete sync and harmony
with what you're writing about. That's why it was easy.

INTERVIEWER

Did you start writing the screenplays because you wanted
to support a family, or because of frustration as a novelist?

PRICE

I started to write screenplays because, as a novelist, I felt
the well was dry. It had been for a while. I'd had a lot of

offers to do screenplays over the years, so . . . let's see what happens. I knew if I stayed with the novel I was just going to kill myself. I was going to fall off a cliff.

INTERVIEWER

How much did the Hollywood people know about you?

PRICE

My first two books were made into movies, neither of which I worked on — *The Wanderers* and *Bloodbrothers*. I had offers because the people out there could see that my novels were very cinematic. I had grown up on TV and movies as much as on books, and it showed — a visual and aural momentum that lent itself very easily to film.

Actually, I didn't literally go out there. I stayed in New York. I came up with an idea about a mailman who wins the lottery and how it changes his life — "Wingo." It was never made but it was pretty good and it got around. Your first script, even if it's good, probably won't get made, but it's the best calling card you can have short of having a movie.

After that, Martin Scorsese was looking for a writer. I met with him for three hours and went off and wrote *Night and the City.* It was too Scorsesian for Scorsese to do, but he saw that I could write; he asked me to get involved with *The Color of Money*, and I got nominated for an Oscar. First time out at the box. Never happened again though. . . . In any event, once one of your scripts is made into a movie, well, it's sort of like being a baseball manager. There are only thirty of you; and even if you're terrible, by virtue of the fact that you have managed a pro team, there will always be a job for you more or less. Once you get something on film, and it attracts any kind of notice, it's never that hard again.

INTERVIEWER

Do you find the lack of control you have as a screenwriter frustrating?

PRICE

It's enough to drive you to write novels. Almost. This is
the immutable law of the business: the only screenplays that
aren't tampered with are the ones that aren't made. Making
a movie is an ensemble act. Writers are not authors out there.
And scripts are not books. They're blueprints. You work with
others, or you're gone.

INTERVIEWER

You wouldn't want to direct your own screenplays?

PRICE

It is sort of a natural law that if you have any kind of significant success as a screenwriter, the next thing to do (according
to Darwin or someone) is to parlay that into some kind of
deal where you'll end up directing. Why would anybody want
to stay a screenwriter, constantly handing your stuff over to
other people to execute? On the other hand, I don't know
anything about directing, but what I've seen I don't like. It
takes over your entire life, physically, mentally, emotionally. If
I weren't a novelist and if I hadn't written *Clockers*, I probably
would've taken a stab at being a director, simply out of despair.
Sometimes the fear of the unknown is not as great as the fear
of things staying the way they are.

INTERVIEWER

Do you want to keep writing both novels and screenplays?

PRICE

Every screenwriter loves to trash screenwriting. It's like
shooting fish in a barrel. They trash the calculatedness, the
cynicism, the idiocy, the pandering. But if they're really honest, they'll also admit they love the action, the interaction.
Depending on whom you're working with, screenwriting is
fun up to a point. And movies have such an impact on people.
Thomas Kenealy once told me about a time he was with the
guerrillas in Eritrea during the civil war in Ethiopia. They were

sitting on the cusp of the desert under the moon. They all had their muskets; they were about to attack some place. Wanting to chill out before they mobilized, they watched *The Color of Money* on video. So every once in a while the hugeness of Hollywood gets to you—the number of people who see a movie compared to the number of people who read a book. So as a screenwriter you keep hoping against hope, "Just because they screwed me the last time doesn't mean they're going to screw me this time." Well, of course they will. They're just going to screw you in a way you haven't been screwed before.

The first draft is the most creative, the most like real writing because it's just you and the story. The minute they get a hold of that first draft it ceases to be fun because it's all about making everybody happy. Raymond Chandler said that the danger of Hollywood for a writer is that you learn to put everything you've got into your first draft and then you steel yourself not to care what happens because you know you're going to be powerless after that. If you do that time and time again, the heart goes out of you.

INTERVIEWER
Do you work on the set?

PRICE
Depends on the director. There are some directors who like to have a writer on a leash, sitting at their feet in case something comes up. There are other directors who feel that a writer on the set is an anxiety trigger. Actors live in a constant state of insecurity, a constant fear of, "Am I going to show my ass out there?" When they see a writer it makes them think about what they are going to say and if it could be better. So a lot of directors would like to keep the writer off the set for that reason. Then there are directors who don't want the writer freaking out because his script is being used only as a blueprint, which is what a script should be. Things are going to come up and the script is going to change in order to make the actor happier. He doesn't want to say what you wrote, he's got

his own take. Yes, it might not be as well-said or well-written as what you had, but what you gain in sort of cutting the quality of the writing a bit is a better performance because the actor feels more in control of what he's doing. Everything's a compromise. The art of movies is the art of collaboration. I always trash how stupid screenwriting is, but the more I do, the more I realize it's really about the art of push-me pull-you, of creative negotiation. It's not about writing. Movies are not scripts; they're living pictures. There's an amazing difference between what works on paper and what works in the flesh. Sometimes what can look like breathless dialogue on the page sounds like "creative writing" in the mouth of an actor. It doesn't make a difference how good the actor is, it's just not human speech. When you read books in which the dialogue seems dead-on and exquisitely truthful to the character you'd be amazed at how artificial those lines would sound if actually spoken by actors. It's remarkable how little can be too much. And sometimes you get better movies off more patchy scripts, because the actor has to reach deeper to make the connection. Whereas, if I write it out, dictate what the actor is supposed to be feeling, telling him to make this gesture, to say it with *this* tone of voice, to take *this* exact amount of time between words, actors can read it and think, "Beautiful, this guy did it all for me." Then they just go through the motions. And oftentimes the end result won't be as good as that other movie they were in where the script was fairly crappy, but the actor had to bring more to the party. It's exasperating, but that's the reality of it. You don't hold the page up to the camera and follow the bouncing ball. It's got to make it into the flesh, and then all sorts of things happen.

INTERVIEWER

What place does the novel have in the world? Why do you keep writing them?

PRICE

Because the novel is *me* . . . what *I* have to say. When people come up and say, "Oh! You wrote *Sea of Love*? That was my favorite movie," I feel like they're talking to somebody standing between me and them. I don't feel like I own it. I ask myself, "What kind of writer am I that I write something and then I don't want to take ownership of the final product?" It's nauseating. I don't mean nauseating in a condemnatory way, I mean that you actually get a feeling of vertigo and nausea about who you are.

INTERVIEWER

Is that why you decided to do *Clockers* next? To get back to the novel?

PRICE

First of all, I got an awful lot of confidence back as a writer because my screenplays were well-regarded. But at the same time I never wanted to be a screenwriter, first and foremost because a screenwriter is not a real writer. You're not an architect; you're a draftsman. I wanted to be a real writer again . . . when I felt like I had something I wanted to write about. Out of my research for *Sea of Love* I found myself in places and with people that moved me as a writer and made me want to write in a way that I hadn't felt for over ten years. And I knew that I had to have control over this material, not some studio. I didn't want to have to buckle under to someone's marketing strategy, be dependent on a director's interpretation, on editing decisions, advertising campaigns, PG ratings. All of a sudden, I found myself in the middle of something. It took a decade to get there. I didn't even know where I was. I just knew I was in the right place. I didn't even have the story. But it was a combination of *where* I was and *what* I was at that point in time.

INTERVIEWER

Can writing be taught?

PRICE

You can't teach talent anymore than you can teach somebody to be an athlete. But maybe you help the writer find

their story, and that's 99 percent of it. Oftentimes, it's a matter
of lining up the archer with the target. I had a student in one
of my classes. He was writing all this stuff about these black
guys in the South Bronx who were on angel dust . . . the most
amoral thrill-killers. They were evil, evil. But it was all so
over-the-top to the point of being silly. He didn't know what
he was talking about. I didn't know this stuff either, but I
knew enough to know that this wasn't it.

I said to the kid, "Why are you writing this? Are you from
the Bronx?"

He says, "No. From New Jersey."

"Are you a former angel-dust sniffer? Do you run with a
gang?"

He says, "No. My father's a fireman out in Toms River."

"Oh, so he's a black fireman in suburban New Jersey? Christ!
Why don't you write about that? I mean, nobody writes about
black guys in the suburbs." I said, "Why are you writing this
other stuff?"

He said to me, "Well, I figure people are expecting me to
write this stuff."

"What if they do? First of all, they don't. Second, even if
they did, which is stupid, why should I read you? What do
you know that I don't know?"

He turned out to be one of these kids in the early eighties
who was bombing trains with graffiti — one of these guys who
was part of the whole train-signing subculture, you know,
Turk 182. He wrote a story, over a hundred pages long, about
what it was like to be one of these guys — fifteen pages alone
on how to steal aerosol cans from hardware stores. He could
describe the smell of spray paint mixing with that rush of
tunnel air when someone jerked open the connecting door
on a moving train that you were "decorating." He wrote about
the Atlantic Avenue station in Brooklyn where all the graffiti-
signers would hang out, their informal clubhouse, how they
all kept scrapbooks of each other's tags. Who would know
that stuff except somebody who really knew? And, it was great.
The guy was bringing in the news. Now, whether it's art or
not depends on how good he is. But he went from this painful

chicken scratch of five-page bullshit about angel-dust killers to writing stuff that smacked of authenticity and intimacy.

That is the job of the writing teacher: what do you think you should be writing about? At Yale I had the same problem. They'd write ten pages of well-worded this or that, but where's the story? I finally came up with an assignment. I hate giving assignments. I hated getting them, and I hate giving them. But—the last of the good assignments—I made them all find a photograph of their family taken at least one year before the writer was born. I said, "All right. Write me a story that starts the minute these people break this pose. Where did they go? What did they do?" We all have stories about our family, most of them are apocryphal, but whether you love or hate your family, they're yours, and these are your stories. On the other hand, Tom McGuane once said, "I've done a lot of horrible things in my life but I never taught creative writing."

INTERVIEWER

What about your work since *Clockers*?

PRICE

I got into writing a script for *Clockers* because it was sold to Universal for Martin Scorsese. I had done three movies with him. Even did a Michael Jackson video with him. So, I spent a year writing a script based on *Clockers*, which is sort of like going from being the parent to the babysitter, because now this story is theirs—they bought it, and I'm just a hired pen. It's like you gave birth, sold the child and then were hired on as the kid's caretaker. And the new parents can give you the boot if they don't like your work. So I was writing for Scorsese, DeNiro was involved too, but ultimately those guys decided to do *Casino* instead.

So Spike Lee jumped in and said, "I read your book, I read all the drafts, and with all due respect I like to write my own stuff." So he took over as the screenwriter. It was a very strange experience. When a movie is made from your own raw material, you come into the movie theater with so much psychic luggage. Everybody else is there just watching a movie, whereas you see what you first wrote as fiction, transformed into script, then changed by Spike, then changed again by the actors, the editing, etc. You're sitting watching a simple dialogue exchange and you trip out down memory lane and the next thing you know twenty minutes have gone by and you have no idea what's been happening on the screen since that little dialogue exchange made you wander off. It's like driving along a highway drifting off, and when you come back to driving consciousness twenty miles have gone by. Who's been driving while you were gone? In a way I can never watch the movie, because everything I'd see would take me out of the movie and back to the script, back to Spike's script, back to the novel, back to the experience that provoked the novel. I could never follow the damn thing, because my mind would keep taking me away. The funny thing is, what I liked best in the movie was the stuff I had nothing to do with — that wasn't in the book — where Spike had to go back and shoot transitional stuff; I had no idea what he was doing. There I felt most like a moviegoer.

INTERVIEWER

Is the process for getting the idea for a novel very different from the process for a screenplay?

PRICE

My screenplay ideas were given to me, or taken from something I've done, or something that's very "surface" for me, like *Mad Dog and Glory*. In Jamaica, I saw a dynamic between two people: one of them a woman from Miami, the other a Jamaican busboy working in a hotel, Lance, with whom I became friendly when I bought some of his ganja. Lance found out that I had a car. He said, "Oh, man. I'll take you into the jungle tomorrow. We'll go visit my grandparents in Sav-La-Mar." To have a car is a treat down there. He said, "We'll take a *ride*." I said okay. He showed up with this blonde, lanky,

gum-chewing woman from Miami named Jody Goldfarb. Jody
was about six inches taller than him, and I couldn't figure out
what they were doing together, except that maybe she's a
tourist who likes to get down with the natives. I spent all
day with them driving around the jungle. They weren't even
talking to each other . . . not hostile, but awkward. I had no
idea what their relationship was. Then by chance she wound
up on my flight back to Miami. I said, "Oh, is that guy your
boyfriend?"

She says, "No, but my friend Lou from Miami came down
to the hotel about a month ago. He got in trouble swimming,
and Lance jumped in and saved him. When Lou got back to
Miami he said to me, 'How'd you like a trip to Jamaica? I'd
like you to be this guy's friend. I owe him one. If you do
something for me, I'll remember it'." She says, "The next thing
I knew I was standing behind the hotel near the employees'
quonset huts in a bikini wearing a sash that said, 'Thanks,
Lou'." She was a human thank-you present. God knows who
"Lou from Miami" was, but it didn't sound good.

That story stayed with me for ten years, but it was not
something I'd really wanted to go into depth with in a novel.
The ideas I have for screenplays are ideas I can hold in my
hand without anything dribbling out onto the floor. Things
that come to me as novels I don't even know how to describe,
because they have no beginning, no end, and I'm not even
sure where the center is. What comes to me as a screenplay
is usually something I can describe in a paragraph.

INTERVIEWER

Is that in the nature of the movie business or of film story?

PRICE

It's the nature of studio business in Hollywood. People there
want something new but familiar; they don't like you to deviate too much from what they've seen before. What they've
seen before has a fiscal track record. If you're going to invest
fifty million dollars in a movie, you would like to know who

the parents are. If you're buying a racehorse, you'd like the bloodlines to include Citation and Whirlaway, not Maude and Mr. Ed. If you tried to pitch *The Crying Game* to a Hollywood studio, you'd have to say, "Well, it's out of *Malcolm X* and sired by *Tootsie*." But if you just say to them, "Look, this is a very small story. It's sort of political. It's sort of a thriller. It's sort of a love story. It takes place in England. It's very small-time people. One of them's a transvestite, the other a terrorist. And, it's *quite* unusual." They'd say, "Great. Go tell it to Miramax."

INTERVIEWER

What did you learn from screenplays that you think might have helped you write *Clockers*?

PRICE

What I learned in screenplays is that I don't have to write about myself all the time. I had a number of assignments for which I had to write about people that were completely outside my sphere, but I learned that if I simply hung out and absorbed their world a bit, I was able to create characters that were compelling and somewhat faithful to their sources. I didn't learn to do that as a novelist. I did it as a screenwriter and that gave me the confidence to take on *Clockers* and all these characters who were not of my personal experience.

INTERVIEWER

Is it easy to go from the novel to screenwriting?

PRICE

The danger of going from screenplays to books, books to screenplays is the danger of movie-addiction. Screenplays are for me like dope. "I'm gonna quit. I swear. Right after this last script." Excuses, excuses. "I need the money. This one's a surefire go. How can I not work with this actor. How can I say no to this director." Three scripts later I'm still writing scripts. That's what happened to me. I went back after *Clockers* and wrote three movies, including *Clockers*, *Kiss of Death*, with Nicolas Cage and David Caruso, and *Ransom* with Mel Gibson.

But now I'm finished with all of that. I'm at work on a new book. I've gone back to the same fictional place as *Clockers*. When I did *Clockers* I went in and saw the urban world in a microcosm in Jersey City and I came out with this huge book. But I also felt I had taken a teaspoon from the ocean, that I could go back to that place and explore various aspects of the urban world for the rest of my life and not make a dent. It's in no way a sequel to *Clockers*. It's about politics and the media. So I'm hanging out again.

INTERVIEWER

I want to apologize for asking a personal question, but would you tell me about your hand?

PRICE

My hand? Well, I was born with a mild case of cerebral palsy. It's no big thing on a day-to-day basis; mostly people get uncomfortable when they have to shake hands with me. What the hell . . . of course, I'd like to be a weightlifter, but I can't.

INTERVIEWER

You'd like to be a weightlifter?

PRICE

Anybody who has something wrong with them physically is kind of obsessed with their appearance, so I'm always dabbling with weightlifting. My left hand's twice as strong as my right hand, so I never get anywhere with it, but . . .

INTERVIEWER

I don't want to get too abstruse here, but do you consider there's any connection between all this and your becoming a writer?

PRICE

If you've got something obviously awry in your appearance
people treat you differently, like you're a special case. It never
stopped me from playing sports. I played handball for my
high-school team. You have to be ambidextrous to be a good
handball player. I developed a backhand to compensate. It
was no big deal. But, then there would be all this drama. The
gym teacher would see me playing with that fouled-up hand
and he'd call me over with tears in his eyes, and he'd say,
"Son, you can always play on my team."

It's not like you walk around thinking about it all day. But
as you grow up with this sense of yourself being singular, in
some way you get hooked on the singularity of yourself. To
be an artist is to be singular. I think, in some people, before
the desire to write there is the desire to be special. That's not
exactly healthy, and there's nothing relevant to creativity in
that. Maybe I was just trying to maintain that sort of special
thing by writing.

My grandmother, who was a big influence on my life, would
take me under her wing because there was something wrong
with my hand. She was a very unhappy person herself, very
heavy, about five feet tall. Really overweight. Like two hundred pounds or more. It was her against the world, and she
saw me as her ally. I think she tended to see herself as a freak.
There was something wrong with my hand, so we were fellow
freaks . . . although she never said that to me. To go to her
house on a Saturday was like getting parole for a day. I didn't
understand how unhappy and isolated she was, but she'd be
all filled with this melodrama about everything. We'd sit and
look out her Bronx kitchen window and watch the East 172nd
Street follies. She'd see a black man who lived across the street
and she'd say, "Oh, this one is a gentleman, married to this
white piece of trash. She goes with anything in pants. She
has him wrapped around her little finger. Do you know how
much of a gentleman this man is? If he goes into his building
lobby to go into the elevator and he sees a white woman there
who's gonna get spooked by him because he's a black man,
do you know what he does? He steps *out* of the lobby so she

can go up the elevator herself. Now, *this* is a gentleman. But that whore he's married to . . . ?"

Then there'd be some other guy. "Oh, this son-of-a-bitch, he's a junkie. Every time he sticks a needle in his arm it's like sticking a needle in his mother's heart. She comes to me, she says, 'Mrs. Rosenbaum, what can I do! What can I do!' Richard, what am I going to tell her?"

It was this constant rat-tat-tat. I'm six and I'm with the fattest, biggest ball of love to me. This is my grandmother. Then we'd go all day to monster movies. She'd be talking back to the screen the whole time.

INTERVIEWER

Monster movies?

PRICE

In a neighborhood you wouldn't go into with a tank. We'd watch *The Attack of the Praying Mantis*, along with *The Crawling Eye* and *The Creature From Green Hell*. She'd be the only person over fourteen in the whole theater. Not only that, the only person over one hundred and fifty pounds. She'd pack up these big, big, vinyl, sort of, beach bags. She'd make sandwiches, thermoses of coffee and chocolate milk, and bring plums and nectarines. If there was a turkey carcass, she'd wrap it in silver foil so we could pick on the bones. We'd go into the movies with all this. We were ready for anything. And when we came out of the theater we'd have those little light dots in front of our eyes because we'd gone in at noon and we'd be coming out at five o'clock. Coming out, she'd walk all hunched over. She was only in her fifties, but she was so arthritic and rheumatic and heavy. We'd walk all the way back home, about one block every twenty minutes with that nonstop commentary about everybody who crossed our path. She lived on the third floor of a walk-up, so that took another hour, one step at a time. Then we get up there, and even after the triple horror feature we'd watch "Zacherly's Shock Theater," pro wrestling, Roller Derby—everything—drama, stories, tragedies, drama, drama.

One time she took me to a wrestling arena in the early fifties
in the height of summer. She had me on her lap and when
one of the villains walked by she jabbed him with a hatpin.
She was what was known as a Hatpin Mary. So, for the next
match, when Nature Boy Buddy Rogers, this peroxide pompa-
doured villain, who wore a leopard-skin Tarzan getup, came
strutting down the aisle, people were looking at my grandmother, and they started chanting, "Stick him! Stick him!"
He heard the chant and stood right over us, daring her. She
was paralyzed, so he took her hand with the hatpin, a woman
who probably felt very unloved by the world, bowed down
and kissed it, said, "Madam." And then he continued walking
toward the ring. At which point my grandmother dropped
me, just dropped me on the floor. I remember ten, fifteen
years later, when I would watch wrestling with my grandmother, every once in a while she'd say, "I wonder how Nature
Boy Buddy Rogers is doing. He's such a nice guy."

INTERVIEWER

Did your mom know about this going on?

PRICE

I guess. My grandmother's house was heaven for me. When
I started writing in earnest I just thought back to the time
with her, all those Saturdays, all those movies, all that commentary on the world under her window, then I started thinking about my friends, about other aspects of my childhood;
the out-of-whack passions, crushes, terrors, and I began writing this sort of magic realism bullshit aka stories about the
Bronx.

As I always told my students, "We all grow up with ten
great stories about our families, our childhoods . . . they probably have nothing to do with the truth of things, but they're
yours. You know them. And you love them. So use them."
And that's what I did. That's what I reached for, to become
a writer.

Now, at this point in my life I've paid all my bills, I've fulfilled all my screenwriting obligations, I'm financially flush, for the next year I have nothing to do but work on this novel without distraction. So, I'm looking at all my notes, at my nice clean desk, my stack of unwrapped ready-to-go legal pads, and all I can think of is that saying: "If God hates your guts he grants you your deepest wish."

—James Linville

Three Poems by James Longenbach

Things You'll Never Know

I was so young that I invented loss,
The image of the mother's face receding
On the far edge of the broken bed,

A child's face, implacable, returning
To a fountain in a foreign city—
Gods and tritons cracked and thin

Behind a chain-link fence that blurred
Into a veil, like the one that draws us,
Following ourselves, into the past.

Not even Rome is consolation for the death
Of children and to think about the future
Is to think of children and to think

About a child is to think of death,
If only since the child is the part of us
That's disappeared: Aeneas, having mixed

The ashes with the wine, surveying all
The future generations' gifts to Rome,
Attends to one tall youth, more beautiful

Than any other but with clouded brows
And downcast eyes, the child we will mourn,
For whom the lilies offer nothing in return.

It would be useful to believe we'd meet
Again, and all of Christianity
Seems poised against its knowledge

That the one who dies is not the mother
But the child, Jesus railing at heaven
And the sky, unanswering, omnipotent,

The image of what every parent feels
In the face of suffering that nothing
We have learned to do throughout the long

And unrewarded climb into adulthood
Can assuage. The possibilities
Are burdensome enough to think of

Much less see: the snowplow sliding off
The exit ramp or blond hair mimicking
A breezy summer at the bottom of the pool.

We're children then ourselves, incapable
Of action or intelligible speech —
A drooling infant sucking on his hands

Like Ugolino, who must hear his children
Whimpering for bread and bear their charity
Our pain will lessen, father, if you eat us —

And do nothing but observe the sunlight
Leaking through the grille as one by one
The children dwindle to the floor and die.

These stories can't be told, as Dante says,
By tongues that babble in a language
Capable of words like *mom* and *dad*.

Our language is the child's world
And when we speak, no matter what we say,
We're longing for a world we've lost forever,

Only to find out, if we begin to poke
Around the dingy corners of the mind,
That it's a world we never could have had.

Some people think they have an easy access
To whatever made them what they are,
And you can watch them, raising children,

As they replicate each long-lost pleasure
For themselves, pancakes wide
As dinner plates, served up with confidence

That what worked once may, recreated,
Work again. These are the parents
Who won't pay the piper once he's rid

The town of rats — the children lost,
Abandoned, past all help, all hurting,
Who will follow him into the hills

Across rat river, where the ghosts of children
Never born will whisper *play with me* —
And we awaken in a sweat and wander

Down the frozen corridor to check
Their beds, their breathing, too embarrassed
To admit that when we dream about their deaths

We want to die. For if the pancakes work —
Piano lessons, weekends at the barn —
The children take the place of loss,

The part that's dead, and no one, having put
The past to sleep, however nurturing,
However fondly we remember it,

Could want to see its specter wandering
That hallway in the middle of the night
To ask for water or to say *I'm cold.*

The truth of how we felt as children
Is the truth of theater: Pandulpho
In *Antonio's Revenge*, when he confronts

The mangled body of his son, admits
That he has acted like a boy who plays
A grown-up part, *speaks burly words*

But when he thinks upon his infant weakness
Is transformed into a child. We play
The roles long before we comprehend them,

But the comprehension only comes
When we admit we'll never understand
The world as we imagined grown-ups might.

The truth of childhood is theater,
An empty bed, our own breath faltering,
As when the old man who refused to grieve .

Before the mangled body of his son
Admits that he has acted like a boy
Who plays a grown-up part, *speaks burly words*

See the body dead than trusting its desires,
Boys afraid of their own loveliness,
A dingy room, the mutilated trees.

We wander through the underbrush,
Survey the bottles and the rusted cans,
And, finding nothing, are confirmed

In the suspicion that we need to lose—
Lose furniture, the books, our clothes,
And all of the generic memories that from

The moment of our birth have worked their way
Beneath the skin—that over time will burst
Like capillaries on our hands and thighs,

A signal to remind us of the world
That we've internalized and can't abandon
Since in losing it, we lose ourselves.

The body cannot tolerate an emptiness,
And as the wound begins to swell, our grief
Replaces what we've lost, grows vast,

Until the grieving seems ridiculous,
Which is the only thing that grief could be.
The notion of the loss, a fantasy,

Can be enough to open wide the sutures
Of an ordinary day, as when a child
Walks the dog alone, and far above

The traffic and the melting slush,
Although we recognize she had to go,
A panic fills the space she left behind.

You are as fond of grief as of your child,
Says a voice inside us, harsh, uncompromising
As the murky sidewalk down below.

But we retaliate, and like the mother
Who begins to grieve before the prince
Is gone, we play a scene, put on a show:

Grief fills the room up of my absent child,
Lies in his bed, walks up and down with me,
And stuffs his vacant garments with his form.

My child plays ferociously with things
We've given her and things she's found
And things she'll never know. I'm not too old

To play along. Before she spoke
I thought I'd come to know her perfectly —
That just by listening, I'd have an answer

For whatever wakes her in the middle
Of the night. But parents have
No special purview on the human heart

And cannot know their children any better
Than they comprehend themselves.
There's one more thing. We tossed

Some lire in the empty pool, and as if
Parched stone could hear us, water burst
From every orifice, the past undone,

And wonder rising through the air like mist.
I don't remember what we wished,
But anything that ever found us was you.

Orpheus or Eurydice

For seven days he sat along the bank
In filthy garments, stained with river mud.
Indifference, jealousy, or recognition

Makes us disregard what happened next,
How he not only made the shrubs and stones
Dance wickedly but dandled shepherd boys

As if no man had ever thought to do so,
Felt their delicate beards against his thigh
Until the men of Thrace all took to boys

But not exclusively, the long nights home
With the women of Thrace, returning for more,
Never the same way twice. And so they pierced

His mouth as he was singing, cheered his head
And lyre floating down the Hebrus,
As so many after him have loved the sound

Of the wind in the acanthus and so paid
For what they loved, the slender bodies
Almost indistinguishable from here,

As if no one remembers pale skin
Beneath the bathing suit, the fleshy parts
Now hard or soft depending not so much

On what you managed to perform but who it was
Behind that scrim of chlorinated sweat—
The interim between the spastic lull

Of childhood and the aggressive threshold
That denotes its end, beside the river
Or the golf course or whatever margin

Comes to mind, a body's means to pleasure
Is not limited by what the parts,
Or so we learn, have been designed to do.

If marriage meant misfortune or he'd made
A promise at her death, then Orpheus
Would seem a moral paragon, not meat,

And nobody would turn from slaying oxen
To a ritual dismemberment
However crazed by animal desire.

Music can't be held responsible
And even sex is not enough to lubricate
The wheels of this narrative — however

Wayward, interspersed with songs of love
Forbidden equally to men and women —
Since behind the bloody rakes and hoes

The story's more familiar than we recognize:
It doesn't take a trip to hell
And back for us to know transgression,

Carrying the extra sets of clothes
We've worn since childhood, the boundaries
And considerations that we'd like to drop

Beside the soiled mattress on the floor,
Aware that while transgressing, we also obey.
It's like the message smeared in pencil

On the bathroom wall: the rough-hewn cry,
The backward glance forbidden in the mind,
Uncertain, gentle, and without impatience

As the memory turns to hobble through
The meadows back into the mind's dark core,
Concealing a switchblade or a smile.

The Faithless Angel

As a child I never bolted, made a scene
Or misbehaved, so every week it seemed
A blank necessity, like waking up

To snow, the boat adrift, or raking leaves.
The sound of worship never reached my soul,
Immune from birth to things invisible,

And having caught from it no wonder
At the pulse of things, the play of light
And shadow or the slow transgression

Of the body's thickening hide, the world
That I inherited was not mysterious,
No void, no presence, echo, no response.

Fishing held no interest for me, bait
No metaphor but stark deception that I knew.
All big ideas, from democracy

To birthday presents, though I practice both,
Were never emptied of their meaning since
I never had a certainty to lose.

And if I ever felt the world existed
To be questioned, scourged, abused
I couldn't revel in the common cause

Since loyalty oaths had long since hung
Along the blackboards in bohemia
When I was old enough to dance to that tune.

The birds don't sing around the bungalow,
They cough, they sputter, congregate and yell.
Maybe if I'd had a dog myself

I'd understand why loose affection seems
To gather in such moments, unforeseen,
Unasked for, like a golden crown descending

On the undeserving pirate's head.
But when I entertained the notion
That the simplest form of human conjuring

Could mend whatever cosmic rift had made
Us mortal, I discovered long before
My mind was capable of understanding

What acquittal of the body's base
Infirmity could mean, that great books
All belie the longing they've aroused

For immortality and recommend,
Too often smugly, that we all get back
Into the boat, return to Italy,

And like the mackerel crowded underneath us
Procreate and die. Our faith is faith
In someone else's faith, said William James,

And watching snow dissolve in the canal,
Dead fish in the window and the waitress
Reappearing with the grappa poured

In two small globes, I could believe
In human pleasure. But as many times
As we retraced our steps we never stumbled

On that restaurant again. It disappeared
Like certainty, a fine ideal, but where
In all this moonlit, dream-infested city

Is it found? Since the body is dogmatic,
Generates belief, we're better off
With anything that leaves us in between,

Humanizes indecision so we learn
To recognize the moment we've become,
Too hopelessly, assertively, ourselves.

The faithless angels who did not rebel
Were sentenced to this place — not hell,
Where the condemned would seem more beautiful —

But to a margin, fed on bitter grass,
And forced to wander through the frozen marshes,
Unremitting plains, until their footsteps

Cut these channels and their voices raised
The sunburnt palace walls that ask from us
No blessing, no condolence, no reprieve.

Shannon Borg

Reclining Woman with Green Stockings

> *Now she is gone. Now I encounter her body.*
> —Egon Schiele

He waited for her the last time
in the Café Eichberger, at their table:
walls the color of chocolate, tiles worn
to a dull sheen. He held the letter
carefully, turning it over and over,
dipping a corner into his coffee,
the stain rising into the white paper.

At seventeen she became his lover.
For four years willing to sit on his table
with her legs apart as he paced
before the easel. She never saw herself
until he finished—her eyes full and dark,
or dull as the Vienna sky in winter,
her red blouse pooled beneath her.

The strokes of black paint contoured
her thighs smoothly at first, telling
of the softness where her hip
met the luxury of her hair. Here
was where his hand touched her
most deeply, as he held the brush
to the surface—seep of paint, sway

of brush. Her skin began to feel
his mood in the bristle's touch—
blackening his mind, yellowing his pain.
His hand stammered over her body.

Angles in her arms hardened.
He turned silk to stone — jagged, piercing
her skin. Fingers awkward and rough.

Eyes staring at nothing. The green
stockings fell around her wooden
ankles. She walked into the café
wearing them that day, newly pressed,
pulled smoothly up her legs. Her hat
barely covering her scarlet hair.
As he pressed the letter into her hand,

the invitation to continue with him
after his marriage — these sketches
emerged in his mind: the hard
geometry of their bodies together,
the flat yellow fields and sky.
As she read, the odors of coffee
and linseed rose from the letter,

scents she had known for years.
He sat in silence as she told him
no — the smoke from his cigarette
rising — in it she saw the blossoming
of her new body, the curve of her arm,
a curl falling onto her cheek flushed
with the color of her own blood.

Two Poems by Corey Marks

Sparrows

My mother wanted to believe she would never lose me,

the way she wanted to believe in Christ
but now maybe all she believes is Thomas,
how he lost the world when the wound opened
to his finger. Thomas knew then
the world changes when the sleeper's eyes turn

into his head and open, dreaming. In his dream
the spear splits Christ's skin and splits his heart
irrevocably, so grief can be real and not faith's failure.
But Christ returned, Thomas traced a finger through the gash
and knew faith and the world conspired against him.

And I want to believe, staring into a tree's branches
where sparrows wake hours before the light,
in how the sparrows' chorus seems one voice
layered over and over itself—
birds so similar they could all be refractions of one bird,

shattered into a hundred selves
as I would shatter, into past and present, into two lives,
to be both child and man rather than the neither I am.
I want to walk into the house and sleep at my lover's back.
I want to stand on the rock in the river where I stood numbly

as a child, my mother looking on from a bridge,
watching my foot twist down the rock's slick face
into the current I thought wanted only to carry itself away.
If I could draw my foot back and suspend the moment
a few years . . . but then,

184

the water simply opened like a wound
and took me in. So I believe in dissolution, my heart's
    vagueness
in wanting everything. Or rather, how through the cover of
    limbs
and leaves I glimpse only the drab flashings
of sparrows and nothing whole,

unlike Thomas who saw their entirety on a roadside.
He left Christ and the crowding Apostles
and walked to where those few sparrows fluttered in the dirt,
dusting their bodies, preening sand into ruffled feathers,
and he thought then if he ever slept what was real would slip

from him to drift in sleep, and the world would reveal itself
changed and inconstant. Or he might simply dissolve into
    dust,
this dust, a patina on the sparrows' backs.
And when another boy pulled me from the river
my mother already knew she'd lost me. I would disappear
    into myself

if she watched, if she didn't.

Solace

It should be a denial, this morning,
the way winter's fallen across those hills so clearly

threatening too much light, a whiteness diffusing a negative
until whatever image it might hold,

trees paled and indistinct like a body's map of nerves,
blurs into the cess of light. Even the train —

where Kappus leans his head on the cabin's paneling,
his eyes narrowed to watch a young woman

thoughtlessly brush her fingers along her breast,
tracing the embroidered, interconnecting pattern of infinities

in the yellow fabric—even the train seems vague
in light and motion, a grayed seam shifting

among minutes and days and the change
of seasons. In Prague, hours before the train would leave,

he walked down one street where most homes
had been knocked out of this world by the war.

He knew the poet had lived here as a child,
and though he imagined that child curled in a window seat

watching a bee walk slow spirals along his arm
as outside the year's first snow began its multiplying variations,

he couldn't find which shattered house had held the boy.
Kappus sleeps on the train, finally, and the woman

disembarks, leaving only a faint impression in the worn
    cushion
across from him. He dreams Rilke

grown old into another life, no longer poet but a beekeeper
in a pear orchard. He dreams that in winter,

because he wanted to forget how enduring fails,
the poet edged briefly into the world

to drag the white-box hives through the wet snow
and into his house to hear in the waking bees' drone

what's infinite. Some crawled the twisted bedsheets,
or ceaselessly crossed the rim of a tall glass,

though most fretted circles in the air, describing brief,
dissolving constellations like the properties of heaven

he couldn't own or lose. And when the poet slept,
snoring closer than ever to nothing,

a few bees entered his mouth and dragged yellow stingers
delicately across his tongue. But Kappus, when he wakes,

wants some other solace, wants
light to erase everything but a street where he'll wait

as the woman in yellow steps like light across unblemished
    snow,
brilliant and whole without the world.

Jordan Smith

The Dream of Marlowe

—*for Ruth Stevenson*
after The Reckoning

As in the plays, the body was decor,
Fit embellishment to a scene
Where chance's misrule seemed to have gone as planned:
The author's death, sign
Of an author's hand; a coat of arms
Emblazoned above the door.
A portrait whose eyes flared, then died away.
In knowledge — shared, contemptuous and lost —
Of how conspiracy counts its own cost.

But something stirred,
As if, the curtain fallen, the bearded man
Had leave to stand and go, but did not go.
It was the slough
Where spirit's lost, the undone, the might have been.
And yet, his spirit strode to the window sill,
Looked out on the alley, where two men
Were quarrelling over a keg of ale,
Or that one had called the other's wife a whore
Who claimed she'd not been paid enough.
"Ah," he laughed, "a common
Plenitude of common woes,"
Then turned to me, as if to a mirror
Of his unpresence there.

"Poet," he said, "my body was the script
Certain Powers contrived for their designs,
Spirits neither dutiful nor kind —
Succession, sedition, ambition, spite —

Who come unsummoned, who find
Their ends and ours ill-suited but conjoined,
Like the pursuits of pleasure and of love,
Who promise we might thunder like some god
If we make a masque of their words."

He shrugged.

"As well might the quartered traitor praise
The law that flung his limbs
Afield, like chaff before the wind,
The playwright scratch his lines away
To make himself more clear . . . But I,
I was a stubborn text, in whose every draft
Still spoke the suffering and the damned
Soul who knew how poor,
How dear all knowledge was.
So I came here . . . " He gestured then,
And the room spun,
A compass placed too near some metal thing,

"Why this is hell," I said.

"Come." He drew two chairs
Aside, "We'll have wine,
And a hand of cards to see who pays."
And I was tempted then, to honor him,
Settle his score, and stay.
Yet even as I thought, he had become
My thought,

and was away.

Four Mice

Joyce Pensato

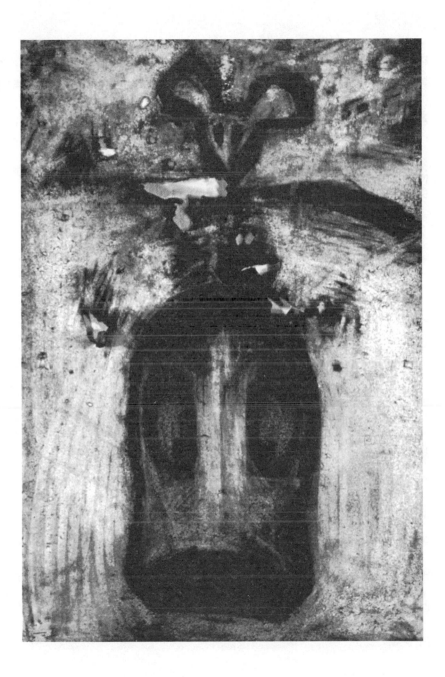

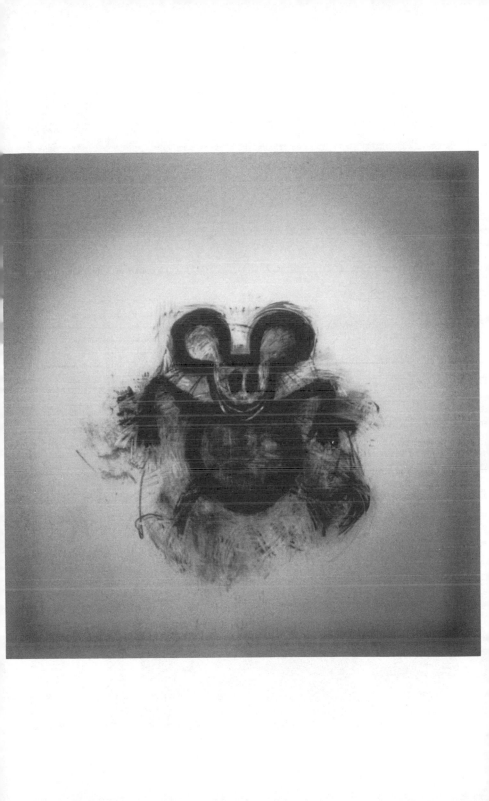

Terry Southern

A Portfolio

Terry Southern:
Introduction

The following pages have been set aside as a kind of tribute to honor the work of Terry Southern, who died last October in New York City — appreciations, reminiscences, critiques, as well as some original work from his files.

A longtime friend, Terry was in a sense largely responsible for the birth of this magazine back in 1953. In the early stages of publishing a Paris-based New Yorker *imitation entitled* The Paris News-Post, *its editors, Peter Matthiessen and Harold L. Humes, were so impressed by the strength of a story submitted by their friend Terry (a section of his novel* Flash and Filigree*) that they decided to scrap the* New Yorker *imitation and start a literary magazine. The story (entitled "The Accident") was incorporated in the first number. Thus,* The Paris Review!

Terry often contributed to the magazine — stories, novel excerpts (a section of The Magic Christian *won the Gertrude Vanderbilt Humor Prize) and an interview on the Art of Fiction with his friend, the novelist Henry Green.*

In appearance Terry was a rumpled, soft-spoken, courtly and rather owlish personage. A distinguishing feature was his speech. Texas-born, he developed a curious, mock high-

*English complete with little harrumphs (What? What?) delivered in fits and starts, with words often abbreviated in hipster style (*fab *for* fabulous*) and marked with qualifying endearments such as "Tip-Top Tony" for Tony Richardson, the movie director — very unique and not unlike how Goofy would sound if born an earl.*

It is appropriate that the Terry Southern material that follows should appear in an issue in part devoted to screenwriting. Toward the end of his interview with Henry Green, his friend told him this: "The novelist is a communicator and must therefore be interested in any form of communication . . ."

When Stanley Kubrick, the filmmaker, impressed by The Magic Christian, *asked its author to come to London and help with* Dr. Strangelove, *Terry temporarily left what he referred to as the "Quality Lit Game" to take on another "form of communication." His work on* Dr. Strangelove *was the first of a number of his contributions to films* (Easy Rider, The Loved Ones, The Cincinnati Kid, Barbarella, *etc.*).

A few years ago Terry Southern was honored by a film society at a huge gathering at Roseland. On a giant screen the famous War Room scene from Dr. Strangelove *was shown, in the early moments of which a scuffle breaks out, stopped by the president of the United States who calls out, "Gentlemen, you can't fight in here. It's the War Room!"*

At the conclusion of the film clip, the audience rose for a standing ovation that went on for minutes. In the manner of an equivalent salute, it is a pleasure for the Review *to offer what follows.*

—G.A.P.

Terry Southern:
An Appreciation

Henry Allen

When word came on the last day of October, 1995 that Terry Southern had died, Henry Allen, a staff writer for The Washington Post, *asked if he could write an appreciation for the next morning's edition. He bicycled home in a rainstorm, six miles, to refer to his collection of Southern work, and in two and a half hours wrote his copy for the following day. It is essentially what appears here, with a few additions.*

Hunter Thompson, with a fresh glass of Wild Turkey, didn't see the Terry Southern question coming. It was 1972. He'd just faxed off another story about fear and loathing on the campaign trail, this one featuring a bellboy beating a snake to death with a vacuum cleaner.

"Have you ever read a book called *The Magic Christian*?" I asked.

Thompson flinched. His face, normally smooth as the leather on a blackjack, wrinkled into a stare, as if he were

about to ask me: "Are you one of . . . US? One of those who
. . . KNOWS?"

I knew.

"Yes," he shouted. "Yes! My God! It was an incredible
influence on me, that last scene with the gorilla running
around on the bridge of the ship, and the smoke pouring into
the staterooms, my God, it was so great."

Indeed. It was about a cosmically ironic multimillionaire
named Guy Grand who went from chapter to chapter sowing
chaos, degradation and fear with wildly expensive pranks. He
bribed the heavyweight champ to break into effeminate pranc-
ing and screaming in the ring. He appalled gourmets at French
restaurants.

This came out in 1959, a little after the novel *Candy*, written
with Mason Hoffenberg, had been a scandal and best-seller
that made Southern famous. Still, he was a connoisseur's taste,
if there can be connoisseurs of a writer who once said that as
a boy in Texas he wanted to rewrite all of Poe's stories because
they didn't go "far enough."

"The important thing in writing is the capacity to astonish,"
Southern told *Life* magazine in 1964. "Not shock — shock is
a worn-out word — but astonish. The world has no grounds
whatever for complacency."

Southern died yesterday at the age of seventy-one. A lot
of his stuff is less printable now than it was in the fifties,
before corsets came off women's hips and got strapped onto
people's minds.

In *Candy*, the pert, cutie-pie heroine ends up writhing
around with a psychotic hunchback.

"'Your hump! Your hump!' she kept crying, scratching and
clawing at it now.

"'Fuck! Shit! Piss!' she screamed. 'Cock! Cunt! Crap! Prick!
Kike! Nigger! Wop! *Hump*! HUMP!' and she teetered on the
blazing peak of pure madness for an instant . . ."

Southern knew he was outraging puritans of feminism,
mental illness and disfigurement. Southern was way ahead of
his time or way behind it, it's hard to tell. In any case, nobody

astonishes now in this Decade of the Dead, and nobody seems to have any of the fun Southern had.

He was a master of American clichés, expectations and pieties, of a world creaking with irony and alive with a topiary of quotation marks and not quite appropriate exclamation points.

In *The Magic Christian*, Guy Grand takes over a Fifth Avenue cosmetics company and announces the launch of a vile-smelling deodorant to his executives: "Gentlemen, I say this product may well spell *home run* in the hearts of Mr. and Mrs. U.S.A!"

This was language that would have gone over quite nicely at the Rotary meeting in Conshohocken, Pennsylvania, but Southern's audience was in on the joke. Southern was a minstrel of the Hip Age, and the essence of hip was being in on the joke, of spotting the bit of epistemological guerrilla warfare known as the "put-on," which took the form of, say, somebody telling you Béla Bartók's ashes were in Sweet Daddy Grace's safe-deposit box in Harlem, some crazy story, and then somebody else saying, "He's putting you on, man," and then you not knowing which one was putting you on.

Hip was a constant struggle over information and who controlled it, the government, the newspapers, the guy drinking coffee at the next table, if you put him on, you controlled it. Terry Southern took this grim doctrine and made it funny, satirizing both hip and square into a style of spectacular grace, clarity and modulation through all the realities you could bite into like a napoleon, all the flaky layers. Hip put banality in quotation marks, made it a joke, a critical overview, whatever. Hip was also the unchallenged possession of all blacks, who were known as "spades."

In a story called "You're Too Hip, Baby," an American intellectual named Murray takes pride in knowing every black jazzman in Paris. He listens to them, gets stoned with them. He befriends Buddy, a pianist, and his wife Jackie. They can't figure him. What does he want? Sex with her? With him? Piano lessons?

Buddy asks him: "'I mean, just what have we got that interests you?'

"Murray looked at him briefly, and then looked away in exasperation. . . . 'Well, what do *you* think, man?' he demanded, turning back to Buddy. 'I dig the *scene* that's all. I dig the scene and the *sounds*.'

"Buddy stood up . . . and shook his head. 'You're too hip, baby. That's right.' He laughed. 'In fact, you're what we might call a kind of professional *nigger lover*.'"

In a story called "The Night the Bird Blew for Dr. Warner," a renowned musicologist descends into the hip world and writes: "It is significant that the emotional nihilism, or again, the cold satiric intent which has come to be identified with these interpretations . . . " A page or so later he's been clubbed to the ground in an alley.

Southern himself wrote some stories whose nihilism and cold satire verge on the irredeemable. In "Heavy Put Away" a desperate and good-hearted woman is conned into prostituting herself for the sake of her unemployed husband who is suffering at home in a body cast. Not only doesn't she get paid, the john steals her wedding ring.

The narrator, hearing the story from an acquaintance, fails to understand the point. Was it worth weeks of chicanery and persuasion to steal a $100 wedding ring?

"'A hundred tops,' said Art, 'probably less.'

"'Well, that doesn't seem like much . . . for all that trouble.'

"He laughed. 'You've got a pretty *materialistic* slant on things, don't you?'"

With that, Southern goes through the moral air lock into the outer-space vacuum of pure evil, evil for evil's sake. Evil was a sideline with Southern — he helped edit an anthology of writers such as Louis-Ferdinand Céline and Curzio Malaparte, fascists only a decade after the Holocaust ended.

Southern is so good a writer, so good a manipulator of readers' expectations, such a virtuoso of tone and effect, that he makes anything possible. A symbol in someone else's prose is a fact in Southern's. Then he takes those facts and springs them with a tour de force, and we're off into a weirdly parallel universe, hip, hip and away.

He was one of the last of the Paris literati, in those Jean-Seberg-George-Plimpton years after World War II, and one of the first of the postmoderns. He helped write *Dr. Strangelove*, which features the famous "Gentlemen, you can't fight in here! This is a war room!" He was a writer on *Easy Rider* which summed up the whole counterculture-communal-drug fantasy with the line, "We blew it."

There are moments in his books that still astonish you and there are moments that make you feel you probably had to have been there. Along with Thompson, Kurt Vonnegut and Ken Kesey, he's one of the last writers in America to be a culture hero, as opposed to celebrity, which he never was.

After publishing a novel called *Blue Movie* in 1970, he wrote one script and published no books until 1992, when he brought out a coming-of-age novel called *Texas Summer*. It vanished with a very small trace. He couldn't go on being hip forever.

In his heyday, we thought he was helping destroy American hypocrisy and self-righteousness for good. Now, of course, we know we were wrong. In the age of political correctness and sensitivity training, things are worse than ever, which means that Southern seems more outrageous than ever. Maybe the silence of his last twenty years meant he was ahead of his time. And as any hipster knows, when you're ahead of your time, you become your own hardest act to follow.

Making It Hot for Them

Terry Southern

Making It Hot for Them will be my first wholly auto-biographical book. It is organized by era; presented not so much as a narrative, as a sequence of scenes.

Part 1: *Texas.* Born in the small cotton-farming town of Alvarado, 1924. My dad, a pharmacist and descendant of the notorious "Indian lover" and first prez of the Republic of Texas, Sam Houston. Around high-school age moved to Fort Worth and Dallas. Attended Sunset High School, learned how to get girls drunk on the original Grayhound — grapefruit juice masking the taste of vod — followed by the adroit and surreptitious use of sharpened rounded-point kindergarten scissors to snip away that last bastion of defense, the panty crotch panel. At an early age began reading some of the more freaky short stories of E.A. Poe, then rewriting them using classmates and teachers in outlandish roles.

My last novel, *Texas Summer*, explored the racial situation; Dallas was divided by railroad tracks, and we would venture into "Nigger Town" for the great chicken and ribs, and the extraordinary music. Dynamic and eventful pilgrimages. At-tended SMU until drafted for W.W. II, trained, dodged torpedoes all the way to Dover, and buzz bombs all over London. The war gave me a taste for Europe.

Part II: *Europe*. With the liberation of France came my introduction to French culture. I began writing stories while living in Paris on the GI Bill, and attending lectures given by Sartre and Camus at the Sorbonne. The historic cafes, Flore and Deux Maggots, were the meeting places for young writers, and we contributed to publications like *New Story*, *Zero*, *Merlin* and *The Paris Review*. During this time I met Maurice Girodias, and would later, after reading Burroughs's manuscript of *Naked Lunch*, persuade him to publish it. During this period I also knew Charlie Parker, André Malraux, Samuel Beckett, Henry Miller, Peggy Guggenheim, Kenneth Tynan, Ionesco, Mordecai Richler and the Arab, Hadj, who ran a hash bar in Les Halles called Soleil du Maroc.

George Plimpton, Peter Matthiessen and Doc Humes founded *The Paris Review*, and the premier issue published my first short story, "The Accident." I began to be published in other magazines, and completed my first novel *Flash and Filigree*, which, after being rejected by twenty-six U.S. publishers, was published in England, glowingly reviewed by Henry Green and voted Best Novel Of The Year by *The Observer*.

Part III: explores *New York Beat life*. The literary and jazz scene, the dope scene and the underground writing scene, Off Broadway plays like *Ubu roi* and Jack Gelber's *The Connection*, the loft scene, the painting scene, where I knew Jackson Pollock, Jean Tinguely, Larry Rivers, Franz Kline, Bob Rauschenberg and Jasper Johns. I also knew David Amram, Neil Welliver and George Avakian who produced the first jazz LP and was the brother of my best friend Aram Avakian. George got us work writing liner notes for the records of many great jazz musicians of the era, including Diz, Bird, Thelonious and Bud Powell. I wrote a short story about an impressionable young girl in Greenwich Village who gives herself to a hunchback, later to become the heroine, Candy Christian.

I met my first wife, Carol, at a party at Robert Frank's studio loft. Alex Trocchi arrived on the New York scene about this

time and got me a job on the barges. We were towed up and
down the Hudson for almost a year. After that we went to
Geneva where Carol taught at the UN School for Children,
and we lived in rooms above the school à la Kafka's Joseph
K. During a visit to Paris, I started expanding the story of
Candy, in collaboration with an American poet, Mason
Hoffenberg. *Candy* was first published in Paris by Olympia
Press, was banned in the U.S. and Britain, but was smuggled
into each country for several years, until it was finally published
in the U.S. Eventually it would sell over 5 million copies,
appearing on the best-seller list for over a year. We received
the equivalent of about $500 for the book, for reasons which
might be amusing to explain. It was about this time I became
great friends with the English novelist Henry Green, who had
reviewed *Flash and Filigree*, and through him met T.S. Eliot
and Bertrand Russell.

Part IV: *Working in films.* I wrote the novel *The Magic
Christian*, which was also first published in England. Peter
Sellers, a voracious reader, liked the book so much that he
bought a hundred copies of it to give to his friends; one such
person he gave it to was Stanley Kubrick. The filming of *Dr.
Strangelove* had already begun, the script at this point a melodrama based on an RAF officer's book *Red Alert*. *Esquire* sent
me to write a story on the making of the film. Kubrick soon
realized, however, that the destruction of the world could not
be "treated in a conventional manner," and because he liked
the humor of *Magic Christian*, he hired me to work with him
in transforming the film from melodrama to black comedy.
The financing of the picture had been based on Peter Sellers
playing multiple roles, including the pilot, Major Kong, but
he sprained his ankle and was unable to perform the rather
strenuous physical moves required in the role. His replacement
was Slim Pickens, a genuine cowboy and professional rodeo
rider who had never before been outside the Southwest rodeo
circuit. It became my task to translate his heavy drawl for the
others. Stanley and I were driven two hours from London to
the studio (Shepperton) each morning in the predawn darkness. The vehicle was a large Rolls or Bentley, its rear compart-

ment quite luxurious with foldout writing desks, lights, etc.,
and we would rewrite the scenes to be filmed that day. They
proved to be some of the best things in the film. Working
on *Dr. Strangelove* was, of course, an extraordinary introduction to screenwriting for any author.

Soon after *Strangelove*, Tony Richardson, riding high on
his smash-hit *Tom Jones* hired me to work on *The Loved One*.
Tom Jones had been nominated for ten Academy Awards
and had made millions for the studio. Tony, who was under
contract to make a second film for the same studio was locked
into a ridiculously low salary, and vowed to take his revenge
by eccentric (and expensive) behavior — casting an American
(Robert Morse) to play an English poet, shooting the film in
sequence and screening all rushes at the plush private screening
room of the Beverly Hills Hotel, with hors d'oeuvres and drinks
for all.

The Cincinnati Kid, directed by Norman Jewison, presented
me with another all-star cast, and a challenging rewrite (of a
script by Ring Lardner, Jr.). The original director, Sam Peckin-
pah was fired after a horrendous falling out over a black/white
love scene.

I did a great many rewriting jobs on films for which I did not
receive (nor request) credit: William Wyler's *The Collector*,
Alexander Mackendrick's *Don't Make Waves*, and *Casino Roy-
ale* come to mind.

Two of my films that did not fare well were, ironically
enough, adaptations of my own novels: *Candy* and *The Magic
Christian*. I withdrew from the production of *Candy* when a
Scandinavian actress was, over my objection, cast as the heroine, a uniquely American role. A recent experience will also
reveal just how wrong things can go for a writer in the movies.
The Telephone, a highly complex O. Henry-type monologue,
developed for Robin Williams by Harry Nilsson and myself,
was doomed when the producers told Whoopi Goldberg, the
new star of the film, that she could improve on the script by
improvising whenever she felt like it, but neglected to tell
director Rip Torn or myself.

My friends in Hollywood were photographer Bill Claxton, James Coburn, George Segal and Lenny Bruce. Lenny lived on the top of Laurel Canyon, and we would drive down the canyon to Tiny Naylor's. I almost persuaded him to play the role of the Lonelyhearts columnist in *The Loved One*, but he finally decided "to wait and star" in his own film.

Part V: *The sixties and groovy London.* Every era has its place where art can flourish, and London was that place in the mid-sixties. The core of the scene revolved around the Robert Frazer Gallery on Duke Street. Michael Cooper, the photographer on whom Antonioni based *Blowup*, turned the Stones on to the "race records" of the period, and acted as a kind of artistic advisor to Frazer. They gave many pop artists their first shows in Europe, including: Andy Warhol, Rauschenberg, Roy Lichtenstein, Jasper Johns, Jim Dine, Magritte, Peter Blake, Claes Oldenberg, Richard Hamilton, Bridget Riley and Jean Dubuffet. Cooper photographed everyone from that period and created the *Sgt. Pepper's* cover in his studio with Peter Blake.

A Few Stories: By 1966, I had earned so much money writing for the movies that my friend the producer, Sy Litvanoff, suggested I invest in a literary property to develop for the screen which he would produce. With his help I was able to get an option on a book I admired: Anthony Burgess's *A Clockwork Orange*, and did a very faithful adaptation of it. It seemed that everything was set to go — with either Mick Jagger or the star of *Blowup*, David Hemmings, very hot at the time, both keen to do it. But the British Lord Chancellor, who has to approve all scripts produced in England, would not give permission because of the Teddy Boy and Mod Rocker violence in the country at that moment. A few years later, when I could no longer afford the option, Kubrick picked it up and wrote a script of his own. In the new more relaxed social climate, the Lord Chancellor found no problem with the material.

Barbarella was adapted from the famous French comic strip and filmed at Cinecitta in Rome. There are many stories about Roger Vadim's relationship with Jane Fonda, and Dino De-

Laurentis's eccentric production methods. During the filming
in Italy, I was paid a visit by Peter Fonda, who was under
contract with AIP and Roger Corman to do yet another biker
movie. Peter wanted to do something of more substance, and
we began to outline *Mardi Gras*, the story of two disaffected
On the Road types. In New York, Peter, Dennis Hopper and
I had story conferences at my house on Thirty-sixth Street.
At one point, we had them as race-car drivers cutting out on
their exploitative promoters, but when we were reminded that
Peter's contract called for a *biker* movie, we abandoned that
pronto. We wanted Rip Torn to be in the movie, so I wrote
a part for him based on Faulkner's Southern lawyer character,
Gavin Stevens. Rip proved to be unavailable, and the role
went to Jack Nicholson and made him a star. An interesting
aside is that Dennis, who has made many public pronounce-
ments about the film, actually never had a clue as to its real
intent: an indictment of the bigoted American redneck. When
he saw the ending I had written, he implored me not "to kill
'em off." "We gotta save at least one of them!" he kept saying.
He just didn't have a clue.

Part VI: *The late sixties.*   I was sent by *Esquire* with William
Burroughs and Jean Genet to cover the Democratic Convention of Chicago in 1968, and after dodging tear gas, billy-club-
slinging police and the riot itself, ended up testifying at the
Chicago Eight conspiracy trial in defense of Black Panther
Bobby Seal and the Yipster Abbie Hoffman. Allen Ginsberg
was also there, holding forth with his Zen mantras against the
outrageous violence of the Chicago police.

We started shooting *End of The Road* two weeks after Robert
Kennedy was killed. My old roommate from Paris and Greenwich Village, Aram Avakian directed. We could not afford a
regular Director of Photography, so we hired someone whose
only experience was in making commercials; he turned out
to be the award-winning cinematographer Gordon Willis.

Part VII: *Pirated Editions and Ill-fated Projects.*   In the
early seventies, I worked with Peter Beard in adapting his book
End Of The Game to film. The Stones were often at Andy
Warhol's, who was a neighbor of Peter's on Montauk Point,

and after seeing what we were up to, Keith and Mick wanted to do some original music for the film, complete with African rhythms and jungle sounds. Their tour began soon after, and Peter and I went with them. I wrote a book about the tour with photographs by Annie Liebowitz. About this time I also wrote a screen adaptation of Nathanael West's *A Cool Million* for Jerry Schatzberg (*The Panic In Needle Park*) but he failed to find a producer. In 1980, Peter Sellers and Hal Ashby hired me to write a script about the sale of weapons to nations of the Third World. It was titled *Grossing Out* and would have been produced if Peter had not died.

A lot of oddball types have hired me to develop their film projects, and surely the oddest of them was Aletha Flynt, wife of the outlandish publisher of *Hustler* mag, to do a film about Jim Morrison. An extraordinary group was either staying or hanging out at Flynt Manse at that time: Frank Zappa, Tim Leary, Madeline Murray (the "professional atheist" whose Supreme Court case got compulsory prayer out of the schools), Marjo, the ex-child evangelist, G. Gordon Liddy (Liddy and Leary used to practice their "debates"), Chief Russell Means, of Wounded Knee fame (Larry Flynt was running for president and Chief Russell Means was his running mate).

Working at *Saturday Night Live* with Michael O'Donahugh in the late eighties will be one of the closing stories. Many of our best efforts were denied production by the network's outrageous Standards and Practices Dept. — including an epic piece about ratings wars between the networks. In our piece the NBC execs were behaving like Third Reich officers during the closing hours of the war, making desperate attempts to come up with shows that would save the ratings. Such quiz shows as "Look Up Her Dress!" and "K.Y. Madness" were briefly considered, along with the zany sitcom "Sleazy Gyno."

Epilogue: A prominent Washington lawyer, Richard Ben-Veniste, one of the Special Prosecutors in the Watergate Trials, turned out to be a great fan of mine and, through the Freedom of Information Act, was able to get files revealing my IRS persecution because of anti-Vietnam activities. The IRS harassment coincided with my not being able to get screenwriting work from 1966 to the present.

My son has archived my work and is helping me organize this book, and others. Ironic, that I return to the publishing arena in a near full circle, keen to begin anew.

The handsome and interesting face (Mick Jagger type) of
Paul Davis, in half profile, hair stirring in the soft night wind,
is gazing out on a beautiful summer evening, from the terrace of
the casino at Monte Carlo. His POV, silver ribbons of moonlight,
playing in intricate abstract patterns across the sensuously un-
dulting incoming waves of the blue Mediterranean.

An extremely beautiful girl, intriguingly exotic, moves into the
frame. She speaks with a slight accent. "What is it, darling?" she
asks softly, "what do you see out there?" She peers into the night,
looking at the same spot, he's looking at, but not seeing it -- not
the way he does. Back to his POV: the lights dancing in fantastic,
almost sureallistic, refraction -- and we know now that his is an
extraordinary perception indeed, either naturally, or through some
form of induced alteration.

"Please tell me," she says quietly, and she raises a thin bamboo-
paper joint into the frame, to her lips, and draws on it deeply.

"Nothing." he says finally, turning slowly to look at her, then
smiles, "only your eyes."

She takes another drag, and proffers it to him, but instead of
taking it, he gently clasps her hand and presses his lips against it.
She gazes at him lovingly, but with a vague sadness. "You don't need
anything, do you?"

He smiles. "I need you," he says, ". . .sometimes." And he re-
leases her hand.

She sighs and looks back inside the casino, through the terrace-
doors, and into the gaming-room, where the action is -- the glitter
of jewels and jewled chandeliers, the silent movement of elegantly
dressed people across the deep crimson plush.

"Are you going to play some more?" she asks, without looking
at him.

"No," he says softly, looking back at the sea, "not tonight."

WHAM! There is a tremendous explosion, with a SLAM-CUT to the
muzzle-blast of a twelve-guage shotgun, and in the distance, under
brilliant sunshine, a white pigeon falls fluttering into the blue
sea. It is the same terrace, at two o'clock the following day, and
Paul and Count LeGrand are engaged in a pigeon shoot competition,
the birds being released below the terrace and shot at as they fly
towards the sea. The dialogue is in French, without subtitles, since it is quite obvious what they are saying.

The first four pages from an unfinished screenplay.

2

> COUNT LEGRAND
> Les doubles?

> PAUL (shrugs)
> Comme te veut.

> COUNT LEGRAND
> Dix mille balles chacqun?

> PAUL
> D'accord.

An attendant relays the message to the person below, and they begin
shooting doubles -- two birds released at the same time. There are
a dozen or so spectators, sitting around the terrace, drinking, and
watching the match with avid *attention*. Among them are several striking-
ly beautiful women, and their particular interest in Paul is most
apparent. Also looking on is a tall *middle-aged* American, wearing a white Stetson
hat, *and* yellow shooting-glasses; crooked on his arm is a custom-made
elaborately engraved, gold inlay, *double-barrelled* 12-guage. Standing alongside
him is a Saudi Arabian Prince, middle-aged, in luxurious burnoose and *rose-*
colored mirrored-shades. The American is a Slim Pickens-Ben Johnson type, *a*
Texas millionaire, *the* speaks with a heavy drawl and twang.

> SLIM (to the Prince)
> Goddam, that ole boy shoots purty good,
> don't he?

The Prince has a slight accent.

> PRINCE (gravely nodding)
> He shoots the best -- the best of
> anyone.

> SLIM (spits *derisively*)
> Well now, is that a fact?

He looks around at the admiring women, chuckles drily.

> SLIM (continuing)
> *An' ah* just reckon that ain't <u>all</u>
> he's good at neither.
> (nudges the Prince and grins)

> PRINCE
> Yes, so they say.

> SLIM (slightly irritated)
> Well, what <u>else</u> does he do
> -- I mean besides <u>shoot</u> an' <u>fuck</u>?

> PRINCE
> Oh, many things. He is *very much,* how
> would you say, a <u>Renaissance</u> man.

SLIM (snorts) *tellin' me*
Well, that sure ain't ~~sayin'~~ much
-- I'm just askin' what the hell he
does for a livin'!

PRINCE
Oh, for a living. He is a designer of
systems. Highly complex computerized
~~systems. For industry and science.~~ Systems,
and systems within systems. He is what you
might call a genius.

The shooting stops, the Count having given up after losing a great
deal of money. Paul is leaving, with a different girl this time, a
young Grace Kelly type,
and Slim tries to detain him.

SLIM
Say, you're a right good shot, partner.
How'd you like to give me an' ole rusty
here a lesson?
(indicates his extraordinary gun)

PAUL (looks at the gub, smiles)
No thanks, not today.

He continues on his way, and Slim calls after him.

SLIM
What's the matter? Ain't Texas money
good enough for you?

Paul turns and regards him quizzically.

PAUL
Why? Are you giving it away?

SLIM (confounded *and irate*)
I'll tell you what I'm givin', -- I'm
givin' two-to-one odds I can ~~beat~~ yore ass
shootin' doubles!

PAUL (ultra cool)
Oh? What about triples?

SLIM (frowning)
Triples?

PAUL (looks at his watch)
Yes, one set of triples...

4.

~~Hi only got two bands apeed how the~~

SLIM (angrily)
Hell, we only got two bands speed, how we gonna shoot triples?

          PAUL (smiles)
    I guess one of us would have to get lucky.
                SLIM (snort of derision)
    Well, it's the damnest thing I ever heard
    of -- but I'm ready when you are. How much?

Paul takes out the money he has just won -- several thou.-- places
it on the balaustrade. Slim counts it. It is a lot.

                SLIM (shrugs)
    You're on.
                PAUL
    You shoot first.

                  to the Attendant
The instructions are given below; three birds are released. Slim
picks off two, ~~handily~~ but has ~~followups~~ no chance for three.
Paul's turn. The birds are released. We see *them* from his POV --
how the birds emerge, immediately separate, flying in different
directions; it looks hopeless; exactly the same flight pattern
~~taken by the three previous birds.~~ He shoots one, then watches (as do we) as
the two other birds move farther away, then finally (at the last
instant of range) transverse, so that both are simultaneously in
his sights for that instant. WHAM! And a MATCH SOUND-CUT to the
exploding exhaust of a Ferrari *revving up*, ~~being revved up~~. CAMERA IN on the
driver, wearing huge ear-phones and, mirrored shades. It is Paul.
A white overalled x Pit-Attendant *grasps his shoulder — wanting* ~~wants~~ to speak to him, ~~grasping his~~
~~shoulder~~. Paul momentarily lifts one ear-phone, and we get a quick
taste of the BLASTING ROCK (or Vivaldi, Palestrina, etc.) he is driving
behind.

Transcontinental with Tex

William Styron

One of my oddest trips in a lifetime of odd trips was one
that I took with Terry Southern across the U.S.A. in 1964.
At that time I'd known Terry (whom I also called, depending
on mood and circumstance, "Tex" or "T") ever since 1952
during a long sojourn in Paris. Like a patient in lengthy conva-
lescence, the city was still war weary, with its beauty a little
drab around the edges. Bicycles and motorbikes clogged the
streets. *The Paris Review* was then in its period of gestation and
the principals involved in its development, including George
Plimpton and Peter Matthiessen, often spent their late evening
hours in a dingy nightspot called Le Chaplain, tucked away
on a back street in Montparnasse. In the sanitarium of our
present smoke-free society it is hard to conceive of the smoki-
ness of that place; the smoke was ice-blue, and almost like a
semisolid. You could practically take your finger and carve
your initials in it. It was smoke with a searing, promiscuous
smell, part Gauloises and Gitanes, part Lucky Strikes, part
the rank bittersweet odor of pot. I was new to pot, and the
first time I ever met Terry he offered me a roach.

I was quite squeamish. Marijuana was in its early dawn as

a cultural and spiritual force, and the idea of inhaling some alarmed me. I connected the weed with evil and depravity. We were sitting at a table with Terry's friends, the late film director Aram ("Al") Avakian, and a self-exiled ex-New York state trooper and aspiring poet whose name I've forgotten, but who looked very much like Avakian, that is to say mustachioed and alternately fierce and dreamy-eyed. Also present was a *Paris Review* cofounder, the late Harold L. ("Doc") Humes, who had befriended me when I first arrived in Paris and was no stranger to pot. The joint Terry proffered disagreed with me, causing me immediate nausea; I recall Terry putting down this reaction to the large amount of the straight brandy I'd been drinking, cognac being the *boisson de choix* in those days before Scotch became a Parisian commonplace. Terry responded quite humanely, I thought, to my absence of cool. He was tolerant when, on another occasion, I had the same queasy response. In our get-togethers, therefore, I continued to abuse my familiar substance, and Terry his, though he could also put away considerable booze.

I was living then in a room that Doc Humes had found for me, at a hotel called the Libéria which had been his home for a year or so. The hotel was on the little rue de la Grande Chaumière, famous for its painters' ateliers; my spartan room cost the equivalent of eight dollars a week or eight dollars and a half if you paid extra to get the henna-dyed Gorgon who ran the place to change the sheets weekly. The room had a bidet but you had to walk half a mile to the toilet. You could stroll from the hotel in less than two minutes to La Coupole or to the terrace of Le Dôme, Hemingway's old hangout, which also reeked of pot or hash and featured many young American men sitting at tables with manuscripts while affecting the leonine look of Hemingway, right down to the mustache and hirsute chest. I even overheard one of those guys address his girl companion as "Daughter." Terry and I would sit after lunch on the terrace, drinking coffee and smirking at these poseurs.

Terry really was hard up for money in those days, even in a Paris where a franc went a long way. I wasn't rich myself but I was, after all, a recently published best-selling author, and I could occasionally buy him a meal. We ate a couple of times in a cramped but excellent bistro on the avenue du Maine and had such luncheons as the following, which I recorded in a notebook: *entrecôte, salade, pommes frites, haricots verts, carafe de vin, tarte tatin, café filtre.* Price for *two*: $3.60. The U.S. dollar was, of course, in a state of loony ascendancy for which the French have been punishing us ever since; if, in addition, you exchanged your traveler's cheques for the fat rate given by Maurice Loeb, the cheerful *cambiste* who hung out on the rue Vieille du Temple, in the Jewish quarter, you could really become a high roller in 1952. It was one of the reasons the Communists plastered *U.S. Go Home* signs on every available wall.

That June I was busy in my room each afternoon, writing on a manuscript that would eventually become my short novel *The Long March*. One afternoon, unannounced, Terry showed up with his own manuscript and asked me if I would read it. His manner was awkward and apologetic. I knew he was working on a novel; during our sessions on the terrace of Le Dôme he had spoken of his serious literary ambitions. I had met a lot of Texans in the Marines, most of whom lived up to their advance reputation for being yahoos and blowhards, and I never thought I'd encounter a Texan who was a novelist. Or a Texan who was really rather shy and unboastful. The manuscript he brought me made up the beginning chapters of *Flash and Filigree*, and I was amazed by the quality of the prose, which was intricately mannered though evocative and unfailingly alive. The writing plainly owed a debt to Terry's literary idol, the British novelist Henry Green, one of those sui generis writers you imitate upon pain of death, but nonetheless what I read of *Flash and Filigree* was fresh and exciting, and later I told him so. Even then he had adopted that mock-pompous style that was to become his trademark yet I sensed a need for real encouragement when he said: "I trust then, Bill, that you think this will put me in the quality lit. game?" I said that I had no doubt that it would (and it did, when it was finally published) but as usual his talk turned to the need to make some money. "De luxe porn" was an avenue that seemed the most inviting — lots of Americans in Paris were cranking out their engorged prose — and of course it was one of the routes he eventually took, culminating a few years later in the delectable *Candy*. For Tex, success was on the way.

I didn't see a great deal more of Terry in Paris. That summer I went off to the south of France and, later, to live in Rome. But back in the States Terry was very much a part of the quality lit. scene in New York during the next twenty years, frequenting places like George Plimpton's and, later, Elaine's, where I too hung out from time to time. He had great night-time stamina, and we closed up many bars together. He bought a house in the remote village of East Canaan, not very far from my own place in Connecticut. And it was either at this house or mine that we decided to make a transcontinental trip together. I had been invited to give a talk at a California university, while Terry, having collaborated on the screenplay of Stanley Kubrick's *Dr. Strangelove*, a great hit, had been asked to come out to the coast to write the script for a film version of Evelyn Waugh's *The Loved One*. It was a perfect vehicle, I thought, to hone his gift for the merrily macabre. But the catalytic force for the whole trip was Nelson Algren. Nelson had written me, asking me to visit him in Chicago. The two of us had become friends and drinking companions during several of his trips to New York from Chicago, a city with which he had become identified as closely as had such other Windy City bards as Saul Bellow and Carl Sandburg and Studs Terkel. In his letter he said that he'd show me the best of Chicago. I had for some reason never been to Chicago and so Terry suggested that we go west together and stop by and make a joint visit to Nelson, with whom he had also become pals. He had the notion of doing the Chicago-L.A. leg by train since soon, as he astutely predicted, no one would be traveling on the rails except the near-destitute and those terrified by airplanes. By taking the fabled Super Chief of the Santa Fe, he pointed out, we'd be able to get a last glimpse of the great open spaces and also of the sumptuous club c⁻ upon whose banquettes the movie bigwigs and sexy st had cavorted while the prairies whizzed by. It would be a precious slice of Americana soon to be foreclosed to travelers in a hurry, and I thought it a fine idea.

Nelson was in his mid-fifties, one of the original hipsters. He had been telling stories about junkies and pimps and whores and other outcasts while Kerouac and Ferlinghetti were still adolescents, and had nailed down as his private literary property the entire grim world of the Chicago underclass. After years of writing, including a stint with the W.P.A. Writers Project during the Depression and another one hammering out venereal disease reports for the Chicago Board of Health, he hit it big with *The Man with the Golden Arm*, a vigorous novel about drug addiction that won the first National Book Award in 1949 and was made into a successful movie starring Frank Sinatra. Money and fame were unable to go to Nelson's resolutely nonconformist head; down-at-the-heel would have been the politest term for the neighborhood he still lived in, where he took the three of us (my wife Rose having signed on at the last minute) after meeting our plane at O'Hare. It was a predominately Polish faubourg, hemmed in by mammoth gas-storage tanks, and the odor of fatty sausage and cabbage began at the curb, becoming more ripe and pronounced as we labored up the five flights to what Nelson called his "penthouse" — an incredibly cramped and cluttered apartment with only two small bedrooms, a tiny kitchenette and an old-fashioned bathroom with water-stained wallpaper.

The boxy living room was dark and jammed with books. It was fairly cleanly amid the disorder but the pad was the lair of a totally undomesticated animal. I do recall a framed photograph of Simone de Beauvoir, with whom Nelson had had a torrid affair, and whom he still referred to as "The Beaver." That night we partook of Polish cuisine, mystery stew and memorably awful, in a nearby restaurant, where Nelson titillated us with secret hints about the Chicago he was going to show us the next day. With the exception of Rose we all got pie-eyed. I was very fond of Nelson but I always thought he was half-crazy. When he got enthusiastic or excited his eyes took on a manic gleam, and he would go off on a riff of giggles that was not unlike Richard Widmark's in *Kiss of Death*. Terry and I exchanged bewildered glances. I frankly had no idea what we would experience, thinking of such wonders as Michigan Avenue, the Art Institute, lunch at the Pump Room, the great Museum of Science and Industry, the Merchandise Mart, even the celebrated stockyards. That night, we three visitors slept in the same room, Rose and I locked immobile in a narrow, sagging single bed, Terry on a cot only a foot away, where he drifted off to sleep with a glass of bourbon still in his hand, heaving with laughter over Nelson and our accommodations.

Early the next morning, still behaving like a man withholding knowledge of a delightful mystery, Nelson took us by taxi on a meandering route through the city and deposited us at the entrance of the Cook County Jail. He then revealed that he had arranged to have us given a guided tour. This would be our most authentic taste of Chicago. We were all stunned — Terry, wearing his shades, said, "Well, Nelse old man, you shouldn't have gone to all the bother" — but in a way it was something I might have anticipated. Despite the merciless realism that he brought to his subject, Nelson was basically an underworld groupie; he loved all aspects of outlaw life and his obsession with crime and criminals, though romantic, was eclectic to the extent that it also embraced the good guys. He counted among his many cronies a number of law enforcement officers, and one of these was the warden of the Cook County Jail. Despite the drab municipal sound of its name, the Cook County Jail was then, as now, a huge heavy-duty penitentiary, with harsh appurtenances such as a maximum-security unit, industrial areas, facilities for solitary confinement, and a thriving — if the term may be used — Death Row. All this was explained to us in his office by the warden, a thin man with a disarmingly scholarly look, whom Nelson introduced us to before vanishing — to our intense discomfort — saying he'd pick us up later. Clearly none of us could comprehend this sudden abandonment. While the warden fiddled with the buttons of his intercom, Terry wondered in a whisper if I was as hungover as he was; beneath his dark glasses his cheeks were sickly pale and I heard him murmur, "Man, I think this is turning into some kind of weird nightmare." Rose tried to appear happy and self-contained. We heard the warden summon Captain Boggs.

Captain Boggs had a round, cheerful, fudge-colored face and could not have weighed an ounce less than two hundred and fifty pounds. His title was Associate Captain of the Guards, and he would be our guide through the institution. As we trailed him down the corridor I couldn't help being struck by his extreme girth, which caused his arms to swing at wide angles from his body and made his body itself, beneath the slate-gray uniform jacket, appear somehow inflatable; he looked like a Negro version of the Michelin tire man. I was also fetched by his accent, with its rich loamy sound of the Deep South. I thought of Richard Wright's native son, Bigger Thomas, also an émigré from the cotton fields to Chicago, only to become the doomed murderer of a white girl; plainly Captain Boggs, in all of his heftiness, had made a prodigious leap for a onetime black boy. He had a rather deliberate and ornate manner of speaking, possibly the result of many trips with what he called "VIP honorees," and the tour itself dragged on through the prison's depressing immensity, seeming to continue hour after hour. "Dis yere is de inmates' dinin' facilities," he said as we stood on a balcony overlooking an empty mess hall. "Dis yere," he yelled at us at the doorway to a deafening machine shop, "is where de inmates pays off they debts to society." We went down into a cavernous basement, chilly and echoing with a distant dripping sound. "Dis yere is what is called de Hole. Solitary confinement. You gits too smart, dis yere where you pays fo' it." We would not be able to go on the tiers of the cell blocks, Captain Boggs explained, Rose being a distracting presence. "Dem suckers go wild aroun' a woman," he declared.

We did end up, finally, on Death Row. After going through a series of doors, we immediately entered a small, windowless room where we had a most disconcerting encounter. Seated at a table was a white inmate in orange prison coveralls being given an intravenous injection by a black male nurse. Captain

Boggs introduced us to the prisoner, whose name was Witherspoon, a mountaineer transplant up from Kentucky, (and
known in the press as "The Hillbilly from Hell") who had
committed a couple of particularly troglodytic murders in Chicago, and whose date with the executioner was right around
the corner. Witherspoon and his gruesome crimes were of
national interest, his case having made the New York papers.

"Howya doin', Witherspoon?" said Captain Boggs in a
hearty voice. "Dese is two writer gentlemen. Doin' de VIP
tour."

"Howdy," said Witherspoon, as he flashed a smile and in
so doing displayed a mouth full of blackened teeth in a beetle-
browed skeletal face that had doubtless inspired many bad
dreams. "I've got diabeet-ees," he went on to say, as if to
explain the needle in his arm, and then, without missing a
beat, added: "They done railroaded me. Before Almighty
God, I'm an innocent man." Terry and I later recalled, while
ensconced in the lounge car of the Super Chief, the almost
hallucinatory sensations we both experienced when, most
likely at the same time, we glimpsed the tattoos graven on
Witherspoon's hands: LOVE on the fingers of the right hand,
HATE on those of the left. They were exactly the mottoes that
decorated the knuckles of Robert Mitchum's demented back-
woods preacher in *The Night of the Hunter*. Witherspoon
himself had a preacher's style. "I hope you two good writers
will proclaim to the world the abominable injustice they done
to me. God bless you both."

"Mr. Witherspoon," Terry deadpanned, "be assured of our
constant concern for your welfare."

I had undergone a recent conversion about capital punish-
ment, transformed from a believer—albeit a lukewarm believer—into an ardent opponent; hence my chagrin, after we
bade good-bye to Witherspoon, when Captain Boggs walked
us down a narrow corridor and acquainted us with the vehicle
that would soon speed the Hillbilly from Hell back whence
he came. We trooped into a sort of alcove where the Captain
motioned us to stand, while he went to one wall and yanked
back a curtain. In glaring light there was suddenly revealed

the electric chair, a huge hulking throne of wood and leather, out of which unraveled a thicket of wires. I heard Rose give a small soprano yelp of distress. In the lurid incandescence I noted on the far wall two signs. One read: SILENCE. The other: NO SMOKING. I felt Terry's paw on my shoulder, as from somewhere behind me he whispered: "Did you ever dig anything so fucking *surreal?*"

Captain Boggs said: "De supreme penalty." His voice slipped into the rhythmic rote-like monotone with which I was sure he had addressed countless VIP honorees. "De procedure is quick and painless. First is administered two thousand volts for thirty seconds. Stop de juice to let de body cool off. Den five hundred volts for thirty seconds. Stop de juice again. Den two thousand mo' volts. Doctor makes a final check. Ten minutes from beginnin' to end."

"Let me out of here," I heard Rose murmur.

"I always likes to ax de visitors if they'd care to set down in de chair," the Captain said, his cheerful grin broadening. "How 'bout you, Mr. Starling?" he went on, using the name he'd called me by all morning.

I said that I'd pass on the offer, but I didn't want the opportunity lost on Terry. "What do you think, Tex?" I said.

"Captain Boggs," said Terry, "I've always wanted to experience the hot squat, vicariously that is. But I think that today I'll decline your very tempting invitation."

I've recently discovered that the quite accurate notes I kept about our trip, which allow the foregoing account to possess verisimilitude, become rather sketchy after we leave the Cook County Jail. This is probably because our trip further westward on the elegant Super Chief was largely a warm blur of booze and overeating, causing me to discontinue my notes except for a few random jottings, themselves nearly incoherent. (I want to mention, however, while the fact is fresh in mind, that some months after our trip I read that Witherspoon never had to receive that voltage; his death sentence was commuted, through a legal technicality, to life imprisonment.) I thought of Terry recently when I read, in an interview, the words of a British punk rock star, plainly a young jerk, nasty and callow but able to express a tart intuitive insight. "You Americans still believe in God and all that shit, don't you? The whole fucking lot of you fraught with the fear of death."

Terry would have given his little cackle of approval at the remark, for it went to the core of his perception of American culture. Like me, Terry was an apostate Southern Protestant, and I think that one of the reasons we hit it off well together was that we both viewed the Christian religion — at least insofar as we had experienced its puritanical rigors — as a conspiracy to deny its adherents their fulfillment as human beings. It magnified not the glories of life but the consciousness of death, exploiting humanity's innate terror of the timeless void. High among its prohibitions was sexual pleasure. In contemplating Americans stretched on the rack of their hypocrisy as they tried to reconcile their furtive adulteries with their churchgoing pieties, Terry laid the groundwork for some of his most biting and funniest satire. Christianity bugged him, even getting into his titles — think of *The Magic Christian*. Nor was it by chance that the surname of the endearing heroine of *Candy* was — what else? — Christian. His finest comic effects often come from his juxtaposing a sweetly religious soul — or at least a bourgeois-conventional one — with a figure of depravity or corruption. *Candy* was surely the first novel in which the frenzied sexual congress between a well-bred, exquisitely proportioned young American girl and an elderly, insane hunchback could elicit nothing but helpless laughter. ("Give me your *hump!*" she squeals at the moment of climax, in a *jeu de mots* so obvious it compounds the hilarity.) One clear memory I have is of Terry in the lounge car, musing over his Old Granddad as he considered the imminent demise of the Super Chief and, with it, a venerable tradition. His voice grew elegiac speaking of the number of "darling Baptist virgins aspiring to be starlets" who, at the hands of "panting Jewish agents with their swollen members," had been ever so satisfactorily deflowered on these plush, softly undulating banquettes.

In fact, he had a fixation on the idea of "starlets," and it was plain that in Hollywood he would be looking forward to making out with a gorgeous ingenue from MGM, and em-

barking on a halcyon erotic adventure. Toward the end of the
trip we stayed up all night and drank most of the way through
Arizona and southern California, watching the pale moonscape of the desert slip by until morning dawned, and we
were in Los Angeles. Rose and I had to catch a late morning
plane to San Francisco but we all had time, it suddenly occurred to me, to visit the place that was the reason for Terry's
trip. This was Forest Lawn Memorial Park, the "Whispering
Glades" of Waugh's scathing send-up of America's funerary
customs; how could Rose and I leave L.A. without viewing
the hangout of Mr. Joyboy and his associate morticians? Terry
agreed that we should all see it together. It was inevitable, I
suppose, that the studio had arranged to put Terry up at
that decaying relic, the Chateau Marmont; for me it was an
unexpected bonus to catch a glimpse of the mythic Hollywood
landmark before heading out to Whispering Glades.

Terry and I were both in that sleepless state of jangled nerves
and giggly mania, still half-blotto and relying heavily on Rose
and her sober patience to get us headed in the right direction.
At Forest Lawn, in the blinding sunlight, our fellow tourists
were out in droves. They were lined up in front of the mauso-
leum where the movie gods and goddesses had been laid to
rest, stacked up in their crypts, Terry observed, "like pies in
the Automat." Marilyn Monroe had passed into her estate of
cosmic Loved One only two years before, and the queue of
gawkers filing past her final abode seemed to stretch for hundreds of yards. Cameras clicked, bubble gum popped, babies
shrieked. One sensed an awkward effort at reverence but it
was a strain; the spectacular graveyard was another outpost of
Tinseltown. As we ambled across the greensward, vast as a
golf course, we moved past a particularly repellent statuary
grouping, a tableau of mourning marble children and a clutch
of small marble animals. A woman onlooker was gushing fe-
verishly, and Terry said he felt a little ill. We all agreed to
be on our separate ways. "A bit of shut-eye and I'll soon be
in tip-top shape," he assured us as we embraced. We left him

standing at the taxi stop. He had his hands thrust deep in his pockets, and he was scowling through his shades, looking fierce and, as always, a little confused and lost but, in any case, with the mammoth American necropolis as a backdrop, like a man already dreaming up wicked ideas.

A Conversation with Terry Southern

TERRY SOUTHERN

We were barge "Captains," as they called themselves—
rather euphemistically since it was a job so lowly that it was
ordinarily held by guys who had been kicked out of the Longshoreman's Union—old winos and the like, being replaced
now by this new breed, the dopehead writer. It was one of
those classic writer's jobs, like hotel clerk, night watchman,
fire-tower guy, with practically no duties ("Just keep her tied
up and pumped out"). Alex Trocchi found it by chance, wandering around the West Side docks after a few hours at the
White Horse Tavern. The guy who did the hiring happened
to be Scottish, a Scotsman called Scotty, in fact. So he took
a fancy to Alex, Alex being a Ludgate Scholar from Glasgow,
who had boss charm besides. (Scottish accent; "Have ye had
any experience at sea, lad?" "Only with small craft, sir—punt-
ing on the Clyde and the like." "Good enough, lad, I like
the cut of yer jib.") So Alex was in. And about half a dozen
of us—of similar stamp and kidney—were quick to follow . . .
under auspices of The Great Troc.

INTERVIEWER

Weren't they garbage scows?

SOUTHERN

The ones we were on carried rocks. They were hauling huge boulders up to the sea wall they were building, a great ocean-jetty a few miles offshore. Hauling these rocks down from a quarry at the top of the Hudson, about a three-day trip. And you could take people along. It got to be a social must, going upriver on the barge. Nelson Algren came a couple of times, David Solomon and Seymour Krim, Christopher Logue and Jimmy Baldwin. And, of course, Mason Hoffenberg would come along quite often. I remember once, after a great hash rave-up, Jimmy Baldwin just sort of collapsed over the side, and Mason had to pull him back aboard. So life on the barge was not without interest.

INTERVIEWER

What were the accomodations?

SOUTHERN

There was a cabin with a bed and coal stove, and, of course, a deck about the size of a football field. It could accommodate a lot of stowaways, even when it was loaded with these gigantic boulders. Sometimes we would be staked out in the middle of the river, several barges tied together. So we could party. Anyway, it was a good job for a writer in those days.

INTERVIEWER

What was the scene in Paris like in the fifties?

SOUTHERN

Oh it was terrific because the cafés were such great places to hang out, they were so open, you could smoke hash at the tables, if you were fairly discreet. There was the expatriot crowd, which was more or less comprised of interesting people, creatively inclined. So we would fall out there at one of the cafés, about four in the afternoon, sip Pernod until dinner, then afterwards go to a jazz club. Bird and Diz, and Miles and Bud Powell, and Monk were all there, and if not, someone else. Lester Young and Don Byas. It was a period when the Village and *St.-Germain-des-Prés* were sort of interchangeable, just going back and forth. The thing to do was take a freighter—it was the cheapest way to go, a comfortable and interesting way to go because it was long, thirteen days. And the Scandinavian ones had pretty good food. There were only about eight passengers. We'd eat at the Captain's table—and he was invariably some kind of great lush. So you'd get there—St. Germain, and the town was swinging. Once in a while you'd find yourself homesick, for one place or the other, but it was okay, because both were good places to arrive. Sometimes we would save up some money and just take off, *On the Road*-style. Sometimes we had a car, other times we took the train. It was always a gas.

Mason was ultrapersuasive. *Boss persuasion*. Once he convinced me to join a kibbutz with him and go to Israel, despite my complete ignorance of anything Jewish. So we packed some books and clothes and checked into the Holland-American kibbutz freighter, into a dormitory-type situation, with about sixty other guys. The ship was still at the dock, we had a couple of days to wait until they got their full roster. So we were put to work in the hole, cleaning the boilers—an unbelievably shitty job, plunging our arms up to the shoulder into these furnace pipes and bringing out mountains of wet black soot. Gross City. Anyway on the first morning when we woke up, one guy is already awake, breaking out over the fact that thirty dollars is missing from his footlocker. Someone else says, "Okay, we've got to put locks on the footlockers." Someone else says, "No, we've got to trust each other. Whoever took the money needed it." This doesn't go over too well with the guy who lost the thirty bucks. He's still ranting. So immediately this tight-knit and brotherly group is divided into two bickering factions. Hardly the utopian comraderie we had expected. So we split. Went to the White Horse and had a couple of tall ones.

INTERVIEWER

Tell me about *Blue Movie*—the making of the movie from your novel.

SOUTHERN

Blue Movie was based on an idea that Stanley Kubrick had. Somebody came by one day with some porn footage. We looked at it, and he said, "Wouldn't it be interesting if one day someone who was an artist would do that—using really beautiful actors and good equipment." So that was the genesis. Of course I was hoping he would do it as a film. But he's surprisingly puritanical and shy. When he read part of it, still in manuscript, he said, "Congratulations, you've written the definitive blow job." There actually was a tremendous amount of interest in doing *Blue Movie*. It nearly happened a couple of times. Ringo Starr had the option for a couple of years. John Cally, who was a very hip producer at MGM—he produced *The Loved One*, which I worked on, and became the president of Warner Brothers for a brief time—this heavy decision-maker said, "Well now it's time to do *Blue Movie*." He was convinced that the first studio to come out with a quality full-length film showing erection and penetration, using stars, would go over the top. "It'll be like *Gone with the Wind*," he kept saying. Super enthusiastic about it. So he got Mike Nichols to direct. And since John was practically living with Julie Andrews at the time, he was able to get her of all people, as the girl. John's diabolical genius envisioned Mary Poppins getting banged for the world. So Mike Nichols was ready to go. I couldn't believe it. But the whole thing got bogged down in lawyers. The deal fell through, in a grotesque hangup between Nichols and Ringo's lawyers. But if it had been done, with those kinds of credentials, between Nichols and Julie Andrews, it could hardly have been dismissed as shabby porn.

INTERVIEWER

What was the real story of *Easy Rider*? There are so many versions of how, and who created it.

SOUTHERN

If Den Hopper improvises a dozen lines and six of them survive the cutting-room floor, he'll put in for screenplay credit. That's the name of the game for Den Hopper. Now it would be almost impossible to exaggerate his contribution to the film — but, by George, he manages to do it every time. The precise way it came down was that Dennis and Peter (Fonda) came to me with an *idea*. Peter was under contract to A.I.P. for several motorcycle movies, and he still owed them one. Dennis persuaded him to let him (Dennis) direct the next one, and, under the guise of making an ordinary A.I.P. potboiler they would make something interesting and worthwhile — which I would write. So they came to my place on Thirty-sixth Street in New York, with an *idea* for a story a sort of hippy dope-caper. Peter was to be the actor-producer, Dennis the actor-director, and a certain yours truly, the writer. I was able to put them up there — in a room, incidentally, later immortalized by the sojourn of Dr. W.S. Benway (Burroughs). So we began smoking dope in earnest and having a nonstop story conference. The initial idea had to do with a couple of young guys who are fed up with the system, want to make one big score and split. Use the money to buy a boat in Key West and sail into the sunset was the general notion, and indeed already slated to be the film's final poetic sequence. We would occasionally dictate to an elderly woman typist who firmly believed in the arrival, and presence everywhere of the inhabitants of Venus; so she would talk about this. Finally I started taping her and then had her rap about it, *how they were everywhere* — Jack Nicholson's thing with *Easy Rider* was based on that.

So you can see that during these conferences the hippy dope-caper premise went through quite a few changes. The first notion was that they not be bikers but a duo of daredevil car drivers barnstorming around the U.S. being exploited by a series of unscrupulous promoters until they were finally disgusted enough to quit. Then one day the dope smoke cleared long enough to remember that Peter's commitment was for a motorcycle flick, and we switched over pronto. It wasn't until the end that it took on a genuinely artistic dimension . . . when it suddenly evolved into an indictment of the American redneck, and his hatred and intolerance for anything that is

remotely different from himself . . . and then somewhat to
the surprise of Den Hopper (imitates Hopper in *Apocalypse
Now*): "You mean kill 'em both? Hey, man, are you outta
your gourd?!?" I think for a minute he was still hoping they
would somehow beat the system. Sail into the sunset with a
lot of loot and freedom. But of course, he was hip enough
to realize, a minute later, that it (their death) was more or
less mandatory.

INTERVIEWER

Are you saying there was no improvisation in the film?

SOUTHERN

No, no, I'm saying that the improvisation was always within
the framework of the obligations of the scene — a scene which
already existed.

INTERVIEWER

Then how did Dennis and Peter get included in the screenplay credits?

SOUTHERN

After they had seen a couple of screenings of it on the coast,
I got a call from Peter. He said that he and Dennis liked the
film so much they wanted to be in on the screenplay credits.
Well, one of them was the producer and the other was the
director so there was no way the Writers Guild was going to
allow them to take a screenplay credit unless I insisted. Even
then they said there was supposed to be a "compulsory arbitra-
tion" because too often producers and directors will muscle
themselves into a screenplay credit through some under-the-
table deal with the writer. They (the WGA) said I would be
crazy to allow it and wanted to be assured I wasn't being
coerced or bribed in any way, because they hate the idea of
these "hyphenates" — you know, writer-producer, director-
producer . . . because of that history of muscle. Anyway, we
were great friends at the time, so I went along with it without

much thought. I actually did it out of a sense of comraderie. Recently, in *Interview*, Dennis pretty much claimed credit for the whole script.

INTERVIEWER

Writers appear to be treated like the lowest of the breed in the film biz.

SOUTHERN

Yes. Except we still have persuasion.

INTERVIEWER

What was it like working with Kubrick?

SOUTHERN

Working with Stanley was terrific, although the circumstances may seem peculiar—in the backseat of a big car. The film was being shot at Shepperton, outside of London, in the winter. So he would pick me up at 4:30 in the morning and we would make this hour-long trip to the studio. It was a big Bentley or a Rolls, so the passenger part was something like a railway compartment, with folding-out writing desks and good lighting. It would be pitch-black outside and really cold, and we would be in this cozy-rosy compartment, in a creative groove, working on the scene to be shot that day.

INTERVIEWER

Writing it? Or rewriting it?

SOUTHERN

Well, let's say trying to improve it. Kubrick would say, "Now what's the most outrageous thing this guy would say at this point?" and hopefully I could come up with something like, "If you try any preversion in there, I'll blow your head off."

INTERVIEWER

Keenan Wynn to Peter Sellers in the phone booth?

SOUTHERN

Yes. Col. "Bat" Guano ("If, indeed, that *is* your name") to Group Captain Lionel Mandrake. The thing about Kubrick is that he's not only extraordinarily creative, but he will encourage the other person to go all out, and not try to keep a "reasonable lid on it." Stanley's like a kind of chess-playing poet. One side of his brain is very scientific, the other poetic.

INTERVIEWER

Over the years I heard talk of a "missing scene" or a sequence that was deleted from *Strangelove*. What's the story on that?

SOUTHERN

Well that would be the fabulous so-called pie-fight episode. You may recall the scene near the end of the film, in the War Room, after the bomb has been dropped, when Strangelove suddenly stands up from his wheelchair, and says, "Mein Fuehrer, I can valk!" And he takes a step? Recall that?

INTERVIEWER

I do indeed.

SOUTHERN

Well, in the missing sequence, after taking one step he falls flat on his face and starts trying to get back in his wheelchair, but each time it scoots out of his grasp. Meanwhile, parallel to this action, in another part of the War Room, the Russian Ambassador is caught again trying to take pictures of the "Big Board." George C. Scott nails him, and again they're fighting in the War Room. So Scott exposes about eighteen micro-mini spy cameras on the ambassador—in his wristwatch, cuff links, tiepin, on his ring finger, everywhere. But Scott says, "I think these are dummy cameras. I think he's got the real McCoy concealed on his person." And he turns to the detail of MPs who have come in. "I want you to search him very carefully, boys," he says, "and don't overlook any of the six bodily orifices." And the Russian ambassador goes through this quick

calculation, "vun . . . two . . ." and then when he reaches
the last one, he freaks. "Vhy you Capitalist swine," he says,
and he reaches out of the frame, gets something and throws
it at George C. Scott. I should mention that we have previously
established a huge catering table that was wheeled in, laden
with food, so they don't have to leave the War Room during
this crisis. The ambassador reaches out of the frame, grabs
something from the table and throws it at Scott. We don't
see what it is immediately but Scott ducks, and this big custard
pie hits the president in the face. The mere indignity of this
is so monstrous that the president just faints dead away. Scott
grabs him and keeps him from falling, and he's holding him
in his arms like a martyred hero. "Gentlemen," he says to the
others, "our President has been struck down in the prime of
his life . . . by a custard pie. I say Massive Retaliation!" And
he throws something at the ambassador. It misses and hits one
of the other Joint Chiefs. So this immense pie fight begins —
between Army, Navy, Air Force — a bit of interservice rivalry,
if you grasp the innuendo. Now while this pie fight is going
on, Strangelove is still trying to get back into this wheelchair,
moving like a snake across the floor of the War Room, the
chair continuing to scoot out of his grasp each time he reaches
for it. Finally he gets to the end of the War Room, and the
chair is against the wall — it looks like he's got it this time.
But it scoots away again. So Strangelove pulls himself up so
that he's sitting with his back against the wall. He's watching
the pie fight in the distance. Then his hand — his uncontrolla-
ble right hand — reaches inside his coat and comes out with
a Luger pistol and points it at his head. He grabs his wrist
with his other hand and grapples for the pistol, which goes
off with a tremendous bang. Then cut to the long shot of all
these generals in a freeze-frame. Strangelove says, "Enough
of these childish games. We have work to do." So they all
stand there staring at him in complete silence, until Scott
recognizes this is the guy to get tight with, so he walks all
the way across the War Room floor, and says, "Doctor, may
I help you?" And helps him into his wheelchair. He starts
pushing him back across the floor, which by now is so deep

in custard pies it resembles a beach—and sure enough we quickly pass the president and the Russian ambassador sitting there crosslegged like two children, doing sand castles, making mountains. And Strangelove says, "Ah too bad. Apparently their minds have snapped under the strain. Perhaps they'll have to be institutionalized." And so Scott continues pushing him across to this group of officers and CIA types, who are so covered they look like ghosts. And he says, "Well, boys, I think the future of this great nation of ours is in the hands of people like Doc Strangelove, and I think we owe him a vote of thanks. Let's hear it for the good Doctor." And in a really eerie (whispering) voice, they go, "hip-hip hooray, hip-hip hooray." Then he continues pushing him across the floor as they start singing, "For he's a jolly good fellow, for he's a jolly good fellow." Now this counter camera pulls up so you've got this long shot of the ultimate allegiance between this mad scientist and this general from the Joint Chiefs of Staff. Then they cut to the explosion and the song "We'll Meet Again" comes in—and the credits rise.

INTERVIEWER

That was cut?

SOUTHERN

Not without good reason. The problem was that Stanley, great genius director that he is, forgot to say to his actors, "Listen, what we're representing here is interservice rivalry, which is one of the most evil things. Each time there's an appropriation to one group the other says, 'Listen, we've got to have that too.' And there's no stopping the Pentagon on this level. It's viscous." He forgot to tell them it's viscous. So what's happening in this pie fight is that people are laughing, and they shouldn't be laughing. It's supposed to be deadly serious. But it was such a funny situation that people outside the periphery, including Stanley and myself, were tossing pies into the melee, you see. So it lost its edge. It was like a comedy scene when everything else in the film had been played straight, except once when the Coca-Cola machine spurted in Keenan Wynn's face. That's why he decided not to have it in. I saw it again recently and think it holds up well.

INTERVIEWER

Me too. So does *The Loved One*. It recently came out for the first time on video, after all these years. Why did it take so long?

SOUTHERN

For some weird reason, they held it back—it's an MGM film. Haskell Wexler, who was the coproducer and cinemaphotographer, had a copy he sent me, and I got a duplicate made, but you couldn't get it. The casting on that was great. Remember that sequence with Milton Berle and Margarite Leighton, when the dog dies, and she doesn't want to let them bury it?

INTERVIEWER

Yeah. That was played really strong. But Rod Steiger— Joyboy—and his mother were too outrageous to describe.

SOUTHERN

Everytime I see Rod Steiger, rather, the few times I've seen him, he always talks about that. He was carried away by that role, he got into that role so much. He had his hair in rollers on the set. Running around on the set when he should have been resting. Dishing with the girls. It had such a great cast: John Gielgud, Lionel Stander, Robert Morley, Jonathan Winters, Robert Morse . . .

INTERVIEWER

What happened to *The Magic Christian*?

SOUTHERN

Well, I had written a really good script of *The Magic Christian* for Peter Sellers. He and the director, Joe McGrath, were in London, supposedly setting up the film while I finished

working on an adaptation of John Barth's *End of the Road*—
which, incidentally, was one of the most interesting films I've
been involved with. But instead of waiting for me to get to
London, Peter who was always ultrahyper and antsy about
everything, gets Spike Milligan and a couple of his *Goon Show*
cronies to rewrite a few scenes—*without having ever read the
book*. Dig that for gross weird. All they knew was that it was
about an eccentric billionaire who staged elaborate practical
jokes. So they slipped into a bit of infantile self-indulgence,
with some pointlessly destructive behavior by Guy Grand.
Totally out of character. They had him cutting up Rembrandts
for Christsake! So I'm afraid that the film has, in my view, some
serious lapses. Peter Sellers bought a hundred copies of the
book when it first came out in England. He would give them
to friends at Christmas. In fact, he was the one who turned
Stanley (Kubrick) on to . . . this unique brand of humor.

INTERVIEWER

How did growing up in Texas shape you as a writer?

SOUTHERN

Well Texas is probably a good place for a boy to grow up,
in a Huck Finn sort of way, like one big outdoor playground
with a lot of hunting and fishing, Dad-and-Lad stuff going
on. But, as Liz Taylor said, "It's hell on horses and women."
Because it's a cultural desert. Once, when I was seven or eight
and sick in bed, my mother decided to read to me. The book
she chose, for some odd reason, since her own leaning was
more towards Louis Bromfield, was a volume of the great E.A.
Poe—*The Gold Bug*, if memory serves. Well, for a young
Texas lout, E.A. Poe was heady brew. And it was a perfect
turn-on to "Quality-lit," of a weirdo bent. I was hooked on
Poe. And Poe, of course, is the gateway to the greatest. If
marijuana leads to cocaine, Poe most certainly leads to Baude-
laire, Rimbaud, Joyce, Céline, Lautréamont, Huysmans, Na-
thaniel West, Faulkner, Sartre, etcetra, etcetra, *ad glorium*.

—**Mike Golden**

Remembrance

Caroline Marshall

Southern taught screenwriting at Columbia for several years.

His gentle, soft-spoken manner was reassuring. When I got my script back from him highlighted with yellow Post-it notes, I realized his keen perception hadn't missed a thing. A fellow Texan, his masterful grasp and intimate knowledge of Texas slang helped reshape my wacky Texas characters into movie material. I rolled out of my chair with laughter when he crossed out *bazookas* like any high-school English teacher grading an essay and wrote in the margin, "Try hooters, knockers, tits or bazooms." He was a stickler for good grammar. He told me to go for the outrageous, the exaggerated and *never* hold back for good taste. To illustrate this, he crossed out *red dress* and noted in the margin, "Never say just *red dress*. Be specific: ultra-revealing, micro-mini with fringe."

He said not to worry if the story was too way out. It could always be modified later. From then on, I pushed everything beyond the limits of the ordinary and over the edge into the uncharted moonscape of questionable sanity, a place where Terry was obviously comfortable.

I visited him in the St. Luke's Hospital emergency room. He was alert and awake, hoping I could help him escape. Useless on that point, I tried to amuse him with a story I'd written. He changed a rat image to an iguana, then said, "There's a lot of weird stuff happening in here." I offered him an *Esquire* and a *Mad* magazine. He chose *Mad*.

In his room the next day, he was eating, talking and watching TV. He was good-natured, creative, stoic and brave, preparing for a trip to London. I asked him if he was depressed being in the hospital. He said, "Not at all." In fact, he was intrigued by his female doctor, Dr. Villemena, and was thinking up a new script—he wanted to call it "Hospital."

Envoi

Terry Southern's son, Nile, wrote an account of his father's last days in the hospital. The following is an extract from that account, which he calls Grand Dad.

As we stroked Terry's forehead and held his hand, he would casually remove the mask as if about to shave or sleep. Before his oxygenation level fell below 69, I would gently hold the mask before his nose, careful not to let it chafe and crimp him.

"You've got to keep the mask on," my mother Carol said, "it's what's keeping you alive."

At one point he seemed quite determined to get up and out of bed. After slumping back down, he looked at us with a theatrical mask of helplessness.

"What we need is a nurse and derrick!" he said.

"What do we need?" said Carol.

" . . . NURSE . . . and . . . DERRICK!" he said.

When the doctor came round — a woman Terry would have liked a lot, sort of a thoughtful Candice Bergen — she took me aside.

"Your father's heart is huge."

"Yes," I said.

"Even so, it is not receiving enough oxygen, and we're not sure why." She looked at me intensely, both of us lit by the half-light of the darkened corridor and hospital television monitors.

"Has your father ever worked in a coal mine?" she asked suddenly.

"No," I said, trying to imagine his boyhood in a Texas coal mine, "Not to my knowledge."

"How about an asbestos-factory?"

The image of him on an assembly line was just about as un-Terry as anything imaginable.

"His lungs are calcified, and his blood won't oxygenate. It appears to be black-lung disease."

I couldn't help but think of the "What's My Disease" scene from *Flash and Filigree*, where the contestants have to guess the nature of the in-studio victim's affliction. "Can you speak?" was the usual opening gambit.

"What's-the-delay?" he said into the air, sounding like a British squadron leader. He suddenly bolted upright, as if readying himself to get out of bed. "I'm out of here . . ." he said. "Got to GET OUT!"

Lying back exhausted, he said with a resigned urgency, "All right, let's go . . . I'm ready for the next step . . . I've had enough of this."

I asked him if he could sleep.

"Yes . . . yes . . . time for a bit of shut-eye . . . *bedways is rightways now.*"

The final night nurse was named May, and she was a very peaceful Filipina woman with a serene smile. Before turning off the machine, for her own peace of mind, she tried to get a response of any kind from Terry and could not. Terry looked radiant — his long silver hair and sharp-angled nose — the angelic trickster, laid to rest.

A Businessman Disappears

Jaime Collyer

1

The last thing I heard about Cerutti was that he'd died (which is, of course, the last thing we hear about anybody). In Africa, or more precisely, in Kangala. I knew the country — and Malabo, its capital — personally and had run into Cerutti there in late 1982. His death, reported without fanfare in the international section of *Le Monde*, made me remember him from campus days. His wanderings, though, ran in the opposite direction: from the university to the savanna to the teletypes and then to that report in *Le Monde* with the photo of his body stretched out in a room in the Malabo Palace on the day Mokoena's victorious troops entered the capital to establish socialism — or whatever it was — in the Soviet or Chinese style, depending on whichever side Mokoena was leading at the time.

We had met back in Chile, at a big campus assembly during the time of tear gas and wild street demonstrations. I remember getting along well with him from the start. There was talk about a revolution that was sure to explode — so they said — across the continent, beginning in the altiplano and from there spreading down the Andean massif to surrounding areas,

including Santiago, Buenos Aires, São Paulo, the most important urban centers, more or less as Guevara predicted. Cerutti
scoffed at these grandiose predictions with studied sarcasm:
he wanted to know the name of the leader (the man who
would guide the people down from the altiplano), how many
guns were available and where the capital of the new socialist
republic would be (for the de rigueur triumphal entrance). I
kept quiet, my silence an early warning sign of my future lack
of commitment.

Cerutti and I were both strangers to urban life. He came
from the Argentinian pampa and enjoyed surrounding himself
with an air of mystery. I came from the South too, from the
country next door, where no one makes you hurry and the
days pass mostly indoors, with a curtain of water on the window, beyond which there is nothing but mud, some ram-
shackle outbuildings, with hens and cows numb from the cold.

Along with some other nostalgics from the provinces, we
both lived in a boardinghouse near the university. It was far
from paradise, partly because of the monotony of the menu:
mounds of cabbage and soup, and spaghetti day after day.
Cerutti sat at the head of the table in silence, head bowed,
hands crossed in front of his plate as if in prayer.

"Well," he would finally say, emerging from his silence and
abstraction. "Turn your forks, guys. What's important is to
keep turning things around."

And he would stick his fork in the pasta, sauce and cheese,
and wind the spaghetti around it solemnly. We turned our
forks around the way he did and felt at one with him, as
though we belonged to something, even if it was just that
meal, our peculiar version of the last supper. In his own way
he was a born leader—although a few of our tablemates, indifferent to his influence, had already started bolting down
their spaghetti without such formalities.

Our friendship within the underground didn't last long.
The proletarian revolution was taking its time, and each
would-be rebel in the area eventually ran off to work at a bank
or at a government agency under the pretext of "infiltrating"
the system and weakening it from within. I have a vague
memory of Cerutti's being expelled from the university after
making some comment in public about the rector's mother

and having to go back to Argentina. Before his departure we drank a lot of maté in the backyard of the boardinghouse, where a grimy hammock had hung under the Southern Cross since time immemorial. The murmur of water boiling for coffee or maté served as both pretext and prelude for talks that lasted until two or three in the morning, sometimes even later, when the only thing left was silence, an occasional siren in the distance and the burden of idle hours.

"This thing isn't working, man," he concluded one night, stretched out in the hammock, hairy belly showing below his shirt. "These people waste their time on meetings and petitions. What with party discipline and death squads, we won't have any militants left. It's just like what happened during the Inquisition, man—everybody wants to get in on it. Everyone lights their own little fire!"

"So what are you going to do?"

"About what?"

"About the party, the class war . . . all that crap."

"I'm getting out of here as soon as I can. That's what I have the pampa for."

"And the cows," I added.

"Exactly. An Argentinian without his cows is like a dog without fleas, you know. Another maté, man? Stir it well."

Several months later he sent me a postcard from his new location: he was sick of cows, prairies, gauchos and barbecues. He was up to his ears in pampa. He was headed for Paris, "where being an Argentinian is always an advantage," and from there to Africa, where the blacks had just freed themselves from the last of the European colonials. "Must be seen to be believed, man."

2

The Sunday after his death, *L'humanité* published a page-and-a-half feature in its weekly news summary. Not about Cerutti—he was no big deal—rather, the article focused on Mokoena, the new man in charge of Kangala, and his talk about international credit and austerity—although it was impossible to imagine any greater austerity than the people of

Kangala were already practicing, at least at the gastronomic level.

The article's author, a correspondent for one of the government agencies, did include an inset, however, in which Cerutti was mentioned as the Argentinian mysteriously assassinated at the Malabo Palace. The text ended: "Malabo's police have been unable to establish responsibility in the death of the Argentinian citizen found under suspicious circumstances in the most expensive suite of the Malabo Palace on the same day the rebel army entered the capital, and just as the government officials were rushing to eliminate all proof of their shady deals in the ministries of the old regime, and its deposed leader, Moses Rashola, was starting his journey into a pleasant exile, considering his hefty bank accounts in European institutions."

The dead man in shirtsleeves ("of fine Italian silk, obviously expensive, bought in a shop for foreigners") had a bullet hole in his chest with an exit wound at the back. The bullet had lodged itself in the mattress, according to the correspondent's report. It was from a heavy caliber weapon, the sort used by the guerrillas. Could the killing have been perpetrated by the winning side? Or by the vanquished, motivated perhaps by some obscure grudge? This fundamental uncertainty led to other questions. What was an Argentinian citizen with an expired passport doing in Malabo on Victory Day, dressed in fancy clothes, just bought at Burberry's, the store of choice of the British colony? Was it a case of espionage? Or maybe a political crime? The police officer assigned to the case didn't seem particularly eager to solve it. Mokoena's victorious troops were busy thinning out the ranks of police that the tyrant Rashola had left behind. So his primary concern was saving his own job — if indeed his own neck. As for the Argentinian, the sooner they buried him several meters deep, the better.

But it was impossible to bury him. A week later, according to a final cable from Malabo, someone had stolen his corpse from the morgue. "He's not the first Argentinian to disappear in recent times," the Argentinian consul in the capital of Kangala commented to the Agence France Press. The brief report included, for the first time, a picture of Cerutti's body. A maid in the hotel had found him close to noon on Saturday, Victory Day, when she entered the suite to make the bed and tidy up the room. It was just after the rebel troops had marched past the hotel. He was lying spread-eagle across the sheets, still warm, she told the *Gazette de Kangala*. I read the story, looking at the picture while having an evening drink on the terrace of the Estoril in Paris. The camera had caught him from the chest up. His emaciated face, half-closed eyes staring off in the distance, the detail of his slightly open lips, scraggly beard, sunken cheeks, dark circles under the eyes—and yet for all that a certain air of nobility—shook me. The myth was revived: he looked like a recent but less solemn version of Guevara in the Bolivian mountains.

3

I remember the day he arrived at our shack, sometime around 1982. I was living with Theresa on the outskirts of Malabo, by a river that wasn't a river anymore, on whose dried-up bed, turned to powder by the drought, deluded local flamingoes and ostriches gathered. He'd put on weight. I became aware of it when I saw his exhaustion from negotiating the rocky trail that led to the riverbank (without a river) on his way from the nameless settlement where Theresa and I bought kerosene for our lamps, the local bread and canned goods that had been brought in from Malabo to feed the Protestant missionaries who'd come from Brighton and scattered far and wide. With his conspicuous belly, open *guayabera* shirt, greasy neckerchief, muddy shoes, once-white slacks and untrimmed beard, Cerutti was hauling two trunks on a handcart with balky wheels. He'd left Nigeria four or five months before, trekking through four or five more or less identical countries, full of tall and bony guerrillas with berets and rope sandals, regular soldiers halfheartedly patrolling useless checkpoints, women with jars of water on their heads, babies with swollen bellies, grumpy oxen, snakes and flies.

We greeted each other without any fuss. We'd both expected

to meet again. Maybe we'd sought without ever saying so to talk about rain and everyday trivia in the midst of the African drought. He'd come with a decent supply of maté. By the third day of sipping through a metal *bombilla*, I began to wonder.

"How did you find me?" I asked.

He thought a minute. "There are no secrets in Africa."

On the fourth day Theresa joined us, squatting nonchalantly by the fire, where the mosquitoes attacked her glossy brown skin. She went through life wearing a loincloth and nothing else.

"Hey, man, that girl . . . " he said suddenly on the fifth day, "she's not bad."

"No."

"To tell you the truth, she looks pretty good."

"*Very* good."

"You won't mind if I offer her a little maté?"

"No."

Theresa accepted his offer readily. She'd been captured in the bush by a British functionary in shorts with a cricket-enthusiast wife so that Theresa could pick up their china and prepare their evening gin fizz. I caught a glimpse of her during one of the Commonwealth celebrations at her master's house. She was carrying a tray of olives and Scotch. The small starched apron couldn't hide her wild voluptuousness. I met her on my way to the bathroom at the end of the evening. We drifted into garbled English, smiling back and forth.

An international philanthropic organization had approved one of my projects for building a well on the outskirts of Malabo. Theresa agreed to go along with me. Before long, we forgot about the well, and she went back to walking around in a loincloth. I lost myself between her shiny thighs.

Within her peculiar cosmogony of wide velds, volcanoes and antelopes, I slowly learned that I fit into a sort of bird-man category, sent by divine intervention to return her to the savanna and her natural habitat. Her grandfather—or maybe it was the tribe's medicine man—had predicted all this. She seemed pretty sure about everything until Cerutti showed up with his trunks, sweating like a pig. Theresa then wondered whether he might be her prophesied bird-man rescuer. Like all African women, she was very pragmatic.

For the time being, Cerutti's behavior remained well within the bounds of our friendship: he barely said a word to her. It may have been a matter of loyalty. Or maybe it was because Theresa had no interest in what he was talking about—the Boca Juniors soccer team, Perón or the Malvinas. I only half-listened to him, intoxicated by the fragrant twilight and the call of wild animals in the distance and the last drops of our stock of Ballantine's.

The African night gradually enveloped us as we sat by the fireside. Theresa had wrapped herself in a blanket, like a curled-up cat taking refuge in sleep—free of numbers, theorems, "honor" and all the rest. As we listened to her breathing by the glowing embers, Cerutti and I surrendered ourselves to silence and waited for dawn, when the sky would be lit anew with shades of pink gleaming in the distance, and flocks of cranes and flamingoes would cross the heavens. During that luminous hour, it seemed as if the river by our shack might fill up again with water; it almost seemed as if all our dead might come back and finally rest in peace.

4

After a week had gone by, I asked him about the trunks.

"What trunks?" he asked.

"The ones you dragged in."

"Oh, yeah! The trunks."

He kept silent for a while, *bombilla* between his lips, sipping maté every now and then. He liked to give himself airs with these little stalling maneuvers, like a religious leader meditating over a disciple's question.

"Uniforms," he finally replied.

"What sort of uniforms?"

"For guerrillas."

"Guerrillas? What guerrillas?"

"Whoever. The ones who are winning. Or maybe the losers,

as consolation. Preferably whichever ones pay cash. It's the law of supply and demand."

"Where'd you get them?"

"They're British navy surplus. They gave me the shirts half-price and threw in the pants for free."

"What about the rest?"

"There's a set of berets in maroon or black. No boots, but that's okay. Africans get corns. They'd rather hunt rhinoceros barefoot. Themselves and the rhinoceros, both barefoot."

"So what'll you do?"

"Sell them. I'm meeting with Mokoena tomorrow."

"Agamemnon Mokoena?"

"That's the one. Who gave him that name, anyway?"

"He's Greek on his mother's side."

"Black?"

"As the night. Colored genes are dominant."

"Agamemnon . . .," he repeated, bemused. "Which one? The one from Mycenae?"

"Beats me," I said.

Cerutti came back a week later, still dragging the trunk, sweaty and disheveled, unshaven and a bit skinnier.

"What a shit, man!" he burst out. "I'd rather beg than negotiate again with that guy!"

While he fixed his maté, he told us what had happened. That Mokoena was a pain. He idolized the Greek world and its hellenistic legacy. He wanted to found a real democracy, just like the original, with all the people joining together in an assembly, maybe in the Malabo stadium, reproducing Attica, Athens and the Parthenon. Cerutti couldn't see where the problem was: he was offering *British* uniforms from the navy and the army, two guarantors of one of the most unbroken parliamentary monarchies on the globe, where authentic Athenian ideals were incarnated better than anywhere else today. So why not wear their insignias and shirts? The berets could be left out, of course. This was a once-in-a-lifetime opportunity, it was now or never. Otherwise he'd pack it all up and sell the whole lot to Sefatsa's Maoists. . . .

The deliberate reference to his rival upset Mokoena, who

forbade any further mention of the name of that "traitor on Peking's payroll." Cerutti accepted the prohibition with reservations. Mokoena reminded him that his was a triumphant revolution, and he would soon enter Malabo victorious. So much the better, replied our friend; this was one more reason to buy the uniforms, since it was important to make a good show when entering the capital. Mokoena lost his temper again; it would be a big mistake if Cerutti thought Mokoena was going to be satisfied with just the capital. He planned on continuing north, to liberate the Sudan, penetrate into Egypt, reach the Mediterranean and build a city bathed by its waters, with a lighthouse and a library or an avenue of columns. Cerutti reminded him that Alexander had already done this without its having made much difference. Nobody, Mokoena responded, had ever dared to insult his mother before.

Cerutti was baffled. Mokoena inquired calmly whether he would rather be shot or force-fed his uniforms one by one, along with the trunks. Shooting would be quicker. Cerutti suggested that maybe they'd rather put him in a big pot and cook him over a slow fire, the old-fashioned way. At this point Mokoena kicked him out of the tent, trunks and all. "I have a revolution going on," Mokoena shouted at him from inside.

I said, "So what are you going to do now?"

"Sleep," he concluded resolutely.

And that's what he did, for a whole week, completely out of it in a corner of the shack. Theresa and I stretched out by the fire that night and the next. On the third day, she slipped out of my arms and went to join Cerutti. She didn't come back.

5

I dedicated myself to digging the well by the river, four hours in the morning and about that many in the afternoon, but the soil had hardened. Like a bird with its wings cut off, that's how I felt—like one of those disheveled flamingoes roaming the dried-up riverbed, no longer drawn by thirst, resigned to their stiff, ungainly gait, their absurdly haughty posture.

When he was done resting, Cerutti took his trunks and left while I was working inside the well. He'd gone to look for Sefatsa and his troops. Theresa curled up again under a bush, preoccupied and remote. This time he wasn't gone for long. He was back three days later, even thinner, with one of his trunks on his shoulder.

"You sold something," I guessed.

"The berets," he reported, and Theresa clapped her hands like a little girl.

The esteemed Duma Sefatsa was something else. Cerutti couldn't understand why he was at such a disadvantage. Maybe it was because of the Chinese, who'd never financed a guerrilla operation worthy of the name. This unreliable backing was exactly why Sefatsa and his people needed to change their image, to do something that might revive their hard-earned reputation as fighters—a set of berets, for instance, maroon or black. Sefatsa had listened to him with a paternal smile, exchanging knowing looks with members of his joint command. Then he dredged up a quotation from the Great Leader about rain pitter-pattering on the Great Wall. Cerutti figured that he was on the right track. At dinner in the guerrilla camp, with his brain stewed in apple brandy, he accepted with pleasure a promissory note to be paid in the city in the presence of an officer of the embassy of the People's Republic of China.

"This Sefatsa is something else," he concluded on his return.

The next day he left for Malabo to cash the promissory note. He returned at dusk, cursing. The Great Leader, or rather his Pekinese successors, had refused to open an embassy in Malabo. There had never been an embassy from the People's Republic of China.

That evening by the fire, Cerutti chewed the promissory note methodically, washed it down with Ballantine's, and Duma Sefatsa passed instantly into the same category as Mokoena in his private hierarchy.

6

The last chance, the final customer, was Rashola, Moses Rashola, top dog in Malabo, guarded by his police force and a handful of regular soldiers on the verge of deserting.

"They already have uniforms," I warned him. "The British themselves put them in uniform years ago."

"Yeah, I know, many years ago. All the better, man. You know that, with all those maneuvers, uniforms wear out."

I criticized his plan to deal with the military. "They're like vultures who feed on carrion," I declared. "They fill their bellies by living off the dead."

He shrugged his shoulders. "So what?" he retorted. "Vultures suffer from bad press, that's all. We do practically the same thing. Or do you eat your cow while it's still alive?"

He didn't even wait for an answer. He went into the shack to rest; Theresa followed. I stayed by the flickering fire, muttering to myself about "high-tech international crime," "dogs of war," second-rate mercenaries and sneaky homebreakers invading humble African homes, showing up one day with trunks full of berets and epaulets, slowly drinking up all your whiskey, taking over your shack, your woman, your hammock and blankets, who don't think of offering to pick up a shovel and help dig the damned well that some international organization approved ages ago, only to file the project away among their least important documents or on the most insignificant chip of an obsolete computer stored on the top floor of a building in Geneva or Brussels, where the project and the well were described in great detail, far from the flies and starving flamingoes who kept looking in vain for a well by the dried-up bed of a river in Kangala, a country where honorable men were left at the mercy of the elements without due warning, forced to listen until dawn — between one's own impotent insults — to an unlikely couple fooling around shamelessly in the obliging darkness of the shack, one's very own shack, while the rhinoceros that sometimes showed up at night browsed through piles of discarded tin cans . . .

It was the end, time to leave and say good-bye to each other before we got hurt. There was only a package of spaghetti and a can of tomatoes left for our farewell dinner. Theresa brought several dubious-looking mushrooms, thyme and caraway seeds and other herbs. The spaghetti was ready at noon. Cerutti installed himself at the head of the table.

"It's the same old story, man," he said, lifting his fork ceremoniously. "You've got to keep turning things around."

He left for good at naptime, dragging the handcart. At seven o'clock, I packed up my knapsack with all the stuff I'd brought with me—next to nothing—and headed toward Malabo.

Theresa was the only one to stay behind. When I reached an open spot, I turned around for a last look. She was dazzling in her loincloth, one arm raised, savanna all around her, smiling by the well.

7

I never went home. I was surprised to learn of Rashola's defeat—along with Cerutti's death—almost two years later. It took Mokoena and Duma Sefatsa, who had joined forces in a last-minute agreement, that long to unseat him.

During the next few months we received new reports from Kangala. But after the cable about the disappearance of his corpse from the morgue, there was no follow-up. The situation in Kangala was a mess. The smell of new carpeting and government offices soon sparked old rivalries between the two guerrilla leaders. Sefatsa threatened to go back to the savanna; Mokoena, that he'd chase him the whole way if he didn't. These developments prompted the news organization ORTF to assign a film crew to Kangala, which I joined at the last minute.

With Mokoena and his people in the government, things seemed pretty much the same. At the airport, the tricolor flag of the faction Mokoena himself had led flew with unfounded optimism next to the Kangala emblem.

My ORTF colleagues spread out through the ministries to

get as many interviews with the revolutionary hierarchy as possible. I broke away from the film team as soon as I could and, hailing a cab, a decrepit relic from the *ancien régime*, I headed for the capital's residential area. I knew exactly where to go: the Argentinian consulate, which shared a floor with other diplomatic bureaus on the old Rashola Avenue, now called Liberation Avenue.

My ORTF ID card paved the way to the consul. He was an affable sort, with Arab features: unkempt salt-and-pepper beard, big nose and lips, thick hair and massive hands, ready for bone-crunching handshakes. He looked like a Bedouin monarch, free at long last from his camels and ensconced now behind a desk, eager to make a good impression: the mark of a true Argentinian!

"From French TV, right?" he began, pointing to an arm-chair. "Don't tell me you've come to ask what happened to that Cerutti guy."

He knew all about the case, down to the last detail, because he'd conducted the investigation.

"Nothing ever happens here, you know. In all my seventeen years as consul, I've never been so bored. First off, you need to understand that I go way back in this business. Before the dead bodies and all, the 'disappeared' people, whatever. I'm a career man. Dead people all look the same to me, red or yellow. It was my job to investigate while the body was still at the morgue. You already know it disappeared after that. It was lifted right out off the slab. Maybe it's been eaten. Seems likely, with all the hungry rebels on the prowl these days.

"Who killed him?"

"No one."

"No one?"

"If you want to know," he said, "I was as puzzled as you about the cause of death. It was straight out of Agatha Christie: a guy shot through the chest in a five-star hotel, lying on the bed with an assortment of half-empty champagne bottles on the nightstand, clothes straight off the rack from Burberry's, where only the British can afford to shop."

He hesitated a moment behind his desk.

"It was simpler than I thought," he concluded. "The guy was selling uniforms, undercover. Three days before Rashola was overthrown, he sold a bunch of British navy shirts to the dictator's troops, after he'd hounded the minister of finances for over a year. Most of the troops deserted, taking the shirts with them, but since Rashola paid cash, they went in style and filled Cerutti's pockets at the last minute. This explains the luxury suite at the Malabo Palace: he went there to celebrate. A couple of days later, Mokoena and Sefatsa entered the city, their men on trucks shooting their guns in the air. They'd just driven by the hotel when the cleaning woman found Cerutti."

"Then . . ."

"One of those shots in the air," my informant continued, "made a hole through the Malabo Palace windows, a hole so small that no one spotted it at first. The bullet ricocheted off the ceiling and hit my compatriot in the chest. Better than Agatha Christie, don't you think? Even without counting the body's disappearance a few weeks later. This isn't the first Argentinian, however, to disappear in recent times. I can't imagine where he could be."

I took a bus out of town that afternoon, bound for the past, but not the past I'd imagined. I discovered this as soon as I got off the bus and headed toward the river. I expected to find a rickety shack built of scrap lumber and sheetmetal. It had been rebuilt board by board. I expected emaciated ostriches and flocks of smaller birds in an atmosphere of desolation; in their place were chickens, a corral and a vegetable garden. I expected an empty hole by the dried-up riverbed; the hole was still there, but the savanna had taken care of filling it — water had finally risen up from deep underground, and someone, some tireless hand, had turned it into a well. I expected a barren landscape, but there were other huts nearby, with gardens and corrals. I expected absences, the implacable silence of the savanna; instead, Theresa's face — lined but still youthful — watched me with quiet satisfaction from the threshold of the hut. Next to her a small black boy — very young, two years old at the most — was blithely picking his nose without taking his eyes off me. Close to the hut, there was a wooden gravestone with flowers all around it.

That night we slept by the well, in each others arms. The next day, while Theresa was visiting neighbors, I sat beside the gravestone for a while. Then I drew a bucket of water and, with the child by the hut watching my every move, I drizzled some over the flowers. I deliberately poured some of the water on myself, and the child burst out laughing. It was Cerutti's laugh. Or mine. Theresa never managed to clear this up for me. It was the uninhibited laugh of a survivor in the heart of Africa . . . with a dead man to honor with our memories and flowers beside a gravestone, and an abundant source of water close by.

A week later, I quit ORTF over the phone. I never went back.

—translated from the Spanish
by Lillian Tagle and Carolyn Brown

William Hunt

Likely Images

With Pelléas and Mélisande, Claude
Debussy turned to sleeping figures:
the garden was growing cold, its trees
pancake hatted, leaned Orient-
wards· but otherwise bare chested:
gesture absented melody,
gesture absented memory.
No mirrors. No history.
Voices alive to themselves alone.

Music can't be itself
like a thought can be itself the gesture
in the glass shaped like itself: music
wakens the heart, skips or weakens the head.
He said: me too at times its charm rubbed raw:
its wayward grace wronged,
distracted, was made indistinct, pallid
as a boat or bar of soap
glistening where it rises to the surface
and floats sitting up.

His legs outstretch doll-like, while Chou-Chou
beside him on the lawn busies herself in prayer;
she is a child and it is understood prays for herself
alone and doesn't know someone takes this photo,
nor why Daddy's eyes and heart and hands grow cold.
It would be simple now for him to pay his debts,
but in a short while he won't have to.

Two Poems by S.X. Rosenstock

Rimininny!

> *And they read no more that day.*
>
> —Dante

If you can't fuck me while I read, fuck off.
You're not the best of what's been thought or said,
Not yet. But youth, with genius, is enough.

Ménage à trois is greatness, not rebuff,
If you gain art from what art's represented.
If you can't fuck me while I read, fuck off.

I want you, and I want a paragraph
Of lengthy James; he does go on. My love,
Can you? I shouldn't praise his length? Enough

Of him? The body of work's living proof
We're all rare forms, and living . . . in the dead.
If you can't *A Little Tour in France* me while I read, fuck off.

I signal lusts by *title*, not handkerchief,
Since I'm the sex of all that I have read;
Sometimes I write this sex. Kiss me enough,

And well enough, that I may bear the snub
That reading's not a *sexual preference*.
If you can't fuck me while I read, fuck off,
Or rave how *I'm* a work of art enough.

Walk This Way

Did their Catullus . . .

—W.B. Yeats

I. *O rem ridiculam,* . . . Redux

Hey, Coco, here's a joke, or what
To reckon with the brain and twat.

Please chortle everywhere for me
If you love S-E-X (*sans* E).

Today nearby the Beverly Center,
I saw this weird guy break, and enter

Such a nice girl. I shouted some
Flow Chart; of course he couldn't come.

His dick slipped out, all small and pink.
I act, you know, quick as you think.

He had his pants down, and he tripped:
I fucked him with my manuscript!

I rolled it tightly and, fast, tried
To smear it with some Astroglide

I had on me. I heard him grunt.
"This Snapple's not a lubricant,"

I hissed, and poured his tea up him.
And counseled more time at the gym.

I then retrieved my dirty book,
Gleaning the awe in his "hurt-me" look.

To who do I owe . . . "It's to whom!" *Who?*
"Ms. Veronensis, Ass, to you."

II. ANTISTROPHE: Sonametric

The battered sex;   the face like a bad scrape;
The khaki skirt too reminiscent of,
Now, his bad pants;   the death of physical love
In woman's nomenclature of escape
Valves, means to leave culture's many wrongs and shape
Fresh culture's dreams; (We're only made by troves
Of culture's treasures turned eros in the swerves
Of our cultured capacity to leap
Libidinized, *née* grandiose, at change.)

The hope of yourself demolished in rape;
(You thought you'd fall in love after you fell
In love with your career and you'd compelled
A small—your own!—apartment, sky, fawn, maize,
To softly represent what one can't say—
I'm wonderful!—about oneself.)   the hell
Of crisis intervention's, martyr's, help
That makes a woman feel so torn, agape
To victimhood; in debt to the poor thing:

I have attacked and ridiculed he who
Was rank brutality. Art can *make* well;
But must it make you well? The literal,
Rank usefulness, harms what I want for you:
The nerve of your imagination to be true
As is. Curl up with, in, this book. I smell
His crap. But my hard *labor* works this spell:
Come through—Art bears this.—birth's dilation, new.
Art, love; it must be one of these: come through.

Two Poems by John Kinsella

Rat Tunnels

Like monks tunneling into desert
mesas, a vibrant hermitage surrounded
by a moat of sand, rats have tunneled
deep into the walls of the horse-dam.

But their science is flawed—it's Autumn
now and the rains have yet to come,
Summer lies low in the hollowed ground,
a brackish indolent puddle—Winter

will unleash the flood that will fill
the lowest chambers, drive rats with young
blindly towards the upper galleries,
as frenzied as victims in disaster films

who've realized technology is just a mask
to hide a human failing–"we can't be wrong,
we've considered every alternative." But God
makes kingdoms in the strangest places.

Watching the Storm Approach Canning Bridge

Bottleneck or gateway? Where the Swan
& Canning Rivers merge, or as the storm
approaches—a throng of poltergeists

with wicked notions—clash.
Hypnotized or possessed
they hesitate, & then suddenly

erupt as if struck by an irrepressible
freedom, a sundering of all morality.
Clouds hang over the city like strips

of graying flesh, the storm's breath
blown over the waters sulfurous
& angry. Beneath the bridge

the irregular wooden pylons quiver,
& baitfish swim with a wind
that rushes against the tide

thundering through the channel, drawn by
the distant conjectural sea.
These silver minnows remain stationary

by swimming furiously, glittering brightly
just below the surface; medusas
camouflaged brown & khaki

toss past like wind-struck parachutes.
Blowfish race through the school
of baitfish & eat voraciously. On the decking

deadly litters of corpses from the previous night's
fishing. Blowfish receive no mercy.
Those baitfish are lures as the storm approaches,

their brilliance in the murky waters
enough to drag the poet down. Their beauty
the beauty of the storm, now alive

with electricity — blue light arcing out
over the city, sparking of rods
on the city's tallest buildings. Their beauty

an anathema as on the surface the planks
are covered in fishgut & burley.
Their beauty that of the transfigured — stationary

yet vigorous in their stasis, the undead — like a poem.
Another blowie rips through their ranks & the wind
drives the surface crazy. As if atoms within one body —

cold in the bubbling water, dry ice fuming in the crucible —
these tiddlers explode as one, spray fuming
through the wind-slick, the body molten & singing

of Democritus "We are accustomed to speak of heat,
of cold, of color. In reality there are atoms & space."
Their phonaesthemic bodies obey the storm's

linguistic flare, flash, flicker, & flame.
There is a lull, as if the storm, transfixed over the city,
contemplates its course. I am possessed

by a torpor, a child fishing here
with my brother, as guilty as the next kid
stranding blowies in heaps on the deck.

We are watching older kids drink green
ginger wine & smoke Marlboros. Sometimes
fighting, marking their territory.

Old men drink from bottles
shrouded in brown paper bags, use only
small hooks & know all the tricks.

They seem never to move, but bury their catch
in dank hessian sacks. Sunlight breaks through temporarily
& as it nets you through the pylons you try to break free.

The storm stirs & a cormorant fillets the poet's
body—a dark sonaric mass. The storm
tacks its way up the Swan, towards the Canning.

It calls to all fish that move beneath
the bridge: O skippy, O tarwhine, O tailor & flounder,
O bream & KGs, O snook, O flathead & salmon,

O pike, O cobbler & you, great mulloway.
Those dead blowfish, looking like Jules Verne
submersibles—porthole eyes

& cyber bodies, living metal struck by a virus.
The baitfish ignite with the lightning,
the sky is as black as an epigraph.

Two Poems by Richard Lyons

The Blind Man, Twilight Turning Night

Is it cardinals

that separate seed from the yellow blades of rye
the way braille comes up with the fingertips,

those russet *chips*

and silences, scarlet, sharp as flax . . . ?
Soon, next door, the college kids tip their glasses

to the falling stars.

In here, where I see, they're all stars, a slow motion
of blood & bone, a quick harem of browns

then one scarlet slur

curving the sky, my arm between the hand & shoulder
like a magician's long string of silk handkerchiefs

blown from the dark.

Lunch by the Grand Canal

Harry Donaghy, an ex-priest, is telling us
that, after ten rounds, the welterweight was still panting
from a literal hole in his heart.
The fish the waiter lays before me on a white plate

is hissing through its eye, I swear it.
Harry spills out a carton of old photos
between the bread & the vials of vinegar.
The people in the pictures are friends of his aunt, whose body

he's signed for & released, now on a jet lifting from Rome.
He says he's always preferred Venice,
here a Bridge of Sighs separates this life from the next.
One of the photos, he thinks, is of his aunt,
she's no longer young having dropped a cotton dress at her
    feet

so the artist at arm's length might see her beauty
as if it had already slipped away. Across from me,
Paige Bloodworth is wearing a red hat, which looks good on
    her,
but she hasn't said a word, so pissed we missed the launch
to San Michele where Pound is buried.

For her, Harry's unidentified relatives
posing on the steps down to the Grand Canal
are lifting stones from their pockets
and pelting the poet's coffin as it eases out
on a black boat, chrysanthemums hoarding their perfumes.

I'm stroking the curved prow of a boat as if it were
the neck of a wild stallion rearing close
for a hidden cube of sugar or a slice of apple.
Miss Bloodworth's hat becomes a figure in memory's contract
as it lifts over water the color of tourmaline.
Harry's big hands trap all the photos, spilling the wine.
It's the winter of 1980, just warm enough
to sit outside as I remember. The rest of that year
no doubt is a lie.

Two Poems by Rick Hilles

Visions of Captivity: Neulengbach, 1912

—after Egon Schiele's Prison Diary

1. Crude Hours Which Pass Over Me like Animals

Even now I do not understand
the spat and hissed and murmured words
strangled out of throats in distant cells;
harangue of murderers

and petty thieves washes over me
each night, until it is too wet to sleep,
and I paint these prison walls to dry.
Only later do I garn

the content of their noise: the story —
Why have I been buried here?
By morning my chronicle disappears,
pulled into masonry

by some animal of unknown origin,
without name. Dust, webs, bile, sediment
from sweat and soot cover the plaster
of this cage. Stains darkest

where my bed touches the wall and white-
washed lime rubs off and comes unsheathed.
It's frightening. Now, even a fire
in my cell would be

beautiful. Tomorrow, the guard
will let my friend bring watercolors.
Thoughts diffuse after dusk. I hear
Trieste, the sea, and open.

2. The Room in Which an Orange Is the Only Light

I paint the cot in my cell,
the corridor, and rubbish of inmates.
Draw the organic movement

of the water-pour, the unsightly chair.
Smudging color to give them shape.
Last night: hoarfrost; the trembling.

Moans—distant, soft; desperate.
At last the minor angels of apathy
stretched out their numb and fragile limbs

upon the frightened dying, dressing them
in sleep. The eye of every other god
now far from here or gazing elsewhere.

Not even their dander falls to us.
Herewith the stink of sweat and lye,
the rot of wool and linen, an orange.

V. brought it yesterday. Last night, it was
my only light, that small indefatigable.
It did me unspeakable good.

3. The Trial: Lord, Open Your Jewelled Eyes

The irretrievable hours have sifted.
A courtroom near Vienna. A gavel
slams. Order. Uncharged and held
without bail, here I learn my crime:

Impropriety. That young vagrant
haunts me still. She came to my room
one night, disrobed, insisting she work
for rent; and though underage, unlovely,

I obliged. Now the judge manhandles
my designs, intrudes the parchment
of her, the study confiscated when
they pulled me from my bed. Lifted

to his lamp, he thumbs the parted legs,
the darker creases of her sex, where it
did not reach light. He adjusts the wick,
beholds her from within. *Pornography.*

This unfinished nude   not my best,
unnerves me. I could show them things;
they would bury me alive. Above,
the paper seal glows amber over

flames and air looms, fragrant. I've
known whores whose hair smelled like
this, burning in bedside lamps.
What the judge does now is willful,

sleight of hand. The darkening parchment
gains circumference like a black hole
he threads the fire through. His moon
enlarges rapidly—a monk's hairline

instantly receding at the crown, taking
in its flame, her skin. Embers sprawl
to the bailiff's box, wind scattering
her crushed bones like mice in white scrawl.

Novalis

—Moravia, 1801

The fever kept him working, waking, writing
warded off the other realm, even as it distilled
the room made fragment by larkspur and woodsmoke.
He stoked the fire, ink plumed in his moving —

the heat from him warmed the night he wanted
to expose. At twenty-five, he nearly did, died
ploughing the hours. He watched them burn
in daybreak's furnace. Not enough, he had to learn

the afterlife. His first Virgil was a dream,
it dreamed to him — he died and came back
to life climbing a rocky gorge, scree crumbling
at his feet. He tumbled down a shaft

and found an unmined passageway. Steam
hissed off the walls. Sparks on alluvium
and groundwater played about the cavern
and his feet. The light hove cold and blue,

and higher cliffs arose with brighter veins. There
he saw it, the blue flower, though it altered
as he approached to take it. The corolla dissolved.
His coughing woke him, wrecked him (or his father's

hammer did) and broke the spell like molten iron
that flares red till it is beaten sideburn white,
sehnsuct melted to a silver ounce of meteor,
star-chipped light, now fallen through a crater

in the firmament. A piece translated from the sky
like crystals formed where lightning strikes.
Inverted celestial. What might have flowered
from *Heinrich* and his apprenticeship mining

the grotto, snaps synapse, flashes out of vision.
Consumption darkened his Eurydice, ink-line broken,
(he wrote) *Each is the midpoint of an emanation* —
the certain flourish of a stallion now hemmed in.

Three Poems by Michael Eilperin

Budapest, 1945

Who can't but love a soldier wearing mums
In his helmet? A colossal private
Produced a flask of something and toasted
The derring-do of the Soviet troops.

We hadn't seen Russians since ambassador
Beksadian came by to warble
Airs from Rossini's "Sins of My Old Age."
He claimed he'd invented a nine-tone scale.

Once, in particularly high spirits,
He spat a gold filling across the room.
We admired its minute, solar glow
Before he popped it back into the tooth.

He resigned before Stalin could reach him.
After certain countries turned him away,
He settled with a people who taught him
To whistle like a thrush, only louder.

Thin Walls

The trout-boned woman upstairs
Wakes my wife and baby daughter
With her early baths. The pipes ache,

Tremble, and swoon rushing water
And God knows what else: plucked lashes,
Sick tissue, a river of age.

I'm ordinary, and worried.
Up, and tuck blankets around her—
I could wring the black out of night.

Aesop, Who Received a Mighty Blow to the Head

"In Roanoke there lives a toad whose head
Resembles caked mud pies. Thus unnoticed,
He mourns his lost gills and tries to account
For the landscape's coarse exaggerations."

. . . My worst patient. I cannot discharge him
Soon enough. Observe the buckshot pupils,
The reluctant locks piled up in a bluff.
Good bones, but he walks a three-legged gait.

We've shaved the skull to a caramel swell.
Note the roseate, cardinal designs
Traced by routed blood, the forms which rise
As his pulse travels its sizeless orbit.
Has eloped with the rain and sprouts blind wings.

They reproach us from the middle distance.

Mark Irwin

Juvescence of Autumn

At dusk the ambulance came
pulling all the way up onto the lawn
like a red speedboat drifting

* * *

ashore. She was old.
She had fallen and broken her pelvis
while picking apples. She had

* * *

pruned that tree so many times
it appeared as a dark
hood. About it her white

* * *

head moved. The attendants, unloading
the gurney, argued about whose turn
it was to buy the pizza. I had been

* * *

sitting outside, reading beneath the yellow
leaves. I heard the thin
cry. She said to call, but that she

* * *

was okay, except for the pain. Then there was
nothing to say. We stared at the apples
still nested in their thick green hive. Then she talked

* * *

of a daughter, her grandchildren, her
dead husband, Karl. Still she stared
at the tree, talking as if the fruit

* * *

restored memory. That was the day a *streaker*
ran all the way down BellHower Lane.
The sudden white breasts, — the pale shadow

* * *

between legs. Now I finally remember
what I wanted to say. — The silver thread
of the siren the ambulance followed

* * *

away. And that tree, the swollen
green crown, on which the apples were cities
opening onto an invisible blue world.

Gregory Fraser

Still Life

My mind long gone, having forgot to shut the body
off, I will lie in some spare room,
some former nursery, entranced by waiting for death
to take me, but death will only take
its time. May will tap the pane, bring flowers like

no visitor, and by the day the votive
candle of summer smolders out, and the leaves catch
flame, my dying will have taken on
a life of its own. I can hear my hollow cough, smell
my stench, decades away. Can you?

Can you tell me why we dare go on, knowing the end
is full, like the beginning, of gibberish
and drool? Early evenings in the living room, steeped
in shadow, the room of the living,
the daughter duty wills me to, some cardinal virtue

or old guilt consigns, will hear
a shallow moan, an infant tide, rise up through my
throat. It must be the third or
fourth year of my dying. She will patiently turn down,
like a bed, a page in her magazine,

mount the stair, and a boy to whom my name
has fallen, like some dashed twig,
will help her tend my dying, clear the feeding tube,
spittle off my lip. He will be told to
fetch warm water from the sink, and my wrinkled

white suit of skin will be cleansed,
moot dignity preserved. Perhaps one night the boy
will search my eyes, as his mother
(divorced by then, fed up with my living!) swabs
away the sour milk of age, or raise

the shade and gaze outdoors at trees, donning the dark
like priests, and ponder what awaits
on the other side: blinding void, or rapture, or both
as in this life. Maybe he will pass
some time with tattered books, that lost year of

my dying, borrowed from my shelf.
Light in August will be his choice, no, *The Grapes
of Wrath*. He will journey back to
farms closed down like half my face, both arms,
after the stroke, crops that failed

unlike my heart, men and women giving up their
hopes, as my flesh will not (God
knows how much longer) its ghost. And if by chance
he stumbles on the diary I ought to
leave to fire, I pray the kid grows bored, sets

the volume back, before he comes across
the section on my own depression—maudlin, wrong—
starting in my late twenties, learns
what I had thought to do and almost done: end it all,
before anything whatsoever had begun.

David M. Katz

An Ode for William Collins

I

Poor Collins sung the gradual, waiting,
Praying for Eve to arrive. And, while bidding
    For her, sure of failure,
    Found her inadvertently.
Where is she now? Without prayer can she
Make us natural, come without ritual
    In these impatient days?
    Can we find the coolest evening
Here, beyond method, beyond practice
In a most despising age? Like thee, I seek
    An inaccessible wing
    Barely seen in heavy shadow
A few feet past measure, as beloved dusk
Descends. Like thee, I seek an intimacy,
    A capacity to speak
    In a small, evasive voice;
Like thee, the beetle, the leathern bat; like thee
The whisper that ceases, in the evening, to aspire.

II

There you were, twisted, disheveled in the sheets,
A permanent shape of disarray. And then:
    "Smith, do you remember
    My dream?" Your eyes, brightening,
Recalled it as a shared schoolboy glory:
    Your one pathetic gesture,

Your failed aspiration.
"Yes of course." The talisman produced for them
Sixteen years ago shone again, that burdened
    And unburdened, polished
    And repolished badge
You offered up. "I was walking in a field
Amid the bending grass, when before me
    There arose the straightest,
    Loftiest tree. Suddenly,
Dangerously, I was balanced at the top.
I reached for a stable branch. But the big bough
    Failed with me, let me fall
    To the floor of the wavering field."
You were safe, but uncannily shattered.
Why? "The tree was the tree of poetry."

III

You were weak before the fact, on the verge
Of something overwhelming that could come
    Only with the strength of time.
    You planned tragedies,
But only planned them. You languished,
Borrowed money, fled bailiffs, finished two odes
    In two years, and waned
    Like a dry slice of moon.
I see you, neurasthenic at the end
Of a tortured day, grieving in a dusky light,
    Able just once to forget
    What could never be done.
The night about to come, about to fall
Decisively down, is suspended
    Above signalling shadows;
    Tentative, departing light
Tantalizes, flashes, subsides . . .
You rise to the large idea of evening,

A sleepwalker awakened
At the edge of the woods, condemned
To wait quietly. But you will not rail
Against silence. You are in her service.
Helplessly you reached for her
And language never faltered.

Shawn Sturgeon

Babylonian Surprise

It was our favorite pastime, to be sure,
those hairs waiting to be split, those pieces
that passed understanding. We thought we'd find
some sense in their words, our hammers harping
against those faces we had so admired,
their hearts simply bursting with expression
as pursuing or pursued they choked on

those sensations—all that vivid color
in our cheeks, their hair just slightly aflame.
And those cities, the ruins, that husbandry
chopped to bits—so very clever, so fine.
And those parchments they made, all those endless
petitions so unnatural to our hearts?
Each thought yielded another thought, until

we simply ran out of definitions!
Their only explanation was they loved
words that had striking force, a sign sounding
in their minds, while ripping out their throats. So,
when they finally finished crying, puzzled,
we made everything mean only itself.
Banging their tombs shut, we made their world real.

it..." Who wrote that?
    (a beat)
Hemingway, right?

TALLY is silent, then nods uncertainly.

               WARREN JUSTICE
F. Scott Fitzgerald.
    (a beat)
Where did he say he'd move you? San Fran-
cisco? No, that's down market. Chicago?
L.A.? Philly?
    (when Tally says nothing)
Philadelphia.
    (another beat)
You'll be up against Marcia Miller. You
try to show her up like you did Rob,
she'll have you for lunch.

               TALLY ATWATER
I thought you'd come with me.

               WARREN JUSTICE
Uh uh. This is a place where I can keep
certain truths self-evident. If it bleeds
it leads.

               TALLY ATWATER
That's a copout.

               WARREN JUSTICE
You got a whole lot left to discover. I
already discovered it. I've heard half
the liars in the world talk about the
people's right to know, then turn around
and feed the people a cartoon version of
whatever it is they have a right to know.
Not that it matters. Since by the time
the next news cycle rolls around the people have forgotten it anyway.

               TALLY ATWATER
That's a copout too.

               WARREN JUSTICE
That being the case... there's nothing
much more in this for either of us.

TALLY looks at him, then turns away toward the window. The CD
is still playing. Tally presses the stop button. After a

A manuscript page from the screenplay of Up Close & Personal
by John Gregory Dunne and Joan Didion.

The Art of Screenwriting II

John Gregory Dunne

The fifth of six children, John Gregory Dunne, the son of
a prominent surgeon, was born in Hartford, Connecticut in

*1932. He went to school at Portsmouth Priory (now Abbey)
and on graduation moved on to Princeton, graduating from
there in 1954. To please his mother he applied to the Stanford
Business School, but changed his mind (if not hers) and instead
volunteered for the draft. He served for two years in the army
as an enlisted man, his overseas service spent with a gun battery
in Germany. He speaks of his years at the Priory (where the
monks were "very worldly") and in the army as being far more
valuable than his time at Princeton. "In the army I was exposed
to people I would not otherwise have known. I learned something about life."*

*Back in the States after his service, Dunne worked briefly in
an ad agency (he was fired), then with the magazine* Industrial
Design. *In 1959 he went to* Time *magazine and worked there
until 1964, the year he married the author Joan Didion. Since
devoting himself to his own work, Dunne has written a number
of novels, including* The Red White and Blue, True Confessions, Dutch Shea, Jr., Vegas *and* Playland *and two nonfiction
books,* Harp *and* The Studio. *He and Didion together have
written over twenty screenplays, seven of which have reached
the screen, including* The Panic in Needle Park, Play It As
It Lays, A Star Is Born, True Confessions, Hills Like White
Elephants, Broken Trust *and, most recently,* Up Close & Personal.

*At present the couple lives in a large sunny apartment on
New York's Upper East Side. One is struck by how neat and
ordered everything is — no sense of confusion, files in neat
piles. The floors throughout the apartment are bare, polished.
The considerable library is in order: the fiction titles only fill
the shelves of the master bedroom.*

*Both have workrooms. When the pair works on a screenplay,
each does a separate draft, and then the two meet, sitting
opposite each other at the desk in John's workplace where they
thrash out successive drafts. Here too are mementos of their
work together. Photographs taken on the set of various movies.
A large police map of the streets of Los Angeles covers one
wall. Authentic, it was used on the set of* True Confessions —
little black dots across its surface where crime-scene pins were

once struck. On the opposite wall, a more serene scene: a blown-up photograph of Joan Didion, standing in the shallows of a quiet sea and holding a pair of sandals. Many photographs are of their daughter, Quintana Roo (named after a state in Mexico), now the photo editor at Elle Decor *magazine. A recent addition in the workroom is a photograph of Quintana and Robert Redford, the costar, with Michelle Pfeiffer, of the newly released* Up Close & Personal.

The interview that follows is a composite — partly conducted at the YMHA before a packed audience, partly at the Dunnes' home on the East Side, with a written portion about the novel Playland, *added by the author himself.*

INTERVIEWER

Your work is populated with the most extraordinary grotesqueries — nutty nuns, midgets, whores of the most breathtaking abilities and appetites. Do you know all these characters?

JOHN GREGORY DUNNE

Certainly I knew the nuns. You couldn't go to a parochial school in the 1940s and not know them. They were like concentration-camp guards. They all seemed to have rulers, and they hit you across the knuckles with them. The joke at St. Joseph's Cathedral School in Hartford, Connecticut, where I grew up, was that the nuns would hit you until you bled, and then hit you for bleeding. Having said that, I should also say they were great teachers. As a matter of fact, the best of my formal education came from the nuns at St. Joseph's and from the monks at Portsmouth Priory, a Benedictine boarding school in Rhode Island where I spent my junior and senior years of high school. The nuns taught me basic reading, writing and arithmetic; the monks taught me how to think, how to question, even to question Catholicism in order to better understand it. The nuns and the monks were far more valuable to me than my four years at Princeton. I'm not a practicing Catholic, but one thing you never lose from a Catholic educa-

tion is a sense of sin, and the conviction that the taint on the
human condition is the natural order.

What about the whores and midgets?

I suppose for that I would have to go to my informal education. I spent two years as an enlisted man in the army in
Germany after the Korean War, and those two years were the
most important learning experience I really ever had. I was
just a tight-assed upper-middle-class kid, the son of a surgeon,
and I had this sense of Ivy League entitlement, and all that
was knocked out of me in the army. Princeton boys didn't
meet the white and black underclass that you meet as an enlisted draftee. It was a constituency of the dispossessed — high-
school dropouts, petty criminals, rednecks, racists, gamblers,
you name it, and I fit right in. I grew to hate the officer class
that was my natural constituency. A Princeton classmate was
an officer on my post, and he told me I was to salute him and
call him sir, as if I had to be reminded, and also that he would
discourage any outward signs that we knew each other. I hate
that son of a bitch to this day. I took care of him in *Harp*.
Those two years in Germany gave me a subject I suppose I've
been mining for the past God knows how many years. It fit
nicely with that Catholic sense of sin, the taint on the human
condition. And it was in the army that I learned to appreciate
whores. You didn't meet many Vassar girls when you were
serving in a gun battery on the Czech border and were in a
constant state of alert in case the Red Army came rolling across
the frontier. As for midgets, they're part of that constituency
of the dispossessed.

You once said you only had one character. Is that true?

I've always thought a novelist only has one character, and
that is himself or herself. In my case, me. So at the risk of

being glib, I am the priest in *True Confessions* and the criminal
lawyer in *Dutch Shea, Jr.* I've certainly never been a cop or
a priest or a pimp lawyer, but these protagonists are in a sense
my mouthpieces. I like to learn about their professions, which
is why I so much like doing nonfiction. I'm a great believer
in the novelist being "on the scene," reporting, traveling,
meeting all sorts of people. You do nonfiction, you get to
meet people you would not normally meet. I'm not a bad
mimic, and I can pick up speech cadences that I would not
pick up if I didn't hit the road.

INTERVIEWER

Do you think novels have a life of their own?

DUNNE

Before I began writing fiction, I thought that was nonsense.
Then I learned otherwise. Let me give you an example. In
The Red White and Blue, I started off thinking the protagonist
would be the Benedictine priest, Bro Broderick. I realized
rather quickly that he could not be, but that I was stuck with
him as a character. He never really came to life until I finished
the book, and went back and inserted his diary, which he had
left in his will to the Widener Library at Harvard. Then for
three hundred pages or so, I thought the leading character
was the radical lawyer Leah Kaye, because whenever she appeared on the scene the book took off. Then when I got to page
five hundred of this seven-hundred-fifty page manuscript, I
realized *she* couldn't be the leading character because she had
not appeared in over two hundred pages. It was only then
that I realized that the narrator, who was the only survivor of
the three major protagonists, would have to be the leading
character. So novels *do* take charge of the writer, and the writer
is basically a kind of sheepdog, just trying to keep things on
track.

INTERVIEWER

Can you say something about the germination of a book?

DUNNE

I think any time a writer tells you where a book starts, he is lying, because I don't think he knows. You don't start off saying, "I'm going to write this grand saga about the human condition." It's a form of accretion. When my wife and I were in Indonesia in 1980 or 1981, we ran into this man who had been a University of Maryland extension teacher during the Vietnam War. He was stationed at Cam Ranh Bay. These GIs would go off in the morning in their choppers, and when they'd come back at night—if they were lucky—he would teach them remedial English. I made a note of it in my notebook, putting it away, because I knew this was a really great way to look at the Vietnam War, and it turned up in *The Red White and Blue*. When I am between books, I am an inveterate note taker. I jot things down mainly because they give me a buzz. I like to go to the library and take a month's newspaper, say August, 1962, and read through it. You can find great stuff in those little filler sections at the bottom of a page. Then, when it comes time to start writing a book, I sort of look through the stuff and see if any of it works. I also write down names. If you have a name, it can set someone in place. I have a great friend in California, the Irish novelist Brian Moore. We were having dinner one night, and Brian said that when he was a newspaperman in Montreal, a local character there was named Shake-Hands McCarthy. I said, "Stop! Are you ever going to use that name?" He said, "No, let me tell you about him." I said, "No, I don't want to know anything about him. I just want to use that name." So the name turned up in *True Confessions*. When I heard the name I had no idea when I was going to use it if, indeed, *ever*. But it was a name that absolutely set a character in cement. We had dinner with Joyce Carol Oates at Princeton once; she was saying that she does the same thing, that she collects those little fillers; she never knows when she's going to use them. She just throws them in a file, and oddly enough, they do stick.

To get back to your question, *Vegas* is the one book for which I can actually pinpoint the moment when it started. I was trying to think of an idea, doodling at my desk while I was talking to my wife, and I drew a heart, then a square around the heart. I found I had written five letters: *V-E-G-A-S*. So, I not only had a subject, but I had a title.

INTERVIEWER

Why is the title of *Vegas* reinforced by the description "a fiction"?

DUNNE

Because I had a contract for a nonfiction book. I always through of *Vegas* as a novel, but Random House said, "It doesn't read like a novel," and I said, "A novel is anything the writer says the book is, and since I made most of it up, it can't be nonfiction." So we ended up calling it a fiction. A lot of it is true. The prostitute did write poetry, although the poetry I used in *Vegas* is not hers. It was actually written by my wife, who as a child had memorized a lot of Sara Teasdale poems. "I can write you bad poetry," she said. So there are two little poems in there that Joan actually wrote.

INTERVIEWER

What is your state of mind when you are writing?

DUNNE

Essentially, writing is a sort of manual labor of the mind. It is a hard job, but there comes a moment in every book, I suppose, when you know you're going to finish, and then it becomes a kind of bliss, almost a sexual bliss. I once read something Graham Greene said about this feeling. The metaphor he used was a plane going down a runway and then, ultimately, leaving the ground. Occasionally, he had books that he felt never did leave the runway; one of them was *The Honorary Consul*, though in retrospect he realized that it was one of his better books.

INTERVIEWER
How much do you know about the end of a book?

DUNNE
When I did *Dutch Shea, Jr.*, I knew the last line was going to be, "I believe in God."

INTERVIEWER
Why did you pick that line?

DUNNE
Because that's the line the man would say as he kills himself. I wanted that most despairing of acts to end with the simple declarative sentence, "I believe in God." In *The Red White and Blue* I knew the last line was going to be either "Yes" or "No," in dialogue, and the penultimate line was going to be "Yes" or "No" not in dialogue. The first line of *Vegas* is, "In the summer of my nervous breakdown, I went to live in Las Vegas, Clark County, Nevada." I knew that the last line of that book would be, "And in the fall, I went home." I don't think it's necessary to have a last line; I just like to know where in general I'm going. I have a terrible time plotting. I only plot about thirty pages in front of where I am. I once had dinner with Ross MacDonald, who did the Lew Archer novels about a California private detective. He said he spent eighteen months actually plotting out a book—every single nuance. Then, he sat down and wrote the book in one shot from beginning to end . . . six months to write the book and eighteen to plot it out. If you've ever read one of those books, it's so intricately plotted it's like a watch, a very expensive watch.

INTERVIEWER
You have said that you have a lot of trouble with plotting a book. What makes it move forward?

DUNNE
I have no grand plan of what I'm going to do. I had no idea who killed the girl in *True Confessions* until the day I

wrote it. I knew it would be someone who was not relevant to the story. I had always planned that. But who the actual killer was, I simply had no idea. Years before, I had clipped something from the *Los Angeles Times* in the small death notices. It was the death of a barber. I had put that up on my bulletin board. I was figuring out, "Now who . . .," getting to the moment when I had to reveal who killed this girl, with not the foggiest idea who did it, and my eyes glommed onto this death notice of a barber. I said, "Oops, you're it." One must have enormous confidence to wait to figure these things out until the time comes.

INTERVIEWER

Do you have great affection for your characters?

DUNNE

You have to have affection for them, because you can't live with them for two years or three years without liking them. But I have no trouble killing them off.

INTERVIEWER

Is there a considerable shifting of gears in moving between nonfiction and fiction?

DUNNE

There's a technical difference. I find that the sentences are more ornate and elaborate in nonfiction, because you don't have dialogue to get you on your way. Nonfiction has its ruffles and flourishes, clauses and semicolons. I never use a semicolon in fiction.

INTERVIEWER

Your latest novel is *Playland*. The background is the movie business.

DUNNE

I lived in Los Angeles and worked in the movie business from the mid-1960s until the late 1980s, but except on the fringes, in *The Red White and Blue*, I had never written about Hollywood and the picture business in fiction. It was like an eight-hundred-pound gorilla. Sooner or later I was going to have to deal with it.

INTERVIEWER

Why did you set the Hollywood part of your novel largely in the 1940s rather than in the period you were working there?

DUNNE

Because I don't think contemporary Hollywood is terribly interesting, and because I don't want any sense of a roman à clef (is your so-and-so really so-and-so?). Mostly I wanted to reconstruct an era from a distance, an era that I kept on getting tantalizing glimpses of from people I knew or worked with who had been there in the 1940s, and had not just been there but had been at the top of the heap.

INTERVIEWER

For example?

DUNNE

Otto Preminger. Joan and I once did a screenplay for him. He was an immensely cultivated man, but he was a tyrant with a volcanic temper. When he lost his temper, the top of his head — he shaved it with an electric razor sometimes during story meetings—would turn beet red. He screamed at most people who worked for him, but never at us; he just got elaborately polite, and he would refer to Joan as "Mrs. Dunne," drawing it out for half a dozen sibilant syllables. He brought us back to New York to work on the script. He said it would only take three weeks tops, but three months later we were still there . . . in this tiny apartment on Fifth Avenue, with our four-year-old daughter and a different babysitter every day. Our daughter called Otto, to his face, "Mr. Preminger with no hair," which he took with good grace. We finally said we were going home for Christmas and we would finish the script there, and Otto said, "I forbid you to go." It was an extraordinary thing to say. We thought he was kidding, but that was the way the studios had always operated and he saw nothing wrong with it. We went back to L.A. anyway, and he threatened to sue us for $2 million. He simply could not understand our lack of deference. It worked out. He paid off our contract at forty cents on the dollar. It was the kind of punishment the old studio system would have exacted. But we always stopped by to see him when we came to New York, because if you were not working for him, he was a charming man.

INTERVIEWER

Who else?

DUNNE

Billy Wilder. In the mid-eighties, he asked me to do a screenplay with him for an idea he had, about a silent movie star playing Christ in a biblical epic. The twist was that the movie star was a dissolute drunk who was screwing everybody on the set, including the actress playing the Virgin Mary, while the actress playing Mary Magdalene spurned him, another twist. Billy wanted him to repent at the end of the picture, and actually walk on water — a gag he would set up throughout the picture, and then pay off at fade-out. Nothing came of the idea, but we had some funny meetings, because Billy has perfect pitch for truly hilarious bad taste. This was a man who won seven Oscars, and he kept them in a closet at his nondescript office on Santa Monica Boulevard. He usually worked with Izzy Diamond, but Izzy was dying or had just died, and Billy always wrote with a collaborator, which is why he had asked me to work with him. Raymond Chandler had worked with him on the script for *Double Indemnity*, and they had detested each other, but they wrote a great screenplay together, which proves you don't always have to like the people you work with. I would ask him about the days of the red scare and the blacklist, and he had this interesting take, which was that no one very good actually joined the Communist party, it only attracted the second-raters. Of course Billy had the most famous line about the Hollywood Ten (or the Unfriendly Ten as they were called) when they had to testify before the House Un-American Activities Committee. Only two of them were talented, he said, the other eight were only unfriendly. We never wrote the script. I had to finish *The Red White and Blue*, and the time did not work out.

Did you work with George Cukor?

I knew George, but never worked with him. We were at a dinner party one night at Peter Feibleman's house. Lillian Hellman was the hostess, and the guests were George, Olivia De Havilland, Willie and Tally Wyler, and then a younger generation — Peter, Mike and Anabel Nichols, Warren Beatty and Julie Christie, and Joan and I. We were very much made to feel that we were at the children's table, there to be seen but not heard. George and Willie and Lillian were all to die in the next few years, and it was as if they knew this was the last time they would see each other, and they wanted to settle a lot of old scores. And boy, did they! The interesting thing was that they all liked the old studio system, and the monsters like Harry Cohn and Sam Goldwyn. At one point in the evening, I made the mistake of asking George about Howard Hawks, my own personal favorite of the old time directors, and he rose up and said, "I despise Mr. Hawks, and I loathe his pictures." Betty Bacall once told me Hawks was a famous anti-Semite; he would talk to her about Yids, not knowing that her real name was Perske, and he wasn't supposed to like gays much either, so needless to say George had no use for him. He'd talk about Garbo and Kate Hepburn, both of whom would stay with him at his house in the Hollywood Hills when they came to L.A. I remember once going to a party at his house. He wasn't giving it, I don't think he was even there;

he had just lent this perfect little jewel of a house to a studio for a press party for some out-of-town distributors. The studio — it was Fox — had dressed the pool area and put up a tent. At the end of the evening, I went to get my car, and as I was waiting for the parking boy, I picked a lemon off a potted tree by the entrance to the house. It occurred to me that it was out of season for lemons, and when I looked at it, I saw that it had been stamped with the word *Sunkist*. What the studio had done was wire lemons to the trees. That's what studios did. They tried to control everything, even the environment.

INTERVIEWER

Blue Tyler's character in *Playland* seems to have elements of Natalie Wood. Did you know her?

DUNNE

Not when she was a child star. When we first got to California, she was just beginning to cross over from a child actress to a grown-up movie star. She had never really been a child star in the sense that Shirley Temple was a star, able to carry a picture all by herself (the way Macaulay Culkin can today), but the transition from child actress to woman movie star was one that only Elizabeth Taylor had made successfully. Margaret O'Brien hadn't made it, and neither really had Shirley Temple. Only Taylor, and now Natalie. About this time, there was a huge eight- or ten-page photo spread on her in *Life* magazine. I remember one of the pictures especially, of Natalie in the conference room at the William Morris Agency, sitting at this enormous conference table, this tiny slip of a young woman, surrounded by her retainers — her agent, Abe Lastfogel, who was the head of the Morris office, her public-relations people and her accountants, all of these middle-aged men focused on managing the career of this twenty-one-year-old child. We met her a few years later. She was an extraordinarily generous woman. She paid for a shrink for her assistant, a young man named Mart Crowley, who wrote *The Boys in the Band*. Mart was a friend of ours, and through him we became acquainted with Natalie and her husband, Richard Gregson, and then later with R.J. (Robert Wagner, called R.J., who was Natalie's first and third husband), when they remarried. I asked her once what it was like being a child star, and she said, "They take care of you," *they* being the studio. One thing I remember about Natalie was how astute she was about the business of Hollywood, about her own worth and the worth of everyone else. She understood money and investment the way a French bourgeoise does. And like most people in Hollywood, she was a fantastic gossip, knew everything, where all the bodies were buried, and under how much dirt. When she died, we went to her funeral, a nastily hot late fall day, with the paparazzi hanging over the walls of the cemetery (the same one where Marilyn Monroe was buried). And afterwards, we stopped by her house, and there I remember two things. First was the family Sinatra sitting side by side on a couch — Frank, big Nancy, little Nancy, Tina and Frank, Jr., as if it were a funeral in Palermo. The other was Elizabeth Taylor, who in the absence of the hostess — Natalie — had taken charge, greeting everyone and to all saying, "I am Mother Courage."

INTERVIEWER

How much of this material made its way into *Playland*?

DUNNE

Specifically only two things really — the photo of Natalie Wood in *Life* at the conference table in the William Morris office, and then Natalie saying that the studio took care of her. This is not to suggest that she was the model for Blue Tyler, because Blue was sui generis, and when I got to know Natalie, she was a twice-married young mother. But with all these people, Otto and Billy and George and Natalie, there was the sense of the studio controlling their lives, their destinies in every aspect, and the concomitant sense that however the studio's subjects — the actors, directors, producers and writers under contract—might have bridled under the idea that the studio knew best, they did not ever really rebel. There is a line in *Playland* when Arthur French says, rather sadly about some lie the studio put out, "People believed studios in those days." What he meant of course was that people were so trusting they even believed the untruths, as they were supposed to. That period, the late 1940s, was the last time that the studios exercised total control and had real power. Television was just a dark cloud on the horizon, and the government had not yet forced the studios to divest themselves of their theater chains. A studio's power was so absolute in those days that it simply would not have permitted a contract star of the caliber of Julia Roberts, say, to marry someone like Lyle Lovett, a funny-looking below-the-title singer.

INTERVIEWER

So, you set out wanting to do a novel about Hollywood in this period?

DUNNE

Actually, no. I started out to do a novel about Blue Tyler's daughter. I thought of her as a contemporary Sister Carrie, but I couldn't make the book work. Then Joan and I were asked to write a screenplay about Bugsy Siegel, which we turned down. But there was something about the idea that intrigued me, and I suggested a story about a New York gangster who comes to Hollywood and falls in love with Shirley Temple. Not Shirley Temple herself, God knows, but a major child star, seventeen years old, trying to cross over into grown-up roles, with the vocabulary of a longshoreman and the morals of a mink. We wrote the screenplay, but it fell between the cracks when the studio we wrote it for was acquired by another studio, which in Hollywood is the kiss of death for projects initiated by the acquired studio. The executives at the new place are scared enough of getting burned by their own projects without having to take the fall for failed projects from another studio. They go out of their way to bad-rap the

Tony Richardson, Joan Didion, John Gregory Dunne,
Vanessa Redgrave in 1990.

other studio's projects. Much of the interplay between the
loathsome director Sydney Allen and my narrator Jack Broderick is a direct result of this experience, although I had no idea
at the time that I was going to make use of it. Then I lost a
year to medicine. First I had open heart surgery, and just as
I was recovering from that, I got blood poisoning.

INTERVIEWER

And it was during that year's hiatus that *Playland* took
shape? Or another shape?

DUNNE

Yes. I rethought it. I had this murder book I had acquired
while doing another picture, the film of my novel *True Confessions*, which had a crucial scene in a morgue. Now I had never
been to a morgue, and so one night at two o'clock in the
morning, the director Ulu Grosbard and I were taken inside
the morgue, absolutely against regulations, by a homicide
detective. We saw the cold room, where the corpses are kept,

and we saw autopsies being performed, and the decomp room, where decomposing bodies are stored — the most God-awful smell, I had to smoke a cigar to get past it. It was quite an experience. Afterward, the homicide cop let us look through old murder files. There was an implicit quid pro quo attached: he wanted to be a technical advisor on *True Confessions* and if we saw something else that hit our fancy, money would change hands. It was on this expedition that I read the murder book of an unsolved 1944 murder. The "murder book" is what cops call the history of an investigation, containing police reports, forensic photographs, autopsies, the questioning of witnesses and suspects, correspondence, updates, all the way to the final disposition of the case, in some instances the gas chamber. The book in this case was still open, as are all unsolved murders. Several things attracted me to it. First was that the victim, who was only seventeen, had gone to the same school my daughter was attending. Second, the apartment building where she lived was one I knew well: it was the home of friends of ours. And third, Shirley Temple was a schoolmate of the victim — her telephone number was in the victim's address book — this was ten years before I even began thinking of writing a novel about a former child star. There was also a riveting forensic photo of the battered and naked girl on a gurney in the morgue. Someone had placed a doily over her pubic area; it was an absurd daintiness considering the circumstances of her death, and the ravages of the assault visible on the rest of her body. The cop said I could have the book for twenty-four hours, so I took it, got it photocopied and the forensic pictures photocopied. It was back in the file the next evening. I suppose one might call the entire endeavor an example of off-the-books free enterprise.

INTERVIEWER

And this is the murder that appears in the book?

DUNNE

Considerably rewritten to accommodate the narrative. I had the file for years, and didn't know what to do with it. I was

not interested in it by itself as a discrete literary endeavor, and
I did not know how to fit it in anyplace else. What intrigued me
mostly were the loops and turns of a criminal investigation,
the number of tangential lives it happened to touch, and how
in the course of the detective work a mosaic of petty treasons,
moral misdemeanors and quiet desperation emerged that had
nothing to do with the murder in question, but only with
permutations of life itself.

INTERVIEWER

Again, it's interesting how much of the book is based on
fact.

DUNNE

Fact is like clay. You shape it to your own ends. For example,
I wanted a namer of names before the House Un-American
Activities Committee who was a sympathetic, and unrepen-
tant, character. So I invented Chuckie O'Hara. Gay. A director. An admitted communist before HUAC. But then a
wounded war hero in World War II. And finally someone
who purged himself by naming names, and then lived out
the rest of his days without guilt. It is about Chuckie, at his
funeral, that I wrote: "Whatever his transgression, in the end
he was one of them. Membership in the closed society of the
motion picture industry is almost never revoked for moral
failings." That is a coda for Hollywood even unto the present
day.

INTERVIEWER

So *Playland* is about this closed society?

DUNNE

I suppose so, yes. Among other things. Like, what is truth?
Because no one in the book ever really tells the truth. Half-
truth is the coin of the Hollywood realm.

INTERVIEWER

Whatever happened to Blue Tyler's daughter, the one you originally thought the book was about?

DUNNE

She appears for the first time on *Playland*'s last page.

INTERVIEWER

To go back a bit, you started off writing for *Time* magazine. Was that helpful? Why did you leave?

DUNNE

It had to do with *Time*'s coverage of the Vietnam War. The *Time* bureau chief, who was doing the war out of Hong Kong before he moved to Saigon, was a guy called Charlie Mohr. Charlie was one of the first to say this war isn't going to fly. He was by no means a liberal; he just saw it on the basis of his reporting. One week we did a wrap-up on the war, and Charlie sent in a file, the first sentence of which was "The war in Vietnam is being lost." It was a Friday night, and I said to myself, "Uh oh, this is never going into the magazine." I had dinner with Joan, and I said, "I think I'm going to call in sick." She said, "No, you've got to go back and do it." So I went back and did the story based on the file, trying to put in the qualifiers that would get past Otto Fuerbringer, and went home around three in the morning. The next morning the edited copy was on my desk, and on the top it said, "Nice. F." It was the complete opposite of what Charlie's file was and what I had written. Redone from top to bottom. Charlie quit and eventually went to *The New York Times*. I said I no longer wished to do Vietnam. I ended up doing Lichtenstein, the Common Market, realizing that my days there were numbered. Joan and I got married in January. In April I said, "Do you mind if I quit?" And that was it. However, I liked *Time*. It taught me how to meet a deadline, to write fast. It's wonderful training. Writing for *Time* is like writing for the movies: ultimately, what you write is not yours, because you're not in charge of what you're doing.

INTERVIEWER
Joan worked for the Luce people for a while, didn't she?

DUNNE

For *Life*. She had published her first novel *Run River* and
then the essays in *Slouching Toward Bethlehem*, and was
about to publish *Play It As It Lays*, when she got the offer to
do a column for *Life*. I said, "Don't do it. It'll be like being
nibbled to death by ducks." She lasted seven columns. It was
about that time we got asked to do our first movie, so everything worked out.

INTERVIEWER
Had you thought of writing for the screen?

DUNNE

As a matter of fact I started a novel about Hollywood when
working for this industrial design magazine after coming out
of the army. I knew nothing about Hollywood and had never
been there. It was called "Not the Macedonian," and the first
line was "They called him Alexander the Great." That's as far
as I ever got. I used to write a lot of first lines of novels; the
second line was the problem.

INTERVIEWER
How did you come to be asked to do a screenplay?

DUNNE

A wonderful man named Collier Young . . . he was Virgin-
ian, I think, and had married four times. Wives two and
three were Ida Lupino and Joan Fontaine. He lived up on
Mulholland Drive in a place he called the Mouse House. One
year his Christmas card said, "Christmas greetings from the
Mouse House, former home of Ida Lupino and Joan Fontaine."
He was the creator of the television series with the detective,
Raymond Burr in the wheelchair. He got fired three segments
into it, but he still got paid every week because it was his idea.

In 1967, the same year that South African doctor, Christiaan Barnard, did the first heart transplant, Collie came to us and said, "I think there's a movie here." We worked out a story in which a Howard Hughes character, Hollis Todd, needs a heart, and his underlings kill a former Olympic athlete who had become a paraplegic after an automobile accident, and transplant his heart into Todd. All the main characters had last names for first names, I suppose because Collie's name was Collier Young. To our amazement, it sold to some studio, I think it was CBS, which paid us $50,000. I thought I'd died and gone to heaven. The picture was never made, though the screenplay was novelized and called *The Todd Dossier*. The man who wrote the novelization basically took our treatment and just added onto it. That book is still in print. It's sold in seventeen foreign languages.

INTERVIEWER

So you were on your way?

DUNNE

That got us into the Writers Guild and once you are in the Guild you can work. The first screenplay we wrote that was produced was *The Panic in Needle Park*. My brother Dominick Dunne took it to various and sundry places, and it was finally bought by Joe Levine. We were told you had to sell to Joe Levine with one line. The one line that sold it to Joe was: "Romeo and Juliet on junk."

INTERVIEWER

How do you and Joan work when you're doing a screenplay?

DUNNE

With *The Panic in Needle Park* I wrote the first draft in about eighteen days. Joan was finishing up her novel *Play It As It Lays*. When I finished she went over the draft and did her version. Then we sat down and put together the version we handed in. It's generally worked that way with every script we've done. The version the studio sees is essentially our third draft. A movie is so much more schematic than a book: you only have 120 pages, because the rule of thumb is one page equals one minute of screen time, and movies shouldn't be over two hours long.

INTERVIEWER

Why in writing for the screen is a film rarely done without collaboration?

DUNNE

I'm not sure that's so. Bob Towne works by himself. So does Alvin Sargent. Bill Goldman. Larry Gelbart. But I cannot imagine doing a screenplay by myself because so much of it is talking it out first, so you know where the high points are. With a book you can often do riffs, which you can't really do in a movie, unless you're a writer-director. We have never wanted to direct pictures. By the time we wrote our first screenplay, we had written maybe five books between us, which was what we wanted to do because we were our own bosses: with a book you are the writer, director, editor, cameraman. But I can say without equivocation that the movies have supported us for the past twenty-six years. We've written twenty-three books between us, and movies financed nineteen out of the twenty-three. And we like doing it.

INTERVIEWER

Why is it that it's looked upon with such detestation by people who consider themselves serious novelists and who have gone out there to make the money? Do you think they've actually had quite a good time and just don't want to admit it?

DUNNE

Yes, I do. I've never believed in Hollywood the Destroyer. The naysayers are people who would have been destroyed at Zabar's if they never went west of the Hudson. I simply never believed it. Faulkner wasn't destroyed. Hemingway wasn't. O'Hara wasn't.

INTERVIEWER

Have you worked at doctoring other people's scripts? Is it worth it?

DUNNE

Yes. Six figures a week, if you're any good, hundred grand at the minimum. We've all done it. For a long time, I couldn't understand why they paid so much. If you get a six-figure weekly fee, you think it's more money than there is in the world. The studio, however, is looking at a 40-million-dollar picture, and if it doesn't get done, they are out all that money. So they will throw in writers at a hundred and fifty grand a week to put in jokes, put in scenes just to get the picture on . . . they *always* answer with money. The worst thing that can happen is that the project gets flushed, because then they lose all the money spent for development, which can add up to millions of dollars.

INTERVIEWER

Can you give a few examples of screenwriting at its best?

DUNNE

Chinatown. Robert Towne. It was a wonderfully intricate, well-worked screenplay with an enormous amount of atmosphere. Another one: Graham Greene and Carol Reed in *The Third Man*. That is the best collaboration between writer and director I can think of. It is the one movie Joan and I always watch before we start a script, because it is so brilliantly worked out. It's very short, an hour and forty-five minutes. What else? I wouldn't say it's one of the best, but Truman Capote's *Beat the Devil*. Oh, and Quentin Tarantino's *Reservoir Dogs*, a terrifying and funny screenplay; I liked it much more than *Pulp Fiction*, which just seemed to rework *Reservoir Dogs*.

INTERVIEWER
I assume a great screenplay can be destroyed by direction and by acting.

DUNNE
There's no such thing as a great screenplay. Because they are not meant to be read. There are just great movies.

INTERVIEWER
So when you talk about a good screenplay you're really talking about what directors and actors did with it. There's no way one could have a recognizable style as a screenwriter?

DUNNE
What the screenwriter is ceding to the director is pace, mood, style, point of view, which in a book are the function of the writer. The director controls the writing room, and it's in the editing room where a picture is made.

INTERVIEWER
Is there a formula to screenwriting?

DUNNE
Not in general. Specifically perhaps. Bill Goldman once said that you start a scene as deep in as you can possibly go. You don't start the scene with somebody walking through the door, sitting down and starting a conversation. Bill said you start a scene in the middle of the conversation, which I think is a very astute observation.

INTERVIEWER
Would you divide the screenplay into acts, as some people do?

DUNNE
The studio people talk about first act, second act, third act. We don't do it when we're writing. When we were doing *True*

Confessions, Ulu Grosbard came up with a wonderful take. He said the script was a "one-span bridge" and it needed to be a "two-span bridge." I knew exactly what he meant. The screenplay we had went up once and came down, instead of going up twice and then coming down. In other words, we needed a third act.

INTERVIEWER

Is there a connection between a writer who has literary merit and a screenwriter? Is a screenplay such a departure from the novel that one hardly needs to know how to write to become a screenwriter?

DUNNE

What troubles me is that screenwriters today seem to have had no life other than film school. They've rarely been reporters, they've rarely gone out and experienced a wider world. I had the army, I was a reporter for ten years, I'd been to Vietnam, not for long, but long enough to know I didn't like to get shot at, I covered labor strikes and murder trials and race riots. The entire frame of reference the younger screenwriters have is other movies. It's secondhand. And if you steal a moment from an old movie, you can probably bet that the moment you stole was probably itself stolen in the first place.

INTERVIEWER

Would you recommend to a young person a career as a screenwriter?

DUNNE

I'm not sure I would, because you're really not a writer and you're really not a filmmaker. I once said that the most you could aspire to be as a screenwriter is a copilot. If you are going to write movies full-time, and you don't write books like Joan and I do, then you better aim to be a director, because that's the only way you're going to be in charge, and being in charge is what writing is all about.

INTERVIEWER

You sound downbeat about screenwriting.

DUNNE

Look. It pays a lot, and it's fun. It's better than teaching and better than lecturing, the other compensatory alternatives for writers without jobs. But it is hard fucking work. On our last script, *Up Close & Personal*, it took eight years to get it on. We quit three times. Two other writers came on board and left. In all, we wrote twenty-seven drafts before a frame of film was shot, then we worked for seventy-seven days during the shoot rewriting. The picture was originally supposed to be about Jessica Savitch, a golden girl for NBC News who flamed out and died in an automobile accident. She was a small-town girl with more ambition than brains, an overactive libido, a sexual ambivalence, a tenuous hold on the truth, a taste for controlled substances, a longtime abusive Svengali relationship and a certain mental instability. Disney was the studio, and the first thing Disney wanted to know was if she had to die in the end. And they weren't crazy about an interracial love affair she had, nor her abortions, nor the coke, nor the lesbianism, nor the gay husband who hung himself in her basement, nor the boyfriend who beat her up. Otherwise, they loved the idea. Making that work was work. Eight years worth. Twenty-seven drafts worth. Thank God it was a hit.

— **George Plimpton**

The Man in the Back Row
Has a Question II

For this feature the editors have selected answers to a questionnaire sent out to a number of distinguished screenwriters. They are listed below with some of their credits. We are extremely grateful for their cooperation.

Dan Algrant (*Naked in New York*)
Jay Presson Allen (*Deathtrap, Prince of the City*)
Paul Attanasio (*Quiz Show, Disclosure*)
Noah Baumbach (*Kicking and Screaming, Mr. Jealousy*)
Peter Benchley (*How To Sleep, Jaws*)
Michael Blake (*Dances With Wolves*)
John Briley (*Ghandi, White Fang*)
Jean Claude Carriere (*The Unbearable Lightness of Being, The Tin Drum*)
Hampton Fancher (*Blade Runner, The Mighty Quinn*)
Horton Foote (*Tomorrow, Of Mice and Men, To Kill a Mockingbird, Tender Mercies*)
Bo Goldman (*One Flew Over the Cuckoo's Nest, City Hall*)
Winston Groom (The novels *Forrest Gump, Gump & Co.*)
Larry Gross (*48 Hours, Geronimo*)

Jim Harrison (*Wolf, Revenge*)
Steven Katz (*The Alienist, Morningside Heights*)
Callie Khouri (*Thelma & Louise*)
William Kinsolving (*Brother Sun, Sister Moon, Mister Christian*)
Todd Komarnicki (*Skin and Bones*)
Elmore Leonard (*Get Shorty*)
Jay McInerney (*Bright Lights, Big City*)
John Milius (*Apocalypse Now, Magnum Force*)
Tom Schulman (*Dead Poet's Society*)
Jonathan Marc Sherman (*Sophistry*)
Donald Stewart (*Patriot Games, The Hunt for Red October*)
Ted Tally (*The Silence of the Lambs*)
Alfred Uhry (*Driving Miss Daisy*)

List five examples of screenwriting at its best. (Exclude *Hamlet* and other classics.)

Dog Day Afternoon by Frank Pierson, *Network* and *Marty* by Paddy Chayefsky, *Annie Hall* by Woody Allen and Marshall Brickman, *Taxi Driver* by Paul Schrader.
— Dan Algrant

Not in any particular order: *The Godfather, Part II, Jeannie, Some Like It Hot, Rambling Rose, Pulp Fiction, Citizen Kane.*
— Jay Presson Allen

All About Eve (Joseph L. Mankiewicz), *Some Like It Hot* (Billy Wilder and I.A.L. Diamond), *The Hustler* (Robert Rossen), *Network* (Paddy Chayefsky), *The Bridge on the River Kwai* (Carl Foreman and Michael Wilson).
— Paul Attanasio

Greed, Chinatown, Monte Walsh, The Conformist and *In Cold Blood*.
— Michael Blake

Lawrence of Arabia, Schindler's List, Odd Man Out, The Third Man, The Verdict.
—John Briley

Children of Paradise is close to perfection.
—Jean-Claude Carriere

The Dead, Tokyo Story, Dodsworth, Throne of Blood and *The Loneliness of the Long Distance Runner.*
—Horton Foote

Sunset Boulevard, The Godfather, The Godfather, Part II, Singin' in the Rain, Tunes of Glory.
—Bo Goldman

Dumb and Dumber, Debbie Does Dallas, Pillow Talk, Radar Men from the Moon and *Three Ninjas Kick Back.*
—Winston Groom

It Happened One Night (Robert Riskin), *The Rules of the Game* (Jean Renoir and Karl Koch), *La Notte* (Michelangelo Antonioni and Tonino Guerra), *Lawrence of Arabia* (Robert Bolt), *The Manchurian Candidate* (George Axelrod).
—Larry Gross

Jules and Jim, Being There, Butch Cassidy and the Sundance Kid, One Flew Over the Cuckoo's Nest, Il Postino.
—Jim Harrison

It's a Wonderful Life, To Kill A Mockingbird, Midnight Cowboy, The Graduate, A Face in the Crowd, Dr. Strangelove, A Place in the Sun, All That Jazz and almost anything by Horton Foote.
—Callie Khouri

Citizen Kane, Two for the Road, Singin' in the Rain, The Purple Rose of Cairo, your favorite Alfred Hitchcock.
—William Kinsolving

The Seven Samurai, Viva Zapata!, Lawrence of Arabia, The Bridge on the River Kwai and *Treasure of the Sierra Madre.*
— John Milius

Casablanca, The Graduate, Ikira, La Strada, To Be or Not to Be (original version), *The Man Who Would Be King, Ordinary People, The Godfather, Parts I and II, The Bridge on the River Kwai, Sunset Boulevard, The Apartment, All About Eve.*
— Tom Schulman

Reds (period).
— Jonathan Marc Sherman

Stagecoach, Yojimbo, Z, The Maltese Falcon, Sunset Boulevard.
— Donald Stewart

Can a screenwriter create a recognizable style? If so, how?

The most obvious case of a modern film writer with a style is Woody Allen — heavily influenced by his days as a stand-up. *Hannah and Her Sisters* is really like a disjointed Ibsen play, connected by this stand-up monologue which informs the narrative transitions.
— Dan Algrant

I believe that all serious writers (writers who are devoted to language) have a definitive style.
— Michael Blake

Yes, but it's very difficult because so many other people have a say in the final product — Quentin Tarantino obviously has succeeded. So has Woody Allen.
— John Briley

I hope so.
— Jean-Claude Carriere

Fingerprints are all over everything the Coen brothers write. *Miller's Crossing*, gorgeously droll, brilliantly glum. Read *Barton Fink* or *Raising Arizona* and there it is again. Has to do with attitude. The soft sound of Horton Foote permeates his work. Pinter's hardwood surfaces and tea cups and the flick of viper tongues. The personal expression of a writer. It happens now and again if the front office doesn't damage it.

—Hampton Fancher

You shouldn't. But it will come through anyway if you are any good.

—Bo Goldman

A recognizable style for a screenwriter? No. A dependable personal set of mannerisms, tricks and capabilities are of course what any professional will contribute and be hired for—but a real discernible style over a number of films can only be accomplished in collaboration with a director. Robert Riskin, working with Frank Capra, Robert Bolt working with David Lean, recently John Berger working with Alain Tanner, are real examples of a writer's vision meshing with a director's talent and a recognizable style resulting. But a great screenwriter's work like Robert Towne's or Jean-Claude Carriere's looks entirely different as it is handled by different directors.

—Larry Gross

Possibly, if you're sleeping with all your directors until the final cut.

—Jim Harrison

I think a screenwriter can sometimes create a formula. Eszterhas leaps, frighteningly, to mind. A style is harder, since the screenplay is not a finished object, only a kind of long and interactive memo to your collaborators, who may or may not be able to read it.

—Jay McInerney

Certainly. Richard Price has a recognizable style, as does Robert Towne, Terry Southern, David Mamet, many others.

—Ted Tally

Sure, if you're the director as well. Billy Wilder certainly comes to mind, Preston Sturges, Woody Allen, Oliver Stone, et al.

—Alfred Uhry

How is writing for the screen different from writing for other media?

As a novelist I function as the president. As a screenwriter, I have functioned as everything from a janitor on Capitol Hill to my present status as a senior senator.

—Michael Blake

Harder.

—Bo Goldman

Utterly different, convulsively so. Novels, poetry and journalism are acts of language. You see the words first. In screenwriting you have to see the moving picture first. You have to "see" everything you want in the scene.

—Jim Harrison

I've always felt that screenwriting resembles nothing as much as writing some kind of rigid lyrical form—like a Petrarchan sonnet or a haiku. What a producer wants and, especially, what the audience expects dictates the form and content to an extent unheard of in other media. The artistry in screenwriting is a function of both achieving and transcending the formal requirements of the medium.

—Steven Katz

Screenwriting is the only medium where so many others, none of whom are writers, presume to tell the writer what exactly it is the writer means.

—Callie Khouri

There is a sense of freedom in writing prose, especially novels — wandering away from the the plot, letting your people talk as long as they have something to say — that has it all over the rigid requirements of a script. When I write a book I have only myself to please. When I write a screenplay it's work.

— Elmore Leonard

It must be concise. It must be ruthlessly clear. It uses images and relies on them more than words. And one gets paid more for it.

—John Milius

Someone once said that the difference between writing for the theater and writing for movies is that in theater you're trying to get the characters on stage whereas in film you're trying to get them off.

— Tom Schulman

Playwriting is like jumping off the high dive. Screenwriting is like running a long sadistic obstacle course first, so that by the time you arrive at the diving board, you're probably too tired to leap off gracefully and, besides, the water has probably evaporated by then anyway.

— Jonathan Marc Sherman

What kind of stories work well as movies, rather than as novels or plays?

When I was adapting *The Alienist*, people used to tell me all of the time that it was a natural for the movies. And while it's true that the book takes readers into a world they've never experienced before (certainly a prerequisite), actually it doesn't lend itself easily at all to the movies: it's mostly an armchair detective, Sherlock Holmes-kind of story with a lot of interesting characters and locations — but hardly any action. There's an old chestnut of playwriting that each line of dialogue should forward the plot and character; in screenwriting, the best stories are those in which plot and character are forwarded (principally) by action.

— Steven Katz

Raiders of the Lost Ark and *Star Wars* are two examples that spring to mind of stories that would be uneventful if not told through a visual medium.

— Callie Khouri

Babe, with a talking pig as hero, would be a tough furrow to hoe Off Broadway. The filmic setting was so convincing that it was easy to enter into Babe's lair without a shred of disbelief. Making a paranoid goose or a jealous sheepdog sympathetic is a uniquely difficult task; but by using every movie trick at their disposal, the filmmakers were able to tell a truly human story.

— Todd Komarnicki

I really don't think there are stories so specific to the screen that they couldn't be told pretty well as novels, or even as plays. But *Lawrence of Arabia* would strain the resources of most Off Broadway theaters.

— Ted Tally

Have special effects made screenwriters less important?

Probably, but then hi-tech effects wear out amazingly fast. You can only have a monster leap out from between a pair of tits once or twice. After that, yawns are heard.

— Jim Harrison

No. For *Toy Story*, which was an entirely special effects-generated film, not a single writer (nor actor nor anyone else) was put out of a job by a computer. I like the new generation of special effects; I think they represent a great challenge to writers and make it possible to achieve things which could only be imagined before.

—Steven Katz

Regrettably so. Movies today do not follow narrative dramatic form as much as they follow the presentation of amusement park rides. There are even movies that *are* amusement park rides. This is the contribution of my colleagues George Lucas and Steven Spielberg. It is the first significant degradation of storytelling since Homer, but I have faith that it, like gas, will pass.

—John Milius

It used to be that they made movies about people. Now they make movies (many of them quite entertaining) about cyborgs, aliens, germs, you name it. Yes, while developing the story they'll talk about the importance of the dialogue and story, but the story and the dialogue are not the reason the movie is getting made. It's the dinosaurs.

—Tom Schulman

Do you have a particular actor in mind as you develop a character? If so, can you say something about how a particular actor served your vision?

I create all my characters from my experiences in life. Actors like Kevin Costner or Viggo Mortensen may inspire my efforts, but no more so than the agony of dealing with a dysfunctional family member or a bizarre encounter with a tow-truck operator. As a sponge, I absorb all fluids involuntarily.

—Michael Blake

No. But I can say that only two actors have ever exceeded the performances in my head as I wrote. Ben Kingsley in

Gandhi and Liv Ullman in *Pope Joan*. I suspect Al Pacino, Dustin Hoffman and Meryl Streep have given other writers the same thrill.

—John Briley

Jack Nicholson as McMurphy in *One Flew Over the Cuckoo's Nest*. He served it best. Tied with him is Al Pacino as Lt. Col. Frank Slade in *Scent of a Woman*.

—Bo Goldman

Write a script and see if they can find somebody to play the part. Besides, whoever you thought of, they're not going to hire anyway. I mean, the Forrest Gump in my book and early screenplays looked more like John Goodman or Arnold Schwarzenegger than Tom Hanks. So what do I know?

—Winston Groom

One of my earliest lessons in Hollywood had to do with the fact that the first question people will ask when they read your script is: "What movie star can we cast with this?" This dates from the time when my first scripts (the ones that didn't sell) had unattractive main characters or ensemble casts or were written principally with a director in mind. It's just a matter of being realistic to think about actors as you develop characters. I'm also a visually oriented writer: I like to surround myself with pictures of people and places, culled from whatever sources, when I'm writing. So having a specific actor's picture taped to the wall helps me to see and hear him better.

—Steven Katz

It depends on the assignment. Ideally, the writer writes the characters as demanded by the story. If one is hired to come up with the next *Terminator* film, the screenwriter definitely will have Arnold in mind as he writes every single word. If one is given a book to adapt or writes an original script, even then the commercial nature of the business may demand precasting in the writer's mind. There is a terrible tendency when the persona of a particular actor or actress is with you when writing a script; instinctually, the screenwriter will limit a character to the talents and limitations of that star. It is an insidious constraint, no matter how talented the individual actor may be. One star's persona can influence an entire script, thus making it a mere vehicle. This is a danger, although there are myriad examples of scripts written for one star and then played to exalting success by another; however, such a script was probably rewritten for the other actor.

—William Kinsolving

Only rarely I find if I think too much about actors, I lose the desire to write altogether. I did write with Dennis Quaid in mind as the character of Eddie in *Grace Under Pressure*, which the studio then re-titled *Something to Talk About*. It was wonderful because my expectations of what he could do with the character were fully realized.

—Callie Khouri

I wrote parts with Jodie Foster and Meryl Streep in mind, and in each case something of the actor's own fierce intelligence and integrity found its way into the character. If you picture actors of that caliber saying your words, then your words had better be pretty good.

—Ted Tally

I wrote the character of Hoke Coleburn in *Driving Miss Daisy* specifically for Morgan Freeman. He had played it on stage and his voice was in my ears when I did the adaptation.

—Alfred Uhry

What is the state of Hollywood today?

You'd need a Spengler to do justice to that one.

—Jay Presson Allen

Hollywood is as it always has been: a seedy, glitter-soaked, floating crap game in which the most pathetic losers become winners and vice versa. And, as is the case with all gambling enterprises, the house enjoys a huge advantage.

— Michael Blake

Very depressing.

— Horton Foote

Rich, scared and miserable. But it's been very good to me. And as a caveat, I would add the new Hollywood is, I suspect, very much like the old Hollywood.

— Bo Goldman

California.

— Winston Groom

It's the best of times and it's the worst of times. The growth of cable TV and the video cassette market have created enormous opportunities for Hollywood in general and writers specifically. There are new markets, new money and a greater demand for product — which has even resulted, consequently, in a boom in independent filmmaking. On the other hand, Hollywood today is a lot like Detroit was in the 1970s, before the American automotive industry had any real competition: out of touch, complacent, bloated, irresponsible. This, too, at a time when, with the recent spate of media mergers (not to mention the new communications bill recently signed into law), Hollywood studio conglomerates are acquiring potentially 1984-ish power.

— Steven Katz

In the bad old days, the studios were run by old men with no taste but who knew what good taste was and wanted to be associated with it. They were lowbrow guys striving to make highbrow art. Now, executives are highly educated men and

women who want to make lowbrow movies—because that's
what sells.

—Tom Schulman

**Screenwriters seem to be gaining respect in Hollywood; how
are they treated generally by producers and the others in the
film industry?**

A friend of mine, a real Hollywood pro, told me about
being hired to rewrite a script before the original writer had
turned his version in! I think the Guild protects writers from
this now.

—Dan Algrant

A screenwriter is generally treated with respect and courtesy
until the day he is fired.

- Paul Attanasio

I don't even want to hear how screenwriters are generally
treated. I have been lucky. Of course, I have always tried to
work with the most talented people who would have me. The
degree of talent is largely in direct proportion to the degree
of the director's confidence in his craft. I have found that the
more talented, the more confident and relaxed he tends to
be, the more latitude *I* am allowed.

—Jay Presson Allen

It's a whore's game: take the money, do the work, suffer
the abuse, take more money, swallow more abuse, proceed
with your life. No satisfaction, no recognition, no pride of
authorship. You're an expensive cut of meat, sold to folks for
whom money is no object and who don't much like meat.

—Peter Benchley

I'm in one sense not a Hollywood writer, as I rarely work
for the major studios, but I hear from writers that work for
the studios and their stories make my hair stand on end.

—Horton Foote

I don't see any particular gain in respect for screenwriters. We're a necessary evil and embarrassment because they can't make up their own stories. I've always been treated rather well out there with a few nasty exceptions, but when I arrived I was already a novelist and poet. Also, I've never lived out there, so I haven't pissed them off by overexposure. Frankly, there are a lot of likable people in the business, and especially early on I got along well with the older moguls like Ray Stark and John Calley. I've had much better offers but I've stayed with Sony because I like my producer, Doug Wick. It's the same reasoning that keeps you with a publisher for years. It's an intensely visceral industry and easy to be stomped bloody in a thirty minute meeting, so it's better to stay with identifiable human beings.

—Jim Harrison

Before writing the first draft, you're a star; after that, your status can become questionable. When Jay McInerney and I appeared on "Good Morning America" together, just before he went out to Hollywood to write his first screenplay, I said, "Don't let them pick you up in a limo. If you decide to walk out of the meeting you might need your own transportation."

—Elmore Leonard

In my experience screenwriters are treated in the early stages of a project like girlfriends, then, after the first draft is handed in, like wives, and finally, like ex-wives.

—Jay McInerney

Screenwriters are treated like the weak swine that they are. They're thrown their slop, and then the producers and executives laugh as they fight over it. Speaking of which, there is a joke in which a rich Arab comes to town, hires a limo and goes to the latest club. He tells the driver to go in and bring him the most expensive whore in the place. The driver comes back with a screenwriter. Have you heard about the Polish starlet who fucks the writers? The reason screenwriters are treated so poorly is because they have no balls, no vision anymore, no character. They have lots of money but nothing they value. They will do anything to be hot, to be judged so by the scum-sucking parasites that run the place. The thing that is frustrating is their stupidity — they could be kings because they are the ones who write it down. They are the creative force. I've done most things in this business (directing, producing, even a stunt once) and writing is the most difficult, the rarest talent. The fools! I spit on them generally because they have no spirit, no code, no espirit du corps — no *Bushido!*

—John Milius

Just as bad as ever, thanks

—Donald Stewart

Why is collaboration so common in screenwriting, and how does it affect the integrity of a script?

There are two kinds of collaboration, intentional and unintentional. Partners find each other because it's faster to write with someone; you always can feed off the energy of the other person. Also, feedback is very important in screenwriting . . . does an idea make sense? Does an idea come across as intended? It's a very dumb medium.

The collaboration between two writers when one of the writers is the director is a great thing, because it really allows for specificity. When Martin Scorsese works in a room with Jay Cox and they talk about a scene, the scene can be voice-over, but Marty knows what the images are right then, and Jay can work off that, and they can get a synergy that really is appropriate for the medium. Fellini would get in a room with three writers, and they all would act (write) different parts . . . fantastic, but not really possible without Fellini.

Then there's the collaboration that happens when a writer is fired and another is hired by a producer or a studio. There are some funny stories of people meeting on the podium to accept their shared Oscar never having met before. This is not necessarily bad — and happens sometimes simply because screenwriting is really difficult. Even great writers don't hit it all the time. Most often they need a second chance, or a little more time, which they unfortunately don't usually get.

—Dan Algrant

Because, especially today, a screenplay has to please such a multiplicity of people, often people with different visions. Often people with no vision whatsoever. Also, it all *costs* so much. Where is this Guy Grand who's going to declare that the buck stops with him? Please him alone, and the light is green. I'll tell you where Mr. Grand is. In Forest Lawn for a couple of decades.

—Jay Presson Allen

Because filmmaking is a team sport.

—Paul Attanasio

I have no opinion about this. I have never collaborated.

—Horton Foote

Because it's common to film. I've always considered myself not a screenwriter but a filmmaker. Filmmaking is a collaborative art. And if you want to become some solo operative, working out of a cabin in the woods or from a loft in NoHo, movies are not for you.

—Bo Goldman

I suppose so one person doesn't have to take all the blame.

—Elmore Leonard

Making movies is such a communal activity that I suppose many writers don't want to feel like the only lonely person working on the thing. And studios and directors, of course, tend to create collaborations, on the theory that two heads must be better than one (or, in the case of *The Flintstones*, thirty-two heads). I myself don't like to collaborate with other writers—why split the credit or the money—but I'm perfectly

happy to have the input of a director, producer or actor. I
need all the help I can get.

—Ted Tally

Is screenwriting a literary form?

If I thought of my job as a "literary form," I couldn't write
a word.

—Paul Attanasio

No. A script is not the terminal point of a literary venture.
It's the beginning of a cinematographic process. The caterpillar
to become a butterfly.

—Jean-Claude Carriere

Screenwriting is as much a literary event as a play. Donald
Ogden Stewart's screenplays read much better than his published novels or plays, the same with Frank Nugent or Nun-
nally Johnson. Dorothy Parker, F. Scott Fitzgerald and William Faulkner weren't very good at it. But because they
received a great deal of money and failed, they were contemptuous of movies. I would feel the same, as would Billy Wilder
or Robert Riskin or Herman Mankiewicz, if we were rewarded
for writing lousy novels or plays.

—Bo Goldman

I don't consider screenwriting a literary form except in a
very few hands, people so devoted to the genre they'd write
screenplays even if they weren't getting paid. I can only think
of a couple of scripts that approach the "literary event" stage:
The Third Man, Being There, Five Easy Pieces. That level.

—Jim Harrison

I doubt that I've ever read a script for fun.

—Elmore Leonard

Should one be aware of certain pitfalls in writing for the screen?

The pitfalls sneak up on you.

—Paul Attanasio

Just try to work for talented directors. All else is anguish. The two times I acted on the principle of *Take The Money and Run*, I barely crawled away from the wreck. I got the money, but it shortened my life.

—Jay Presson Allen

Yes. Optimism.

—John Briley

Interior monologues, wobbly narratives and tire tracks on a page (long speeches). I believe it was Lillian Helman, and she was being perceptive and not facetious, who said, "You've got to get them [the audience] with their finger up their nose wondering what's going to happen next." And that does not mean action movies only; all movies, brilliant comedies, dramas of the heart.

—Bo Goldman

The major pitfall is waiting for the first check on a deal to clear. Another is forgetting that this is entertainment. I've suffered for my archness, which is mostly just wallpaper. The fabled scoundrel Elliot Kastner once said, "Cinema buffs can't earn out a movie." I wish I had listened more closely to him at the time. I also gradually found out that he was less of a scoundrel than two-thirds of the producers who called him one. But then there ought to be an academy award for producers because it's the most difficult job out there.

—Jim Harrison

The worst thing that's happened to movies in recent years is Robert McKee and his ubiquitous screenwriter's course. Not only do too many writers take it, but studios regularly enroll their creative executives. The result is a dogmatic, assembly-line uniformity that would bring a smile to Stalin's face. After I took McKee's course, I didn't write a word for six months. Then I ignored everything he taught and wrote a script. It was the first one I sold.

—Steven Katz

A major pitfall is assuming the producers and the director see the story the same way you do.

—Elmore Leonard

Don't ever say, "Well, it's just a movie."

—John Milius

Directors.

—Donald Stewart

Don't write what they tell you they want. They don't know what they want. If you do write what they want, they don't ever like it. The trick is to figure out what you want and make it sound like it's what they want.

—Alfred Uhry

Does literary merit transfer to the screen?

Only in small and uninteresting ways. Generally movies made from great novels are literal and boring unless they're reinvented with a more filmic sense. And I don't know that there's ever been a great film that was written by a great screenwriter, but that was made by a mediocre director. On the other hand, there have been great films made from pedestrian scripts and potboiler novels.

—Noah Baumbach

I think it does. Movies are incredibly powerful, and everyone appears to carry moments from great films as part of their

personal history. I don't think this would be possible without
some semblance of literary merit.

—Michael Blake

No. People tend to equate the script with dialogue. Dialogue is at most 25 percent of what makes a script. The images
that allow the camera to tell the story are what matters. A
writer can put this down brilliantly, and a director, cameraman
and/or editor can make them into poetry. See *Odd Man Out*.
And, of course, literary dialogue is death.

—John Briley

No, the two languages are totally different.

—Jean-Claude Carriere

Rarely.

—Horton Foote

No, but you can't be illiterate either. A friend once asked
me to find a screenwriter job for a novelist-darling of the East
Hampton set whose work, published every ten years, usually
made the cover of *The New York Times Book Review*. "Can't
you get him a screenplay?" she said as if it were like dentistry.
I didn't and he couldn't. But he got a MacArthur Foundation
award instead. As the Lenny Bruce waiter punchline goes, "He
bettah off."

—Bo Goldman

Depends on the literary merit, and how well the screenwriter
can capture each attribute while changing the prose into a
screenplay. The latest Jane Austen explosion supposedly illus-
trates the success of such literary transfer. Even so, the real
question is in the value of what has been excised and what
has been added to the screenplay. It is a delicate exercise and
takes uncommon craft to bring it off.

—William Kinsolving

No. The richer the novel, the more its film adaptation tends to feel reductive, shortchanged. The best adaptations tend to come from short stories, or middlebrow books, or potboilers, or kid's books, where it's easier to encompass or even improve on the original.

— Ted Tally

In some quarters there is a persistent suspicion that films will never achieve the artistic stature of great works of literature. Do you labor under this suspicion, and if so why?

So many films today address, not the mind and the heart, but the blood pressure, so that crotchety suspicion has become well-founded.

— Paul Attanasio

Film seems to have become an art form despite itself. Oddly enough, while the notion of film as art has grown, the level of the mainstream movie has gotten worse. I guess I'd rather not hang out with people who don't take great film as seriously as great literature.

— Noah Baumbach

I don't labor under it, I know it. There is always something ultimately scummy about a major moneymaking enterprise such as the movie business, and the tastemakers of New York as well as English department academia will never let the movies be recognized as the evolving art form it is, unless it's a Chaplin movie in a revival house or Frank Capra in a college auditorium. James Agee knew better.

— Bo Goldman

No. It is obvious that all this crap even at its best will never hold a candle to a good book. You read a book, you see it happen in your mind, which is limitless. You must work your mind to do this, and so the image is yours alone. A movie gives just what is on the screen. It is a lazy way of getting information. No amount of technical virtuosity, loud sound or music can span this gap. It's cheap entertainment. A real writer writes novels.

—John Milius

In a fundamental way, movies will never reach the artistic level of great literature because movies paint their visions in pictures whereas the palate of literature is the reader's imagination. Some writers and directors really work to make the viewer a participant in the story, that is, to make the viewer work to understand what is going on and what meanings are being conveyed. But mostly movies spoon-feed the viewer. That's why many of our favorite movies are so disappointing when we see them a few years later. Our imaginations have imbued them with much more richness and depth than was ever really there.

—Tom Schulman

To what degree are movies affected by commercial considerations? Can you give a specific example?

How on earth could any multi-billion dollar community that refers to itself . . . with justification . . . as the Industry affect quality? What a bizarre notion.

—Jay Presson Allen

Great films are usually made *despite* the film industry, not because of it.

—Michael Blake

I would think that the drive of the industry is generally to make as much profit as possible on the given product. This would certainly affect their chosen choices for good or for bad. Mostly bad, I think.

—Horton Foote

To the same degree the publishing industry affects the quality of novels and nonfiction printed. A lunch at The Four Seasons with some publishing executive is no different from lunch at the Polo Lounge with a studio vice president. Dickens had to make a living through the serializing of his novels, Shakespeare had to cut and shape his plays to the dimensions of the Globe theater and its audience. They were part of industries in a sense, and had to be responsive to the marketplace.

—Bo Goldman

The studio that financed *Bright Lights, Big City*, United Artists, was adamant about cutting out all scenes which showed Michael J. Fox snorting cocaine. The feeling was it wouldn't play in Peoria. The director, the late James Bridges, held firm and threatened to go public with the dispute. I believe, because he had been hired at the last minute after the previous director was fired, that he was able to get the final-cut approval on his contract. At any rate, the coke-snorting scenes, without which the movie would not have made much sense, were trimmed a little, but they stayed. What usually happens is that the studio, and its perception of what will and will not be acceptable and therefore bankable in Middle America, prevails.

—Jay McInerney

An industry owned and operated by corporate bureaucrats will produce mediocre work and will beat down any voice that tries to develop. The product will be uniform, homogenized and marketed to those who will consume it like corn flakes. In the future, individual visions will be seen as unsound behavior, foolish and impolitic. I survived in a different time. I've lived the life of an outlaw, always able to rob the trains in a different state when it got too hot. I slept in a different bed every night and with one eye open. I don't think people will get away with it in the future. People like me will be hunted down and hanged. You get what you pay for.

—John Milius

"Give them what they want" was an oft marketed line from one of the *Badman* movies, but it is really the motto of Hollywood. We live in an anti-intellectual, anti-educational mass culture; a culture that increasingly glorifies youth oriented, gangbanger and "gangsta" values. As corporate Hollywood "gives them what they want," these values become more and more the values reflected in the movies. Everything that *Network* predicted about television applies to movies too, but don't just blame Hollywood; also blame the folks who continue to fork over their money at the box office. They're the ones who sent the messages loud and clear: "No more *Seventh Seal*, we want *Friday the 13th*, parts 1-20." "We're not that interested in more *Ordinary People*'s, give us *Jaws*." Mind you, there's nothing wrong with *Jaws*, except that it devoured *Ordinary People*.

Another industry factor at work is the way theaters and studios divide the box-office revenues. The week a movie opens, the studio gets 90 percent and the theater gets 10 percent of the ticket revenues. The second week the split is 70 percent / 30 percent, and so on. This leads to a cynical but understandable obsession by the studios with opening a movie and less concern as to whether a movie might still be drawing crowds nine weeks later. (Oddly enough, if movie studios were allowed to own theaters again this might change.) Highly recognizable concepts designed to open big—old TV shows, sequels, bestsellers, arcade games, star vehicles, etc.—are thus produced in much greater quantity than more original concepts. Of course, every so often a filmmaker surprises us and miraculously levitates out of the bog creating something bold, original and astonishing, but every year the number of those extraordinary movies gets smaller—a predictable result of the marketplace at work, sucking the originality and quality out of the movies.

Yet every time I sit in a darkened theater and the curtains part, I'm still filled with excitement because once again there's the chance that a movie might take us into a whole new world we never even dreamed existed—and change everything.

— Tom Schulman

Edison, New Jersey

Junot Díaz

The first time we try to deliver the Gold Crown the lights
are on in the house but no one lets us in. I bang on the front
door and Wayne hits the back and I can hear our double drum
shaking the windows like bass. Right then I have this feeling
that someone is inside, laughing at us.

This guy better have a good excuse, Wayne says, lumbering
around the newly planted rosehips. This is bullshit.

You're telling me, I say but Wayne's the one who takes
this job too seriously; he pounds some more on the door,
his face jiggling. A couple of times he raps carefully on the
windows, tries squinting through the curtains. I take a more
philosophical approach: I walk over to the ditch that has been
cut next to the road and sit down. A drainage pipe half-filled
with water. I smoke and watch a mama duck and her three
ducklings scavenge the grassy bank and then float downstream
like they're on the same string. Beautiful, I say but Wayne
doesn't hear. He's banging on the door with the staple gun.

•

At nine Wayne picks me up at the showroom and by then I have our route planned out. The order forms tell me everything I need to know about the customers we'll be dealing with that day. If someone is just getting a 52" card table delivered then you know they aren't going to be too much hassle but they also aren't going to tip. Those are your Spotswood, Sayreville and Perth Amboy deliveries. The pool tables though go north to the rich suburbs, to Livingston, Ridgewood, Bedminster. And lots go out to Long Island.

You should see our customers. Doctors, diplomats, surgeons, presidents of universities, people who dress in slacks and silk tops, who sport thin watches you could trade in for a car, who wear comfortable leather shoes. Most of them prepare for us by laying down a path of yesterday's *Washington Post* from the front door to the game room. I make them pick it all up. I say: Carajo, what if we slip? Do you know what two hundred pounds of slate could do to a floor? The threat of property damage puts the chop-chop in their step. The best customers bring us water and leave us alone until the bill has to be signed. Few have offered us more, though a dentist from Ghana once gave us a six-pack of Heineken while we worked.

Sometimes the customer has to jet to the store for cat food or for a newspaper while we're in the middle of a job. I'm sure you'll be all right, they say. They never sound too sure. Of course, I say. Just show us where the silver's at. The customers ha-ha and we ha-ha and then they agonize over leaving, linger by the front door, trying to memorize everything they own, as if they don't know where to find us, whom we work for.

Once they're gone, I don't have to worry about anyone bothering me. I put down the ratchet, crack my knuckles and explore, usually when Wayne is smoothing out the felt and I can't help. I take cookies from the kitchen, razors from the bathroom cabinets. Some of these houses have twenty, thirty rooms. I often count and on the ride back figure out how much loot it would take to fill all that space up with cherrywood tables, Federal blue carpets and ottomans. I've been caught roaming around plenty of times but you'd be surprised

how quickly someone believes you're looking for the bathroom
if you don't jump when you're discovered, if you just say,
Howdy.

After the paperwork's been signed, I have a decision to
make. If the customer has been good and tipped well, we call
it even and leave. If the customer has been an ass—maybe
they yelled at us, maybe they let their kids throw golf balls
at us—I ask for the bathroom. Wayne will pretend that he
hasn't seen this before; he'll count the drill bits while the
customer (or their maid) guides the vacuum over the floor.
Excuse me, I say. I let them show me to the bathroom (usually
I already know) and once the door is shut I cram bubble bath
drops into my pockets and throw fist-sized wads of toilet paper
into the toilet. I take a dump if I can and leave that for them.

•

Most of the time Wayne and I work well together. He's the
driver and the money man and I do the lifting and handle
the assholes. Today we're on our way to Lawrenceville and he
wants to talk to me about Charlene, one of the showroom
girls, the one with the blow-job lips. I haven't wanted to talk
about women in months, not since the girlfriend.

I really want to pile her, he tells me. Maybe on one of the
Madisons.

Man, I say, cutting my eyes towards him. Don't you have
a wife or something?

He gets quiet. I'd still like to pile her, he says defensively.

And what will that do?

Why does it have to *do* anything?

Twice this year Wayne's cheated on his wife and I've heard
it all, the before and the after. The last time his wife nearly
tossed his ass out to the dogs. Neither of the women seemed
worth it to me. One of them was even younger than Charlene.
Wayne can be a moody guy and tonight is one of those nights;
he slouches in the driver's seat and swerves through traffic,
riding other people's bumpers like I've told him not to do. I
don't need a collision or a four-hour silent treatment so I try

to forget that I think his wife is good people and ask him if Charlene's given him any signals.

He slows the truck down. Signals like you wouldn't believe, he says.

•

On the days we have no deliveries the boss has us working at the showroom, selling cards and poker chips and Mankala boards. Wayne spends his time skeezing on the salesgirls and dusting shelves. He's a big goofy guy—I don't understand why the girls dig his shit. The boss keeps me in the front of the store, away from the pool tables. He knows I'll talk to the customers, tell them not to buy the cheap models. I'll say shit like, Stay away from those Bristols. Wait until you can get something real. Only when he needs my Spanish will he let me help on a sale. Since I'm no good at cleaning or selling slot machines I slouch behind the front register and steal. I don't ring anything up and pocket what comes in. I don't tell Wayne. He's too busy running his fingers through his beard, keeping the waves on his nappy head in order. A hundred-buck haul's not unusual for me and back in the day, when the girlfriend used to pick me up, I'd buy her anything she wanted, dresses, silver rings, lingerie. Sometimes I blew it all on her. She didn't like the stealing but hell, we weren't made out of loot and I liked going into a place and saying, Jeva, pick out anything, it's yours. This was the closest I've come to feeling rich.

Nowadays I take the bus home and the cash stays with me. I sit next to this three-hundred-pound rock-and-roll chick who washes dishes at the Friendly's. She tells me about the roaches she kills with her water nozzle. Boils the wings right off them. On Thursday I buy myself lottery tickets—ten Quick Picks and a couple of Pick-Fours. I don't bother with the little stuff.

•

The second time we bring the Gold Crown the heavy curtain next to the door swings up like a Spanish fan. A woman stares at me and Wayne's too busy knocking to see. Muñeca, I say. She's black and unsmiling and then the curtain drops between us, a whisper on the glass. She had on a T-shirt that said NO PROBLEM and didn't look like she owned the place. She looked more like the help and couldn't have been older than twenty and from the thinness of her face I pictured the rest of her skinny. We stared at each other for a second at the most, not enough for me to notice the shape of her ears or if her lips were chapped. I've fallen in love on less.

Later in the truck, on the way back to the showroom Wayne mutters, This guy is dead. I mean it.

●

The girlfriend calls sometimes but not often. She has found herself a new boyfriend, some zángano who works at a record store. *Dan* is his name and the way she says it, so painfully gringo, makes the corners of my eyes close. The clothes that I'm sure this guy tears from her when they both get home from work — the chokers, the rayon skirts from the Warehouse, the lingerie — I bought with stolen money and I'm glad that none of it was earned straining my back against hundreds of pounds of raw rock. I'm glad for that.

The last time I saw her in person was in Hoboken; she was with *Dan* and hadn't yet told me about him and hurried across the street in her high clogs to avoid me and my boys, all of whom could sense me turning, turning into the motherfucker who'll put a fist through anything. She flung one hand in the air but didn't stop. Before that, before the zángano, I went to her house and her parents asked me how business was, as if I balanced the books or something. Business is outstanding, I said.

That's really wonderful to hear, the father said.

You betcha.

He asks me to help him mow his lawn and while we're

dribbling clear gas into the tank he offers me a job. Utilities, he says, is nothing to be ashamed of.

Later the parents go to the den to watch the Giants lose and she takes me into her bathroom. She puts on her makeup because we're going to a movie. As friends. If I had your eyelashes, I'd be famous, she tells me. The Giants start losing real bad. I still love you, she says and I'm embarrassed for the two of us, the way I'm embarrassed at those afternoon talk shows where broken couples and unhappy families let their hearts hang out.

We're friends, I say and Yes, she says, yes we are.

There's not much space so I have to put my heels on the edge of the bathtub. The cross I've given her dangles down on its silver chain so I put the cross in my mouth to keep it from poking me in the eye. By the time we finish my legs are bloodless, broomsticks inside my rolled-down baggies and while her breathing gets smaller and smaller against my neck, she says, I do, I still do.

•

Each payday I take out the old calculator and figure how long it would take me to buy a pool table honestly. A top of the line, three-piece slate affair doesn't come cheap. You have to buy sticks and balls and chalk and a score keeper and triangles and French tips if you're a fancy shooter. Two and a half years if I give up buying underwear and eat only pasta but even this figure's bogus. Money has never stuck to me; it trails away like piles of dry leaves.

Most people don't realize how amazing pool tables are. Yes, tables have bolts and staples on the rails but these suckers hold together mostly by gravity and the precision of their construction. If you treat a good table right it will outlast you. Believe me. Cathedrals are built like that. There are Incan roads in the Andes that even today you couldn't work a knife between two of the cobblestones. The sewers that the Romans built in Bath, England, were so good that they weren't replaced until the 1950s. That's the sort of thing I can admire.

These days I can build a table with my eyes closed and depending on how rushed we are I might build the table alone, let Wayne watch until I need help putting on the slate. It's better when the customers stay out of our faces, how they react when we're done, they run fingers on the lacquered rails and suck in their breath, the felt so tight over the slate you couldn't pluck it if you tried. Beautiful, is what they say and we always nod, talc on our fingers, nod again, a bit wistfully.

•

The boss nearly kicked our asses over the Gold Crown. The customer, an asshole named Pruitt, called up crazy, said we were delinquent. That's how the boss put it. Delinquent. So we knew that's what the customer called us because the boss doesn't use words like that. Look boss, I said, we knocked like crazy. I mean, we knocked like federal marshals. Like Paul Bunyan. The boss wasn't having it. You fuckos, he said. You butthogs. He tore into us for a good two minutes and then *dismissed* us. For most of that night I didn't think I had a job so I hit the bars, fantasizing that I would bump into this cabrón out with that black woman while me and my boys were cranked but the next morning Wayne came by with that Gold Crown again. Both of us had hangovers. One more time, he said. An extra delivery, no overtime. We hammered on the door for ten minutes but no one answered. I jimmied with the windows and the back door and I could have sworn I heard her behind the patio door. I knocked hard and heard footsteps.

We called the boss and told him what was what and the boss called the house but no one answered. Okay, the boss said. Get those card tables done. That night as we lined up the next day's paperwork we got a call from Pruitt and he didn't use the word delinquent. He wanted us to come late at night but we were booked. Two-month waiting list, the boss reminded him. I looked over at Wayne and wondered how much money this guy was pouring into the boss's ear.

Pruitt said he was *contrite* and *determined* and asked us to come again. His maid was sure to let us in.

●

What the hell kind of name is Pruitt anyway? Wayne asks me when we swing onto the Parkway.

Pato name, I say. Anglic or some other bog people.

Probably a fucking banker. What's the first name?

Just an initial, C. Clarence Pruitt sounds about right.

Yeah, Clarence, Wayne yuks.

Pruitt. Most of our customers have names like this, court case names: Wooley, Maynard, Gass, Binder, but the people from my town, our names, you see on convicts or coupled together on boxing cards.

This time we take our time. We go to the Rio Diner. We blow an hour and all the dough we have in our pockets. Wayne is talking about Charlene and I'm leaning my head against a thick pane of glass.

●

Pruitt's neighborhood has recently gone up and only his court is complete. Gravel roams off this way and that, shaky. You can see inside the other houses, their newly formed guts, nail heads bright and sharp on the fresh timber. Wrinkled blue tarps protect wiring and fresh plaster. The driveways are mud and on each lawn stand huge stacks of sod. We park in front of Pruitt's house and bang on the door. I give Wayne a hard look when I see no car in the garage.

Yes? I hear a voice inside say.

We're the delivery guys, I yell.

A bolt slides, a lock turns, the door opens. She stands in our way, wearing black shorts and a gloss of red on her lips and I'm sweating.

Come in, yes? She stands back from the door, holding it open.

Sounds like Spanish, Wayne says.

No shit, I say, switching over. Do you remember me?

No, she says.

I look over at Wayne. Can you believe this?

I can believe anything, kid.

You heard us didn't you? The other day, that was you.

She shrugs and opens the door wider.

You better tell her to prop that with a chair. Wayne heads back to unlock the truck.

You hold that door, I say.

•

We've had our share of delivery trouble. Trucks break down. Customers move and leave us with an empty house. Handguns get pointed. Slate gets dropped, a rail goes missing. The felt is the wrong color, the Dufferins get left in the warehouse. Back in the day the girlfriend and I made a game of this. A prediction game. In the mornings I rolled onto my pillow and said, What's today going to be like?

Let me check. She put her fingers up to her widow's peak and that motion would shift her breasts, her hair. We never slept under any covers, not in spring, fall or summer and our bodies were dark and thin the whole year.

I see an asshole customer, she murmured. Unbearable traffic. Wayne's going to work slow. And then you'll come home to me.

Will I get rich?

You'll come home to me. That's the best I can do. And then we'd kiss hungrily because this was how we loved each other.

The game was part of our mornings, the way our showers and our sex and breakfasts were. We stopped playing only when it started to go wrong for us, when I'd wake up and listen to the traffic outside without waking her, when everything was a fight.

•

She stays in the kitchen while we work. I can hear her humming. Wayne's shaking his right hand frantically like he's scalded his fingertips. Yes, she's a hottie. She has her back to me, her hands stirring around in a full sink, when I walk in.

I try to sound conciliatory. You're from the city?

A nod.

Where about?

Washington Heights.

Dominicana. Quisqueyana. She nods. What street?

I don't know the address. I have it written down. My mother and my brothers live there.

I'm Dominican, I say.

You don't look it.

I get a glass of water. We're both staring out at the muddy lawn.

I didn't answer the door because I wanted to piss him off.

Piss who off?

I want to get out of here, she says.

Out of here?

I'll pay you for a ride.

I don't think so, I say.

Aren't you from Nueva York?

No.

Then why did you ask the address?

Why? I have family near there.

Would it be that big of a problem?

I say in English that she should have her boss bring her but she stares blank at me. I switch over.

He's a pendejo, she says, suddenly angry. I put down the glass, move next to wash it. She's exactly my height and smells of liquid detergent and has tiny beautiful moles on her neck, an archipelago leading down into her clothes.

Here, she says, putting out her hand but I finish and go back to the den.

Do you know what she wants us to do? I say to Wayne.

•

Her room is upstairs, a bed, a closet, a dresser, yellow wallpaper. Spanish *Cosmo* and *El Diario* thrown on the floor. Four hangers worth of clothes in the closet and only the top drawer on the dresser is full. I put my hand on the bed and the cotton sheets are cool.

Pruitt has pictures of himself in his room. He's tan and probably has been to more countries than I know capitals for. Photos of him on vacations, on beaches, standing beside a wide-mouth Pacific salmon he has hooked. The size of his dome would make a phrenologist proud. The bed is made and his wardrobe spills out onto chairs and a line of dress shoes follows the far wall. A bachelor. I find an open box of Trojans in his dresser beneath a stack of boxer shorts. I put one of the condoms in my pocket and stick the rest under his bed.

I find her in her room. He likes clothes, she says.

A habit of money, I say but I can't translate it right; I end up agreeing with her. Are you going to need to pack?

She holds up her purse. I have everything I need. He can keep the rest of it.

You should take some of your things.

I don't care about that vaina. I just want to go.

Don't be stupid, I say. I open her dresser and pull out the jeans on top. A handful of soft bright panties comes out as well, starts to roll down the front of my jeans. There are more in the drawer. I try to catch the ones that fall but as soon as I touch their fabric I let everything go.

Leave it. She stands. Go on, she says and begins to put them back in the dresser, her square back to me, the movement of her hands smooth and easy.

Look, I say.

Don't worry. She doesn't look up.

I go downstairs. Wayne is sinking the bolts into the slate with the Makita. You can't do it, he says.

Why not?

Kid. We have to finish this.

I'll be back before you know it. A quick trip, in, out.

Kid. He stands up slowly; he's nearly twice as old as me.

I go to the window and look out. New ginkgos stand in
fresh rows beside the driveway. A thousand years ago when
I was still in college I learned something about them. Living
fossils. Unchanged since their inception millions of years ago.
You've tagged Charlene, haven't you?

Sure, he answers easily. I take the truck keys out of the tool
box.

I'll be right back, I promise him.

•

My mother still has pictures of the girlfriend in her apartment. The girlfriend's the sort of person who never looks bad.
There's a picture of us at the bar where I taught her to play
pool. She's leaning on the Schmelke I stole for her, nearly a
grand worth of cue and frowning at the shot I left her, a shot
she'd go on to miss.

The picture of us at Boca Raton is the largest—shiny,
framed, nearly a foot tall. We're in our bathing suits and the
legs of some stranger frame the right. She has her butt in the
sand, knees folded up in front of her because she knew I was
sending the picture home to my mom; she didn't want my
mother to see her bikini, didn't want my mother to think her
a whore. I'm crouching next to her, smiling, one hand on her
thin shoulder, one of her moles showing between my thumb
and pointer.

My mother won't look at the pictures or talk about her when
I'm around but my sister says she still cries over the break-up.
Around me my mother's polite, sits quietly on the couch while
I tell her about what I'm reading and how work has been. Do
you have anyone? she asks me sometimes.

Yes, I say.

She talks to my sister on the side, says, In my dreams they're
still together.

•

We reach the Washington Bridge without saying a word.
She's emptied his cupboards and refrigerator; the bags are

at her feet. She's eating corn chips but I'm too nervous to join in.

Is this the best way? She asks. The bridge doesn't seem to impress her.

It's the shortest way.

She folds the bag shut. That's what he said when I arrived last year. I wanted to see the countryside. There was too much rain to see anything anyway.

I want to ask her if she loves her boss, but I ask instead, How do you like the States?

She swings her head across at the billboards. I'm not surprised by any of it, she says.

Traffic on the bridge is bad and she has to give me an oily fiver for the toll. Are you from the capital? I ask.

No.

I was born there. In Villa Juana. Moved here when I was a little boy.

She nods, staring out at the traffic. As we cross over the bridge I drop my hand into her lap. I leave it there, palm up, fingers slightly curled. Sometimes you just have to try, even if you know it won't work. She turns her head away slowly, facing out beyond the bridge cables, out to Manhattan and the Hudson.

Everything in Washington Heights is Dominican. You can't go a block without passing a Quisqueya Bakery or a Quisqueya Supermercado or a Hotel Quisqueya. If I were to park the truck and get out nobody would take me for a delivery man; I could be like the guy who's on the street corner selling Dominican flags. I could be on my way home to my girl. Everybody's on the streets and the merengue's falling out of windows like TVs. When we reach her block I ask a kid with the sag for the building and he points out the stoop with his pinkie. She steps out of the truck and straightens the front of her sweatshirt before following the line that the kid's finger has cut across the street. Cuidate, I say.

•

Wayne works on the boss and a week later I'm back, on
probation, painting the warehouse. Wayne brings me meat-
ball sandwiches from out on the road, skinny things with a
seam of cheese gumming the bread.

Was it worth it? he asks me.

He's watching me close. I tell him it wasn't.

Did you at least get some?

Hells yeah, I say.

Are you sure?

Why would I lie about something like that? Homegirl was
an animal. I still have the teeth marks.

Damn, he says.

I punch him in the arm. And how's it going with you and
Charlene?

I don't know, man. He shakes his head and in that motion
I see him out on his lawn with all his things. I just don't know
about this one.

We're back on the road a week later. Buckinghams, Imperi-
als, Gold Crowns and dozens of card tables. I keep a copy of
Pruitt's paperwork and when the curiosity finally gets to me
I call. The first time I get the machine; we're delivering at a
house in Long Island with a view of the Sound that would
break you. Wayne and I smoke a joint on the beach and I
pick a dead horseshoe crab up by the tail and heave it in the
customer's garage. The next two times I'm in the Bedminster
area and Pruitt picks up and says, Yes? But on the fourth
time she answers and the sink is running on her side of the
phone and she shuts it off when I don't say anything.

Was she there? Wayne asks in the truck.

Of course she was.

He runs a thumb over the front of his teeth. Pretty predictable. She's probably in love with the guy. You know how it
is.

I sure do.

Don't get angry.

I'm tired, that's all.

Tired's the best way to be, he says. It really is.

He hands me the map and my fingers trace our deliveries,

stitching city to city. Looks like we've gotten everything, I say.

Finally. He yawns. What's first tomorrow?

We won't really know until the morning, when I've gotten the paperwork in order but I take guesses anyway. One of our games. It passes the time, gives us something to look forward to. I close my eyes and put my hand on the map. So many towns, so many cities to choose from. Some places are sure bets but more than once I've gone with the long shot and been right.

You can't imagine how many times I've been right.

Usually the name will come to me fast, the way the numbered balls pop out during the lottery drawings, but this time nothing comes: no magic, no nothing. It could be anywhere. I open my eyes and see that Wayne is still waiting. Edison, I say, pressing my thumb down. Edison, New Jersey.

A *Trainspotting* Glossary

When we signed up Irvine Welsh's first novel, Trainspotting, *I joked that it was going to be Norton's first foreign-language publication, so dense is the author's deployment of contemporary Scots demotic, a rich brew of industrial-strength profanity and slang. The book is written with the highest fidelity to the language of the Edinburgh housing projects or "schemes" that Irvine Welsh grew up in — an important factor in the almost nationalistic fervor that the book has engendered in Scotland. So it was with some trepidation that we broached with the author the idea of a glossary for American readers who might feel the need for some linguistic training wheels, but Irvine pronounced himself "agnostic" on the notion — which we took as a green light.*

The following document was begun by my assistant, Sean Desmond and me, who doped out many of the definitions from context, and it was vetted and completed by Irvine Welsh himself. Impress your friends with your correct usage of such terms as radge, square go, biscuit-ersed *and, of course, the all-purpose term of aggression and/or endearment,* cunt *before the film of* Trainspotting *hits American screens this summer. In fact, so closely did screenwriter John Hodge and director Danny Boyle (both Scots, incidentally) hew to the language of the book's characters that one scene uses standard English subtitles to excellent comic effect. It's a barry film indeed and it will unleash a blast of raw Edinburgh energy throughout the world.*

—Gerald Howard, Editor, W.W. Norton

from *Trainspotting*

—Here we go, here we go, here we go . . . ah sais. That cunt jist smiles. He keeps lookin ower it the burds, thit likesay American, ken. Problem wi that rid-heided cunt is thit he's no goat the gift ay the gab is far is burds go, likes, even if the cunt dis huv a certain style. No likesay me n Sick Boy. Mibbe it's wi him huvin brars instead ay sisters, he jist cannae really fuckin relate tae burds. Ye wait can that cunt tae make the first fuckin move, ye'll be waitin a long fuckin time. Ah fuckin show the rid-heided cunt how it's done.

—No fuckin shy, they British Rail cunts, eh? ah sais, nudgin the burd next tae us.

—Pardon? it sais tae us, sortay soundin likes, "par-dawn" ken?

—Whair's it yis come fae then?

—Sorry, I can't really understand you . . . These foreign cunts've goat trouble wi the Queen's fuckin English, ken. Ye huv tae speak louder, slower, n likesay mair posh, fir the cunts tae understand ye.

—WHERE . . . DO . . . YOU . . . COME . . . FROM?

That dis the fuckin trick. These nosey cunts in front ay us look roond. Ah stares back at the cunts. Some fucker's oan a burst mooth before the end ay this fuckin journey, ah kin see that now.

—Ehm . . . we're from Toronto, Canada.

—Tirawnto. That wis the Lone Ranger's mate, wis it no? ah sais. The burds jist look it us. Some punters dinnae fuckin understand the Scottish sense ay humour.

affie — afternoon
bairn — child, baby
bams — jerks
barry — great, terrific
baws — balls
beamer — red-faced, embarrassed
bevvy — drink
birl — turn
biscuit-ersed — self-pitying
bog — men's room
bollocks — testicles
bools — marbles
box — can be "head" as in "ootay yir box" or "asshole" as in "he stuck it up his/her box"
brar — brother
brassic — broke
broat — brought
buckin — fucking
bung — to lend someone money, to tip
buftie — homosexual male
burd — bird, female friend
caird — card
catboy — "my man"
chibbed — knifed, stabbed
chippy — joiner, carpenter, or chip-shop (fast food outlet)
choc-box — asshole
coffin-dodger — senior citizen
collies — drugs
copped — obtained (often female company)
cowpin — shagging, fucking
crack — banter
cunt — all-purpose term for someone else, either friendly or unfriendly
cuntchy — "you cunt that you are"

daft — idiotic, stupid
deek — look
dippet — stupid
dosh — money
doss — real, as in "a doss cunt"
draftpaks — nutters, low-lifes, or a container for alcohol
DS — drug squad
durex — condom
eywis — always
fitba — football, soccer
foostie — rancid, poxy
gadge — guy
gaff — apartment
gear — works or clothes, or stolen goods
gig — the scene, or a concert
giro — government unemployment benefit check
giro-drops — bogus addresses for those checks
greet — cry
gunge — messy fluids
gypo — pleb or scruff
Hearts, Hibs — football teams
hirays, hireys — money
hotchin — abundant, packed full of
jellies, jelly tots — tranquilizers in capsules, often injected intravenously
Joe Baxi — cab
joiner — carpenter
jungle cat — "the man" on the prowl scoping for companionship
k.b.ing — being rejected, given the elbow, turned away
keks — underpants
ken, kent — know, known
knob — penis

labdick — cop
likesay — you know
loupin — stinking
lurve — love
mantovani — chicks
minge — as mantovani
muckers — mates, buddies
nash — hurry
nembies — Nembutals
NME — New Music Express
nippy — truculent, aggressive
nondy — stupid
ootay — out of
pagger — fight
para — paranoid
patter — style
peeve — drink (alcohol)
pips — dialing tone on the telephone
pish — piss
pished — drunk
plukey-faced — soft
plukes — spots
poppy — money
poxy — scabby, festering
puff "on one's puff" is "on one's own" but also short for poof or homosexual
punter — better or, more generally, fellow
rabbiting — talking incessantly
radge — crazy
rat-arsed — drunk
ride — screw
saps — soft persons
scoobies — stops, shuts up, stumps
scouser — native of Liverpool
scran — food

shag — screw
shan — crap
shoatie — watch
shunky — toilet
skag — heroin
skaggy-bawed — too high on heroin to screw
skint — broke
slag — insult or slut, bastard
snaffles — grabs up
smarmy — creepy, cruisy
spawny — lucky
specky — bespectacled
sprog — child
spunk — semen
square-go — fist fight with no knives or barstools
steamboats — drunk
stroppy — ugly
Subbuteo — table soccer game
swedge — fight, brawl
tattie — potato
thrush — minor sexually transmitted disease
tidy — nice
trainspotting — keeping obsessive notes on the arrival and departure of trains
Tron — area in Central Edinburgh
voddy — vodka
wanker — masturbator
waster — bum
Weedjie — native of Glasgow
whinge — complain
wide-o — term of insult
yin — one
yonks — years

NOTES ON CONTRIBUTORS

FICTION

Jaime Collyer is the author of two novels and the forthcoming short-story collection, *People on the Prowl*, his first English publication. This story marks his English debut. Lillian Tagle, who has translated thirty books, including works by Thomas Mann, and Carolyn Brown, an editorial associate at the International Writing Program at the University of Iowa, translated the story.

Junot Díaz received an M.F.A. from Cornell University. His work has appeared in *Story*, *The New Yorker*, *Glimmer Train* and *Time Out*.

Milan Kundera is the author of six novels and three nonfiction works. His story is taken from his novel *Slowness*, which is forthcoming from HarperCollins. His translator, Linda Asher, is a fiction editor at *The New Yorker*.

Brady Udall's collection of prize-winning stories, *Letting Loose the Hounds*, will be published later this year by W.W. Norton.

Irvine Welsh works, rests and raves in Edinburgh. A film version of his first novel, *Trainspotting*, will appear this summer. The novel has just been published by Norton.

POETRY

Christopher Bakken is a doctoral student in poetry at the University of Houston.

Bruce Bond's third poetry collection, *The Anteroom of Paradise*, won the Collady Award form the *Quarterly Review of Literature* in 1991.

Shannon Borg is a doctoral student in creative writing and literature at the University of Houston.

Nicole Cuddeback's poems have appeared in *Cimarron Review* and *Western Humanities Review*.

Madeline DeFrees has published five books of poetry. She has been awarded a Guggenheim fellowship, an NEA grant and the Carolyn Kizer Award from Calapooya College.

Michael Eilperin is a teaching fellow at the Johns Hopkins Writing Seminars and a doctoral student in English at Yale.

Gregory Fraser is a doctoral student in creative writing and English at the University of Houston.

Lise Goett received the 1995 *Paris Review* Discovery Prize.

Mac Hammond is the author of *Mappamundi*, a volume of poetry. He is a professor emeritus at the State University of New York at Buffalo.

Anthony Hecht's new collection of poems, *Flight Among the Tombs*, will be published by Knopf this fall.

Rick Hilles is a Wallace E. Stegner Fellow at Stanford.

Ellen Hinsey's *Cities of Memory* was selected for the 1995 Yale Series of Younger Poets. It will be published this spring.

William Hunt is the author of two books of poetry, *Of the Map That Changes* and *Oceans and Corridors of Orpheus*.

Mark Irwin's collection of poems, *Quick, Now, Always* was published recently.

David M. Katz's first book of poems, *The Warrior in the Forest*, was published by House of Keys Press.

John Kinsella received the Young Australian Creative Fellowship. His collection *Wireless Hill* will be published this fall.

Caroline Knox was a Lannan Foundation Master Fellow in Literature at the Fine Arts Work Center in Provincetown last fall.

James Longenbach's poems appeared in *The Best American Poetry 1995*. He won the 1995 *Nation*/Discovery Prize.

Judy Longley received the 1993 Marianne Moore Prize from Helicon Nine Editions.

Richard Lyons is the author of *These Modern Nights* and *Hours of the Cardinal*.

Corey Marks received an M.F.A. from Warren Wilson College.

A.F. Moritz's poetry has appeared in *American Poetry Review*, *Pequod*, *Hudson Review* and *The Best American Poetry* of 1991 and 1993.

Kenneth Rosen's collection of poems, *No Snake, No Paradise* will be published this year.

S.X. Rosenstock's first poetry collection, *United Artists*, will appear this spring from University of South Carolina Press. Her poems, with commentary by Edward Hirsch, appear in the *Boston Review*.

Stephen Sandy's last collection of poetry, *Thanksgiving Over the Water*, was published by Knopf. *Vale of Academe*, a prose poem for Bernard Malamud, will appear this spring from Holocene Press. He teaches at Bennington College.

Jordan Smith is the author of three books of poems, *An Apology for Loving*, *Lucky Seven* and *The Household of Continuance*.

Shawn Sturgeon lives in Cincinatti.

Pimone Triplett lives in Houston.

David Wojahn's most recent collection, *Late Empire*, was published by the University of Pittsburgh Press.

Mark Wunderlich is a 1995 Arts Administration Fellow at the National Endowment for the Arts.

FEATURES

Henry Allen is culture critic for *The Washington Post*.

Mike Golden is the editor and publisher of the magazine *Smoke Signals*.

Caroline Marshall's illustrations have appeared in *The New York Times* and *High Times*. She wrote three feature comedy scripts with Terry Southern as script consultant.

Nile Southern lives in Boulder, Colorado.

William Styron's most recent work is *A Tidewater Morning: Three Tales from Youth*.

INTERVIEWS

James Linville (Price and Wilder interviews) is an editor of *The Paris Review*, for which he has interviewed Harold Brodkey, Fran Lebowitz and Mark Helprin. His work has also appeared in *Esquire*, *Harper's*, *Manhattan File* and the *Pushcart Prize Anthology*.

George Plimpton (Dunne interview) is the editor of *The Paris Review*. His most recent book, published last spring by W.W. Norton and Company, is *The X Factor*.

ART

Richard Gaffney is a professor of art at Wagner College. His work is represented by the Atlantic Gallery in New York.

Joyce Pensato is represented by the Max Protech Gallery.

Sarah Plimpton is represented in New York by the June Kelly Gallery.

Lorna Simpson is represented in New York by the Sean Kelly Gallery.

Maria Christina Villaseñor writes on art and lives in New York City. She recently co-edited an issue of *Art Journal* devoted to video art.

The Paris Review
Booksellers Advisory Board

THE PARIS REVIEW BOOKSELLERS ADVISORY
BOARD is a group of owners and managers of
independent bookstores from around the
world who have agreed to share with us their
knowledge and expertise.